LEGENDARY LOCALS

OF

COPPELL

TEXAS

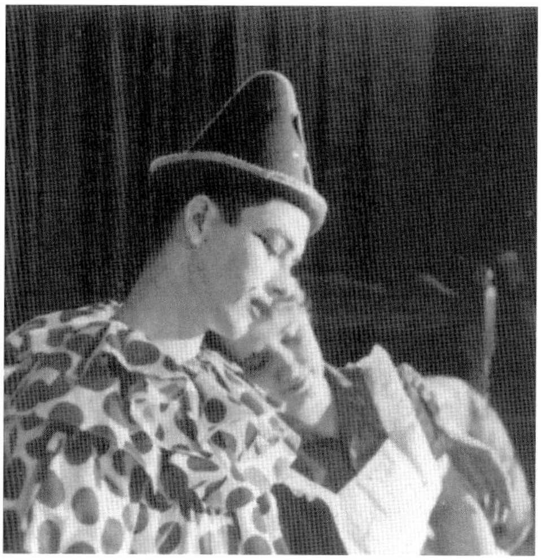

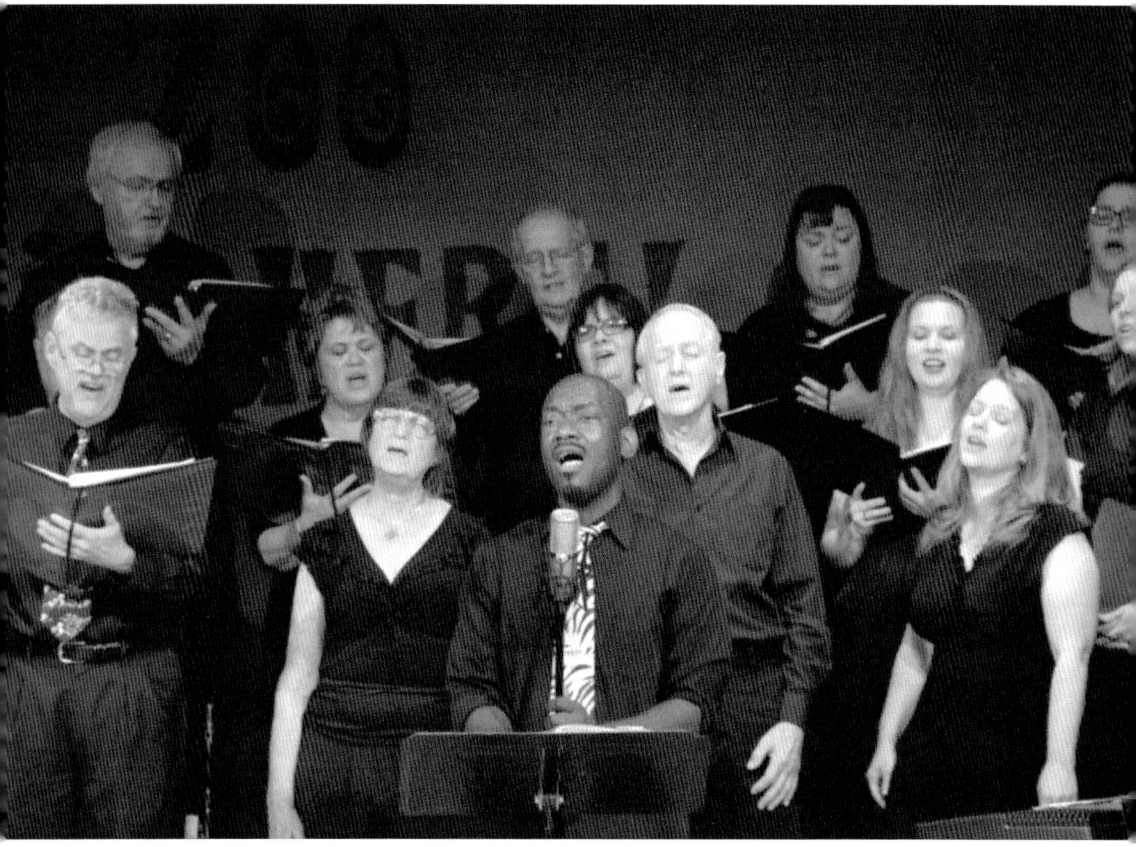

Coppell Community Chorale
Former director Dr. Robert Chalwell (January 2011–May 2014) leads the Coppell Community Chorale in a song from their show *It's a Zoo in Here!* The chorale, one of Coppell's oldest community organizations, stages two shows a year at the Coppell Center for the Arts. At the end of each performance, the chorale welcomes all former members in the audience to join in song onstage. Together, they close the show singing the "Irish Blessing:" "May the road rise up to meet you. May the wind be always at your back . . . and until we meet again, may God hold you in the palm of His hand." (Courtesy of Dr. Robert Chalwell.)

Page 1: Good Bye to the Clown
In 1965, Faye G. Pinkerton, the choir and speech teacher at Coppell High School, encouraged her students to enter a play in the University Interscholastic League one-act play competition. The play would be the school's first production. The selected play was Samuel French's *Good Bye to the Clown*, which featured Wheelice "Pete" Wilson Jr. and Cheryl Huckaby in the lead roles. The cast won a number of awards, including Best Actor for Wilson. It marked the beginning of a life in theater for Wilson, who later led the school's drama department as well as the community theater. (Courtesy of the Coppell Historical Society.)

LEGENDARY LOCALS

OF

COPPELL

TEXAS

SHAUN M. JEX

LEGENDARY LOCALS

ISBN 978-1-4671-0221-6

Legendary Locals is an imprint of Arcadia Publishing
Charleston, South Carolina

Printed in the United States of America

Library of Congress Control Number: 2015936462

For all general information, please contact Arcadia Publishing:
Telephone 843-853-2070
Fax 843-853-0044
E-mail sales@arcadiapublishing.com
For customer service and orders:
Toll-Free 1-888-313-2665

Visit us on the Internet at www.arcadiapublishing.com

Dedication
To my grandmother, Patricia Bernard, who taught me how to listen.

On the Front Cover: Clockwise from top left:
Ruby McDowell, old-time resident (courtesy of the Coppell Historical Society; see page 70), Johnny Dobecka, World War II veteran (courtesy of the Coppell Historical Society; see page 112), Ryan Kate Brandenburg, contestant on *MasterChef Junior* (courtesy of Fox Searchlight; see page 30), Pfc. Carroll E. Kirkland, World War II soldier killed in action (courtesy of the Coppell Historical Society; see page 110), "Old Red," Coppell Fire Department's 1941 Ford (courtesy of the Coppell Historical Society; see pages 78–79), Emily Elbert, Coppell musician and recording artist (courtesy of Emily Elbert; see page 28), Floyd Harwell, longtime Coppell barber (courtesy of the Coppell Historical Society; see page 14), Dash, official fire department mascot (courtesy of the Coppell Fire Department; see page 81), Jacob Schick, veteran of Iraq War (courtesy of Jacob Schick; see page 117).

On the Back Cover: From left to right:
Todd and Tara Storch with family, founders of the Taylor's Gift charity (courtesy of Todd and Tara Storch; see page 104), John and Sara Stringfellow, pioneer family who donated land for Coppell's first church (courtesy of the Coppell Historical Society; see pages 48–49).

CONTENTS

Acknowledgments	6
Introduction	7
CHAPTER ONE Business	9
CHAPTER TWO Art	25
CHAPTER THREE Schools	33
CHAPTER FOUR Church	47
CHAPTER FIVE Neighborhood	59
CHAPTER SIX Government	85
CHAPTER SEVEN Service	99
CHAPTER EIGHT Heroes	109
Index	127

ACKNOWLEDGMENTS

This book would not have been written without the help of many people. Chief amongst these is my wife, Kara Jex. She encouraged me, provided feedback and ideas, and photographed several of the pictures included. A big thank-you also goes to my children, Hayden and Kaitlyn, who showed great patience while Dad was busy doing research. Special thanks to my parents, Brian and Kathy Jex, who nurtured and encouraged my writing talents. They also provided the technological access their semi-Luddite son needed to complete the book. Also, a heartfelt thanks to my sister Janelle Jex for her unwavering support and a patient tolerance for her older brother.

Pete Wilson was invaluable in answering questions, helping me find photographs through the Coppell Historical Society archives, and sharing anecdotes.

Jean Murph of the *Citizens' Advocate* also answered countless questions and gave me access to the archives of her newspaper.

Jane Darling of the William T. Cozby Public Library was a gift, eager to research the library's archives and share her findings.

Cecil Dobecka, Richard and Barbara Lee, Sgt. Sammy Lujan of the Coppell Police Department, and Chief Matthew Uppole of the Coppell Fire Department all provided extensive information and access to personal and historical records.

A note of thanks to my first creative writing teacher, Becki Stevenson of Coppell High School, who took a spark of passion for writing and fanned it into a flame.

Erin Vosgien and the staff of Arcadia Publishing deserve special mention. An entire book could be made of my questions sent to Erin. She was more than patient in answering them all.

Finally, special thanks to all the residents, past and present, who made themselves available to answer questions and share stories.

INTRODUCTION

On a warm February morning, I found myself sitting on the back porch of the historic Kirkland House in Old Town Coppell. Coppell native Wheelice "Pete" Wilson Jr. sat next to me in a rocking chair. We were both sipping cups of lemonade while Pete told stories of Coppell's past. It was the type of scene that you wouldn't believe in a work of fiction. Too picturesque and sentimental. Too Norman Rockwell.

Researching this book has led to many such moments. Sitting in Wesley Hall of the First United Methodist Church of Coppell, I listened as Fred Conger described the perils of playing piano in the church's old building. It seems that the floor of the church was slanted, and when pianist Norma Infeldt sat down to play, she had to position her feet so she would not slide off the bench. In later conversations, Fred waxed poetic about the catfish nuggets served at Dolly's Café, a greasy spoon that has been closed for decades.

Sitting in a two-chair barbershop, I listened as owner Joe Shirley talked about his passion for photography. Later, while local businessman John Taylor got his hair cut, he described the phone museum that he operates out of his home. Give him a call and Taylor will give you a tour of his collection, which covers over 100 years of telecommunications history.

I heard from various residents that Pastor Lou Brown had the funniest funeral that anyone ever remembered attending. The longtime pastor of Coppell's First Baptist Church had a penchant for comedy. After retiring from ministry, he wrote humorous Christian books and made a recording of himself that was played during his funeral. Tears and laughter intermingled freely.

Sitting at her dining room table, Mindy Helsley described how she picked mint from her backyard garden as a little girl. When she had gathered enough, she would walk from her house to the Gibb's Station restaurant, offering it to owner Morris Salerno for use in his iced tea. She also recounted winning a competition that allowed her to throw a pie in the face of town orthodontist Dr. Frank Stitch.

While looking through a box of church history, I learned that the windows of the Methodist church were left open when the congregation sang hymns so that the nearby Baptist church could hear how "Methodists do it." I also learned that attendance dipped so low that, at one point, the pastor asked members with two cars to drive both to the service so the parking lot would not look so empty. Interspersed with these written memories were photographs of potluck dinners held on the church grounds.

Of course, no town is free of its controversies. For every Grover's Corners moment I had while researching this book, I met with just as many that could have been pulled from Edgar Lee Master's *Spoon River Anthology*. One resident told me that the story of Coppell was one of "corruption and greed." Others spoke of the turmoil in the 1980s during the mayoral terms of Andrew Brown Jr. and Lou Dugan. Though over 30 years have passed, many of the wounds still seem fresh and incite passions.

The 1960s were an equally tumultuous time for the town. Only a few years removed from incorporation, some residents began petitioning to dissolve the town. One segment of town was eventually dis-annexed. It attempted to form a new town under the name Jamestown, was unsuccessful, and eventually became part of Coppell again.

In this book, I have chosen not to dwell on the controversies. There is plenty of material available in the library, old newspapers, and town records of city council minutes. These are available to anyone curious enough to search them out. The individuals presented here are recognized for the contributions they have made to Coppell's continually evolving story. As with any story, there is never just one side and the issues are rarely as black and white as either side would have you believe.

To my great delight, most residents have not only seemed receptive to the idea of sharing stories but hungry to share them. Because of that, the research has been remarkably easy. People have, with very little prompting, dug out old photo albums and family stories and put them at my disposal. Some even wrote multi-page histories of their lives and the lives of their families.

Perhaps one of the most difficult aspects of writing a book like this is the simple march of time. Several of the people featured in this book (such as Foy Layton, Bettye Parker, and Juanita Barfknecht) passed during the writing. The number of "old-timers" in town is rapidly dwindling, and with them goes a wealth of history. I hope in some small way that I have honored them with this book.

As with any work of this kind, it is impossible to include everyone. Every person in town and every person who has lived in town has played some part in its story, and each has a unique story to tell. Time and space make it necessary to pick and choose. In addition, lost or nonexistent records have made some portions of town history particularly difficult to relate. For instance, while it is known that F.N. Camp was the first doctor in town and that E.C. Bechtol was the first music teacher, nothing else is known about them. Likewise, records indicate that the Rev. J.B. Bennett was the first pastor of Coppell's first house of worship, but there are no additional details in regards to his birth, death, or family history. In such cases, though the figures are significant, I have had to exclude them.

That said, I hope I have done Coppell justice in the pages that follow. I have called Coppell home since I was eight years old. I attended Richard J. Lee Elementary and played on the playgrounds at Andrew Brown Jr. Park. I graduated from Coppell High School and got engaged at Coppell's Grapevine Springs Park. Today, my own children are growing up and playing at the same grounds that shaped my life over the years. This book is a small attempt to give back and say thank you.

CHAPTER ONE

Business

Michael Dupey lived in Coppell from the late 1970s until his death in May 2010. In those years, he was described with a number of superlatives. He was called a maverick, a retail genius, and a visionary. A 1985 article in the *Coppell News Weekly* described him as "three-fourths boy and one-fourth merchandizing tycoon." A wildly successful businessman, he was known for recognizing industry trends well before his competition.

Dupey's business ventures began while working the family's five-and-dime. He was given the job of running the business and gradually turned it into a craft store, changing its name to Michael's Arts and Crafts. The concept was successful and led to the opening of additional stores over the following years.

In 1983, Dupey's father sold the company to businessman Sam Wyly. The deal provided that Michael Dupey would retain rights to the company name in Dallas. This led Dupey to develop the MJ Designs stores with corporate headquarters located in Coppell. The new stores proved equally successful, leading to the creation of over 50 additional locations by 1997.

Through the 1980s and 1990s, Dupey was also known in town for his elaborate Christmas displays. The displays were moved to Dupey's front yard after his Christmas store concept was abandoned. The decorations contained close to 100 moving animals and 5,000 Christmas lights. Each year, lines of cars would wind through his neighborhood while passengers viewed the spectacle.

Throughout its history, commerce has played a central role in Coppell's development. Business tycoons, such as Dupey and former Dallas Mavericks owner Don Carter, have called the town home. Coppell has also produced a wealth of small, family-owned businesses. They are the favorite haunts that only locals know and that give the town its flavor. Each is tied to a story and a personality, and each helps to tell a piece of the story of Coppell.

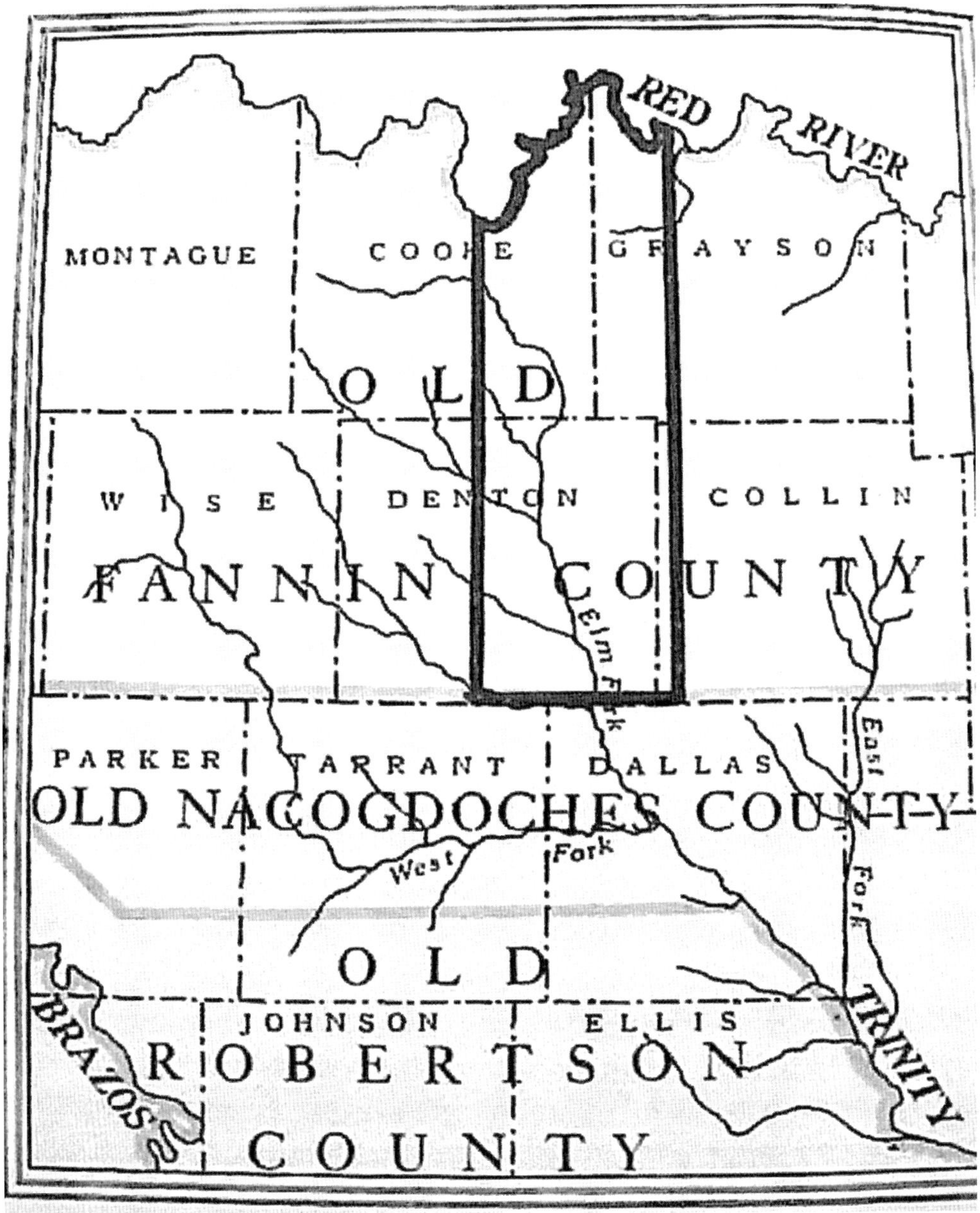

William S. Peters

Though William S. Peters never lived in or visited Coppell, he was instrumental in its founding. Born in 1770 in Devonshire, England, Peters moved to the United States when he was 48 years old. In 1839, he moved to Louisville, Kentucky. He joined his son William and son-in-law Serval Browning in running the music firm Peters, Browning, and Company.

In February 1841, Peters and his associates were granted an impresario contract to colonize in North Texas. The contract specified that Peters had to recruit 200 families within three years to settle the area. It granted 320 acres per single man and a maximum of 640 acres for a family.

The result became the Peters Colony (pictured). Among the early settlers was the James Parrish family, who settled on land that would come to be known as Coppell. (Courtesy of the Coppell Historical Society.)

George Coppell

In 1892, the town of Gibbs officially changed its name to Coppell. However, for many years, no one knew exactly why. A popular theory held that the name was given to honor an engineer who worked on the Cottonbelt Railroad that passed through town, but there was no evidence to support the claim.

It was not until 1988 that the research of resident Pete Wilson began to uncover clues to the most likely identity of the man behind the town name.

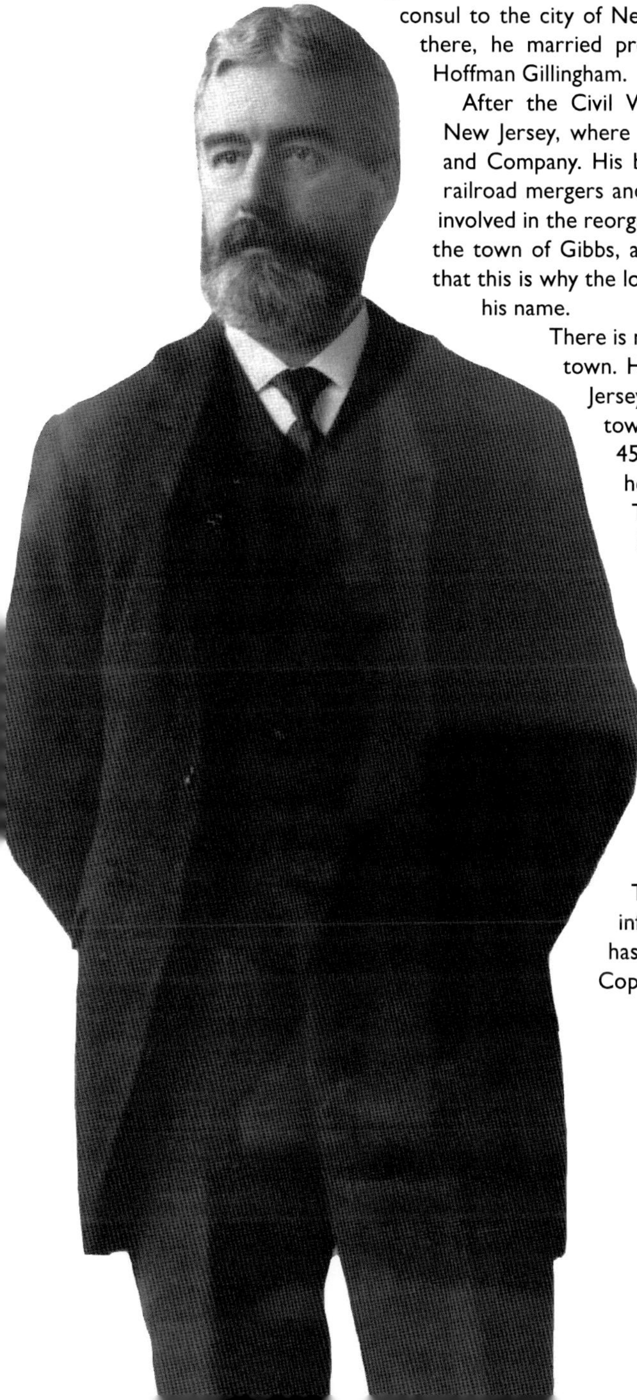

George Coppell was a wealthy New York banker born in 1838 in Liverpool, England. He came to America in roughly 1859 and served as the British consul to the city of New Orleans during the Civil War. While there, he married prominent New Orleans resident Helen Hoffman Gillingham.

After the Civil War, Coppell and his family moved to New Jersey, where he began working for Maitland, Phelps, and Company. His business money came primarily through railroad mergers and bankruptcies. The work led him to be involved in the reorganization of the railroad running through the town of Gibbs, and while it is not certain, it is believed that this is why the local depot and later the town were given his name.

There is no evidence that Coppell ever visited the town. He continued to make his home in New Jersey. He owned several mansions in the town of Tenafly. The first was a sprawling 45-acre home named Birchwood Knoll that he later gave to his son as a wedding gift. The second was a five-acre residence known as the Towers.

Coppell died in 1901 and was buried in the Woodlawn Cemetery in New York.

Despite all of this information, there is still some doubt as to George Coppell's connection to Coppell, Texas. A letter from the St. Louis Southern Railway in 1988 verifies that a railroad was opened through Gibbs in 1888 but states that the railway has no records of anyone named Coppell. The letter further states that any possible information was either never recorded or has long since been lost. (Courtesy of the Coppell Historical Society.)

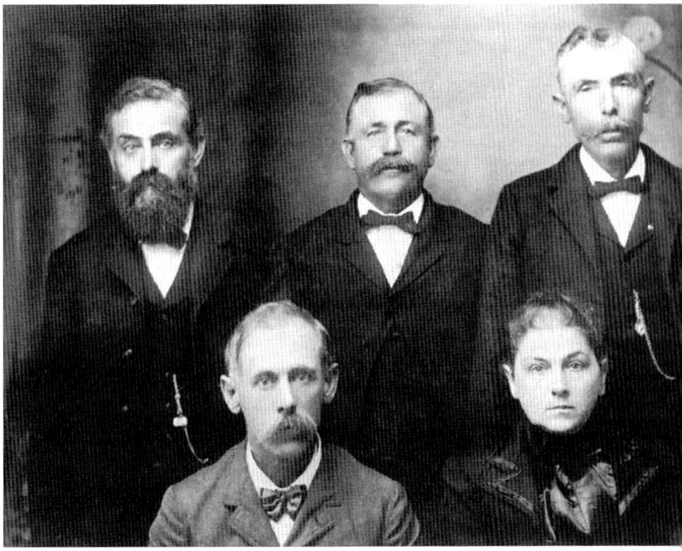

Jonathan Harrison
Prior to moving to the Coppell area, Jonathan Harrison (second row, left) was a Civil War veteran who fought for the Confederacy and was wounded at the Battle of the Wilderness with Britton's Brigade in 1864. He came to Grapevine Springs in 1873 and, in 1874, opened the town's first mercantile with his brothers T.J. (second row, right) and W.O. Harrison (first row, left). The first post office was located in the store with W.O. serving as the town's first postmaster. (Courtesy of Bennett Ratliff.)

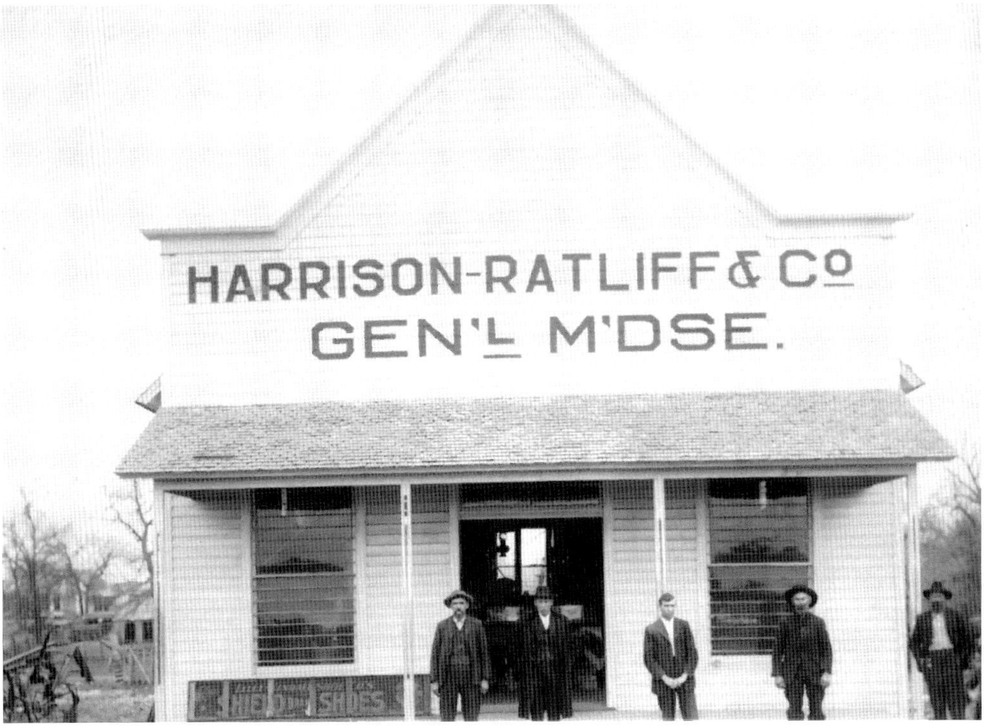

Harrison Ratliff General Store
In 1896, T.J. Harrison and John Ratliff were charter members of Coppell's Baptist church. In 1901, Ratliff married Harrison's daughter Nora and entered into the family mercantile business. The exact date is unknown, but shortly after, the company changed its name to the Harrison-Ratliff General Store. In later years, Ratliff became a Baptist and preached and served the Coppell Baptist church from 1913 to 1915. (Courtesy of Bennett Ratliff.)

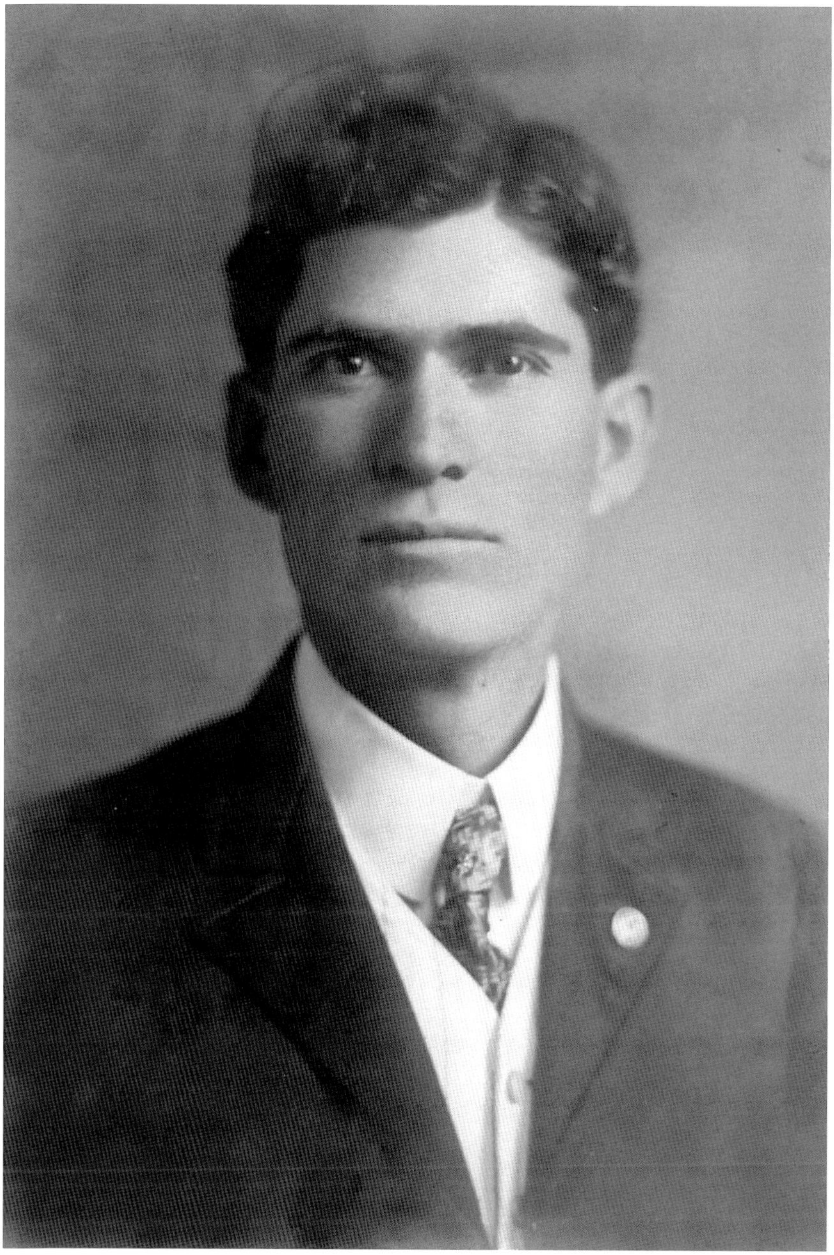

Dr. Jesse C. Bennett

Though he was not the first doctor in Coppell (that honor goes to F.N. Camp, who came to the area in 1890), Dr. Jesse Carroll Bennett was soon to follow. Born in Grapevine in 1878, Bennett married Dora Lee Bullock in 1899 before moving to Coppell and opening his first practice. The office remained open until 1917 when Bennett returned to Grapevine, though he continued to serve the Coppell area until moving to Fort Worth in 1930.

He was an active member of the Grapevine Baptist Church as well as the Grapevine Masonic lodge. Bennett died at the age of 52 and was buried in the Grapevine Cemetery in a service that included over 50 honorary pallbearers. (Courtesy of the Grapevine Historical Society.)

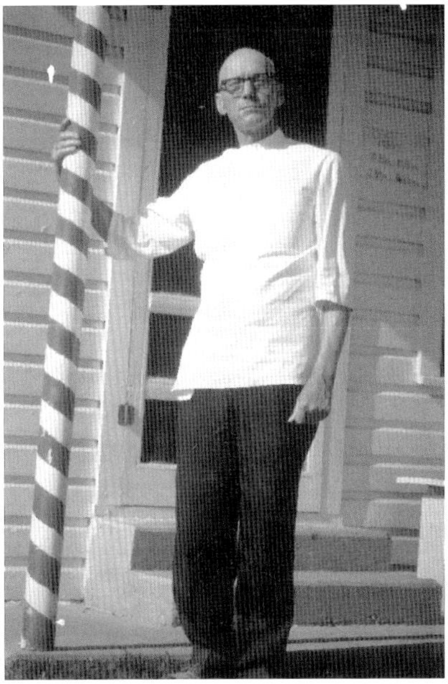

Floyd Harwell

Floyd Harwell was the original proprietor of the Bethel Road Barber Shop. He began the business with his brother Lloyd. The shop offered haircuts and shaves for 35¢ and 10¢, respectively. Around 1930, the original shop was destroyed in a fire. Floyd moved the shop into a service station. In later years, the shop was located in his home until the 1950s when it opened in its current location.

Floyd was passionate about baseball. He umpired games at Grapevine Springs Park and in surrounding towns. In addition, Floyd claimed to have been acquainted with Bonny Barrow of the notorious Bonnie and Clyde, stating that the two once shared a dance. Floyd aided the fire department in its early years, answering the emergency line at the fire station across from his shop and delivering the information to the town's volunteer firefighters. (Both, courtesy of the Coppell Historical Society.)

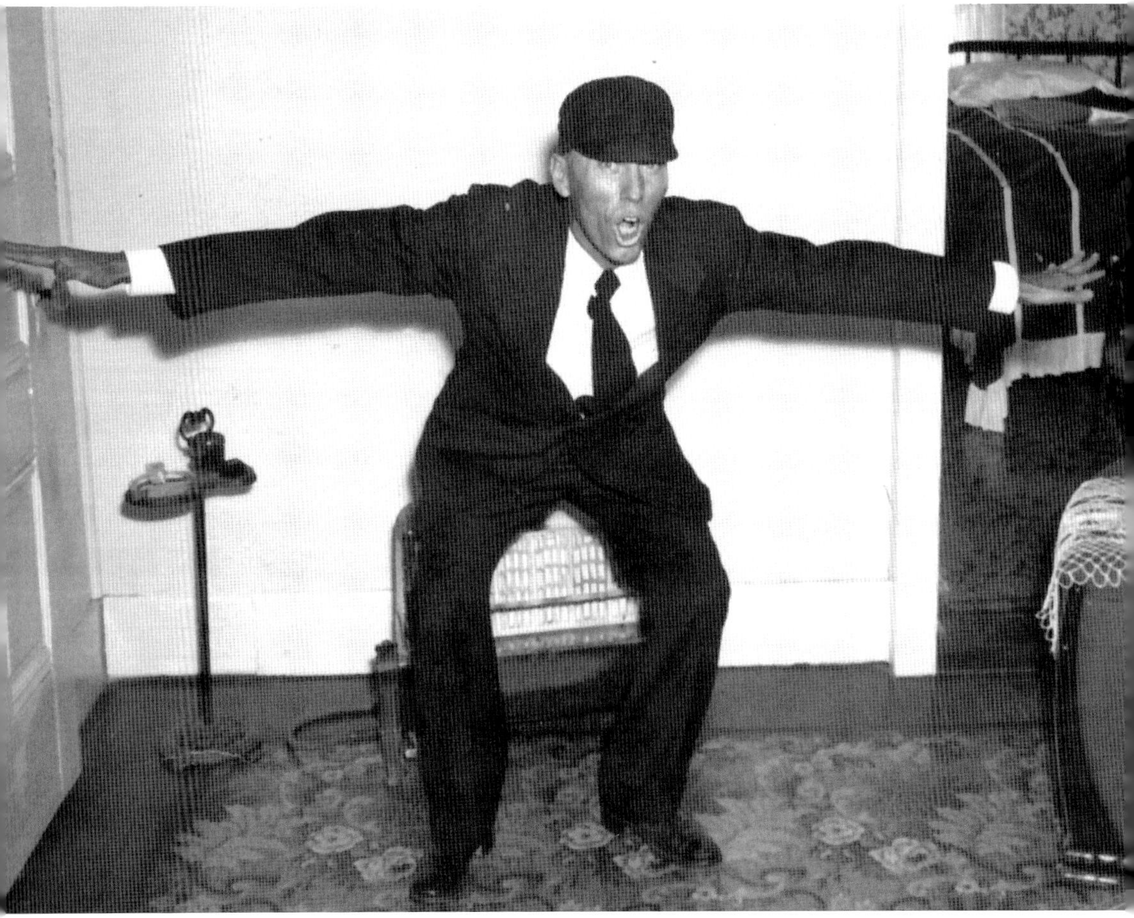

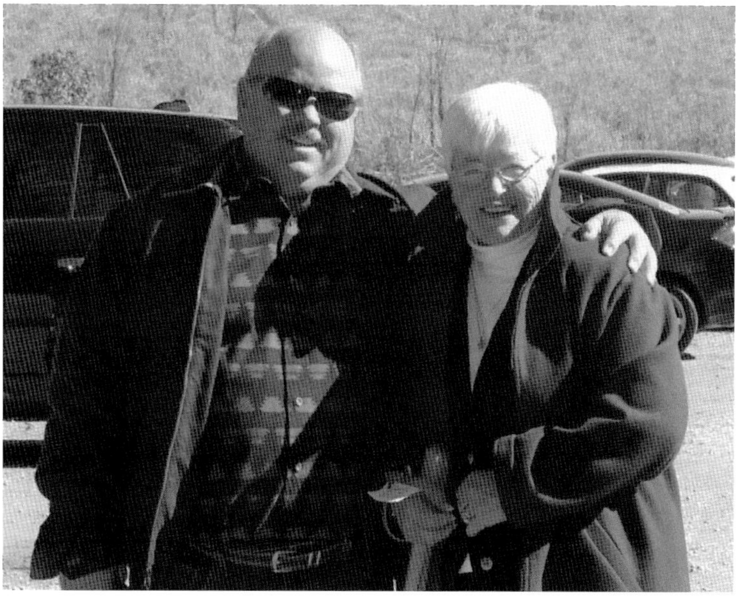

Bettye Parker

Bettye Parker was born in 1931 to Dave Pruitt and Ruby Belle Thweatt. She was the third of four children for the couple. In 1948, she graduated from Carrollton High School and, in 1951, married Coppell resident Herbert Parker (who later held the curious distinction of being elected to the school board without running for the office).

In the late 1960s, Bettye opened a small diner in the old post office on West Bethel Road. The restaurant was known as The Hitchin' Post and served daily lunch specials and hamburgers. It became a favorite eatery for local youth before football games. When Bettye sold the diner to Iola Harris a few years later, the name was changed to Dolly's Café.

Bettye is pictured above with her son Ronnie and below with granddaughter Adyson. (Both, courtesy of Evonne Parker.)

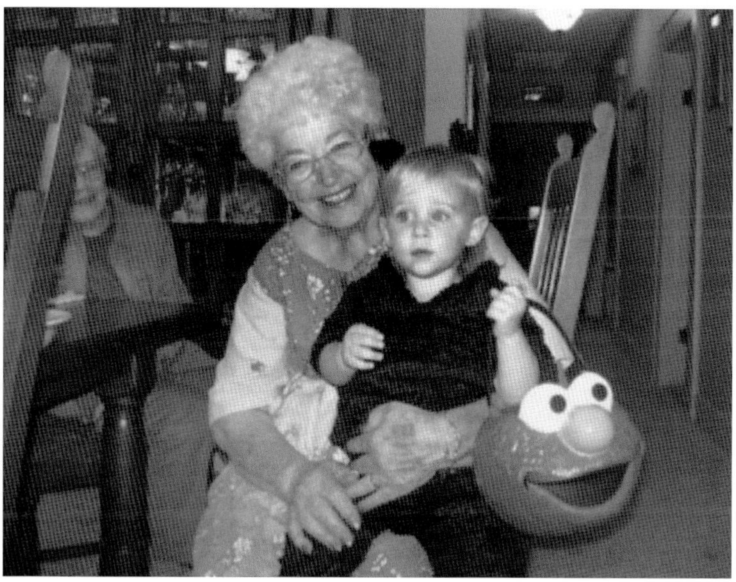

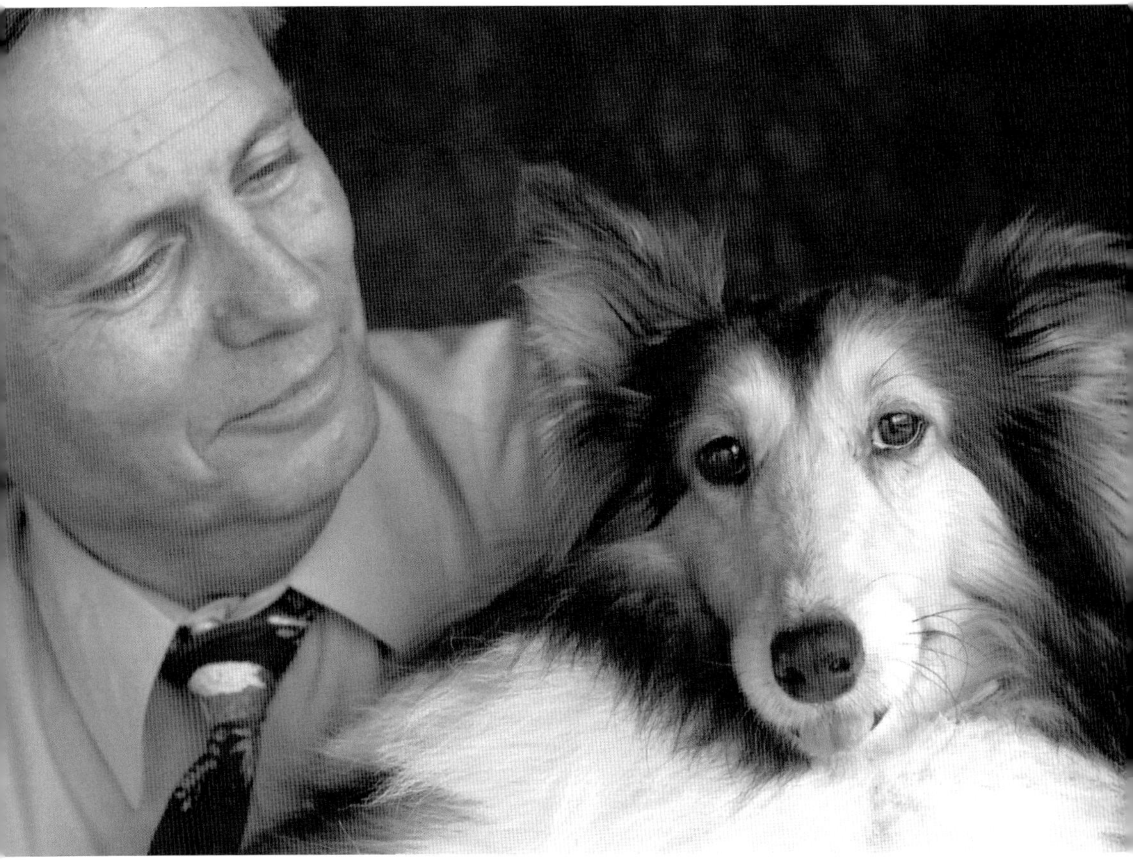

Dr. William Stearman

William Stearman grew up on a ranch near Hico, Texas, before going on to study veterinary medicine at Texas A&M University. In 1978, he opened his practice in Coppell. At the time, the town was still primarily a rural area and the majority of his work revolved around horses. As the community grew, Stearman restricted his practice to dogs and cats. He maintains an active business in Coppell and was honored by *D Magazine* as one of the area's best veterinary practices.

In addition to his veterinary work, Stearman is an avid sailor as well as the past president of both the Coppell Chamber of Commerce and the Coppell Rotary Club. (Courtesy of Dr. William Stearman.)

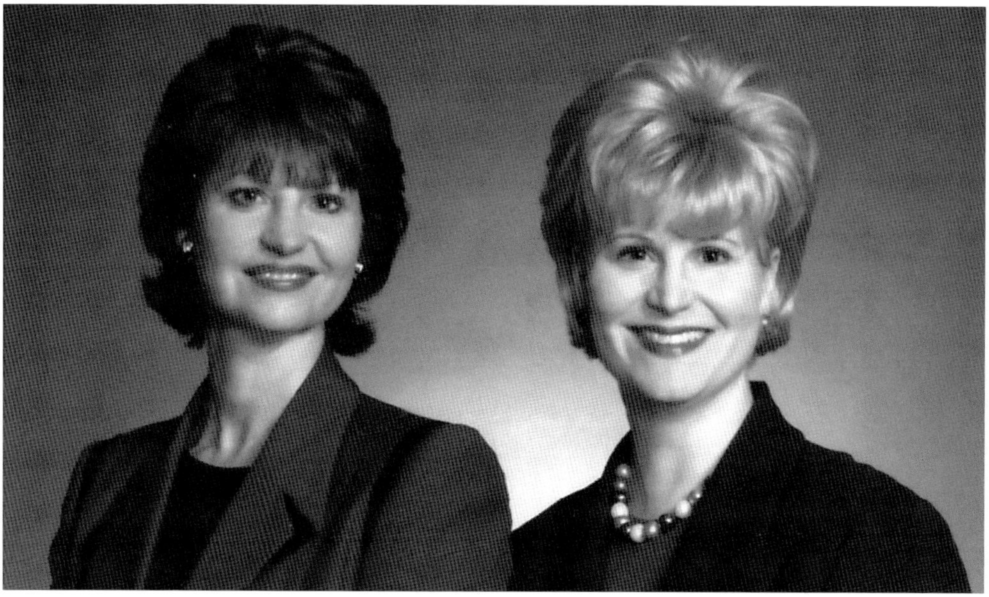

Gretchen and Lisbeth Minyard

In 1981, Minyard Food Stores moved its corporate headquarters to Coppell. Opened in 1932 in a clapboard building near the Minyard home in Dallas, the company had grown to a successful chain when it moved to town. After the passing of chief executive officer M.T. Minyard, control of the company passed to Gretchen and Lisbeth Minyard, who were known locally as the "Minyard Girls."

Increased competition from national chains eventually took its toll on the business and, in 2004, the sisters sold to an investment group. In 2007, the company's distribution center in Coppell was closed.

Minyard Food Stores still maintains a presence in town with a replica of the early store now located in Coppell's Heritage Park. Visitors can get a feel for the store's early days through docent-guided tours. (Above, courtesy of Gretchen Minyard; below, courtesy of Kara Jex.)

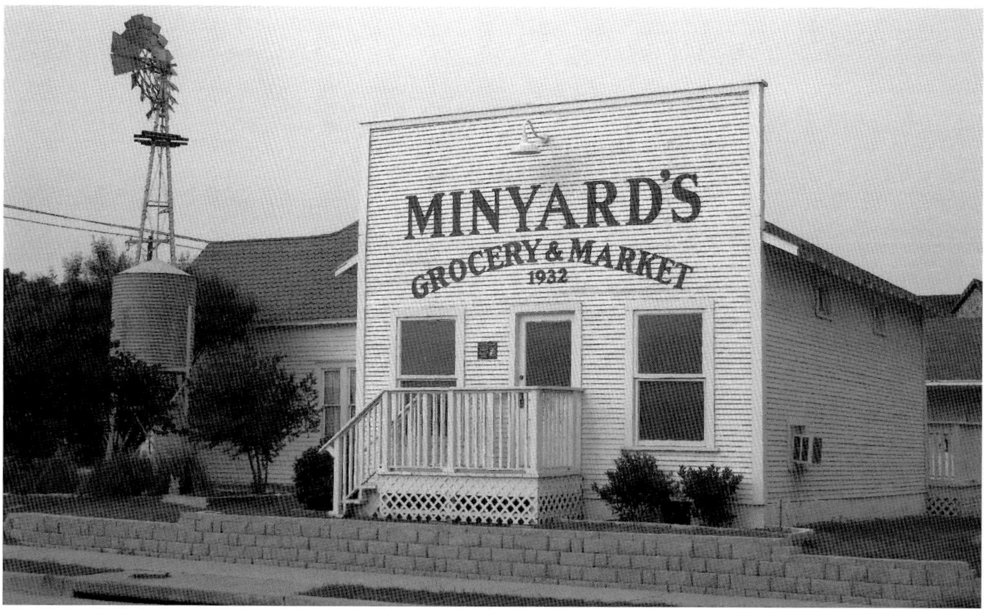

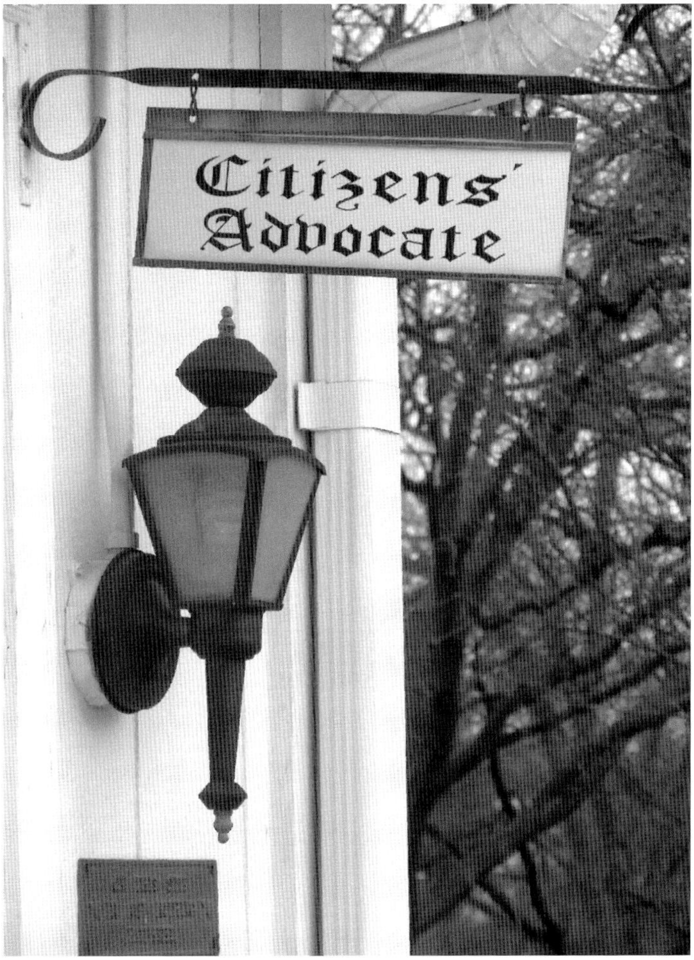

The *Citizens' Advocate*

The *Citizens' Advocate* newspaper was opened in 1984 by Jean Murph, daughter of former Texas governor Price Daniels. The paper was born after the closing of the *Coppell Star*, where Murph was working several days a week.

While working for the *Star*, Murph began covering city hall. With the help of Councilman Walter Pettijohn, she began a series of articles about open record and open meeting violations taking place in local government. Advertisers began leaving the *Star*. The paper fell into financial straits, and Murph offered to buy it. However, a rival group purchased the paper and subsequently closed it down.

Murph then decided to begin her own paper, despite having no publishing experience and no advertisers for backing. The first issue was released on March 26, 1984. The name *Citizens' Advocate* was chosen to reflect the paper's philosophy of being a true people's paper.

During earlier years, the paper focused heavily on the happenings at city hall and became deeply involved in the 1985 mayoral election, with the paper endorsing Councilman Lou Duggan against incumbent mayor Andy Brown Jr.

In the years since, the *Citizens' Advocate* has become the premier newspaper in Coppell. It still focuses on community matters and attempts to keep the public aware of the inner workings of local government. In addition, the *Advocate* works with the Coppell High School journalism program, giving students the chance to intern at the paper and gain professional experience. The *Advocate* has also worked to preserve Coppell history, publishing a special historical journal. (Courtesy of Kara Jex.)

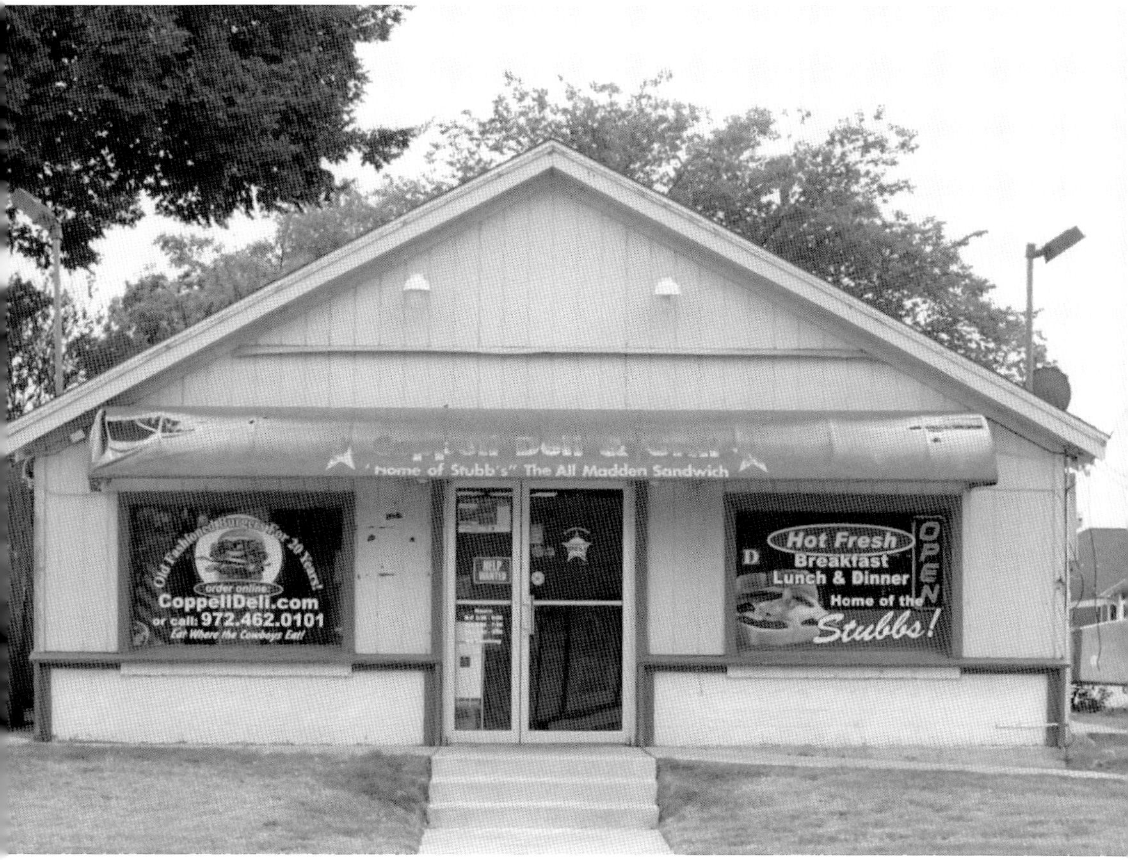

Jay Khorrami

In 1989, the Dallas Cowboys were a 1-15 team. Fortunately, that was the year that Jay Khorrami opened the Coppell Deli. Building his deli in the remains of a World War II grocery store, Khorrami established himself as a unique personality in Coppell. After the opening, he reached out to Cowboys guard Nate Newton and promised that if the Cowboys began eating the deli's food, they would begin to win. The team started showing up, and before long, they were Super Bowl champions. Khorrami remembers children lining up at his door to meet notables such as Troy Aikman, Jimmie Johnson, and Danny Stubbs. This eventually caught the attention of NFL coaching and broadcast legend John Madden. He was so taken with Khorrami's food that he added the Stubbs Sandwich to his All-Madden team.

The popularity of the diner led Khorrami to open a second location in Coppell called the Deli Man's Grill, where he continues to feed the Cowboys as well as hordes of hungry locals. (Courtesy of Kara Jex.)

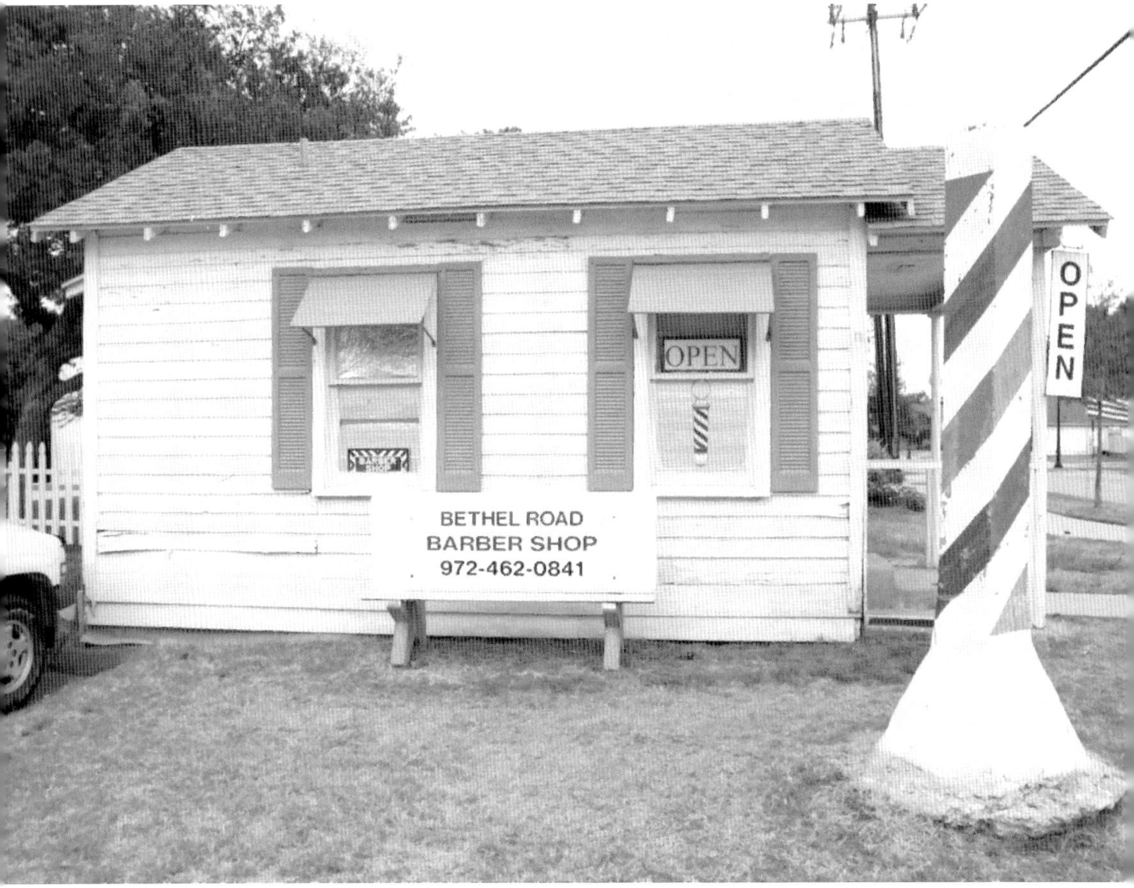

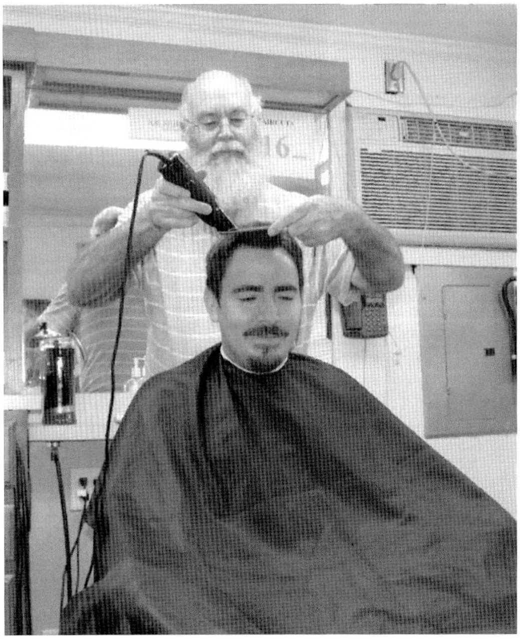

Joe Shirley

Since 1995, the Bethel Road Barber Shop has been run by Joe Shirley, who purchased it from the original owner, Floyd Harwell's widow. Despite pressure to update, Shirley has opted to keep the building as close to its original state as possible. The shop has two chairs and a pad of paper on the wall where walk-ins can sign up for a haircut. No appointments are accepted.

Prior to his time as a barber, Shirley served in the US Navy and worked as an engineer in the oil industry. He is also trained in mathematics and physics. Though seemingly overqualified, Shirley has a passion for the job as well as preserving town history through photography. Customers can come any day of the week, and Shirley is happy to stay open beyond business hours if necessary. (Both, courtesy of Brian Jex.)

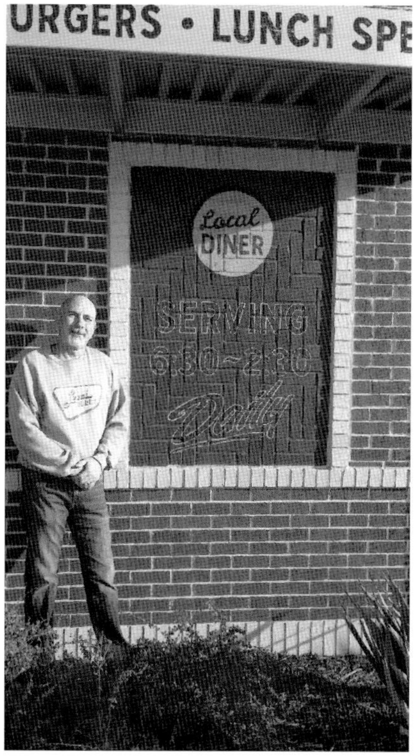

Frank Brightwell

Frank Brightwell first learned to cook at the side of his mother and later honed his skills in a variety of short-order cooking jobs. He worked through college in various restaurants. Though he graduated with a degree in education, Brightwell could not resist the call of the kitchen and returned to the food industry.

In 1989, Brightwell opened Local Diner in neighboring Carrolton and, a year later, opened a second location in Coppell. Since that time, he has maintained an active presence in town by sponsoring school activities, fundraisers, local parades, and chamber of commerce events. Brightwell notes that the Coppell location has been open long enough that children of former employees now work there. (Both, courtesy of Frank Brightwell.)

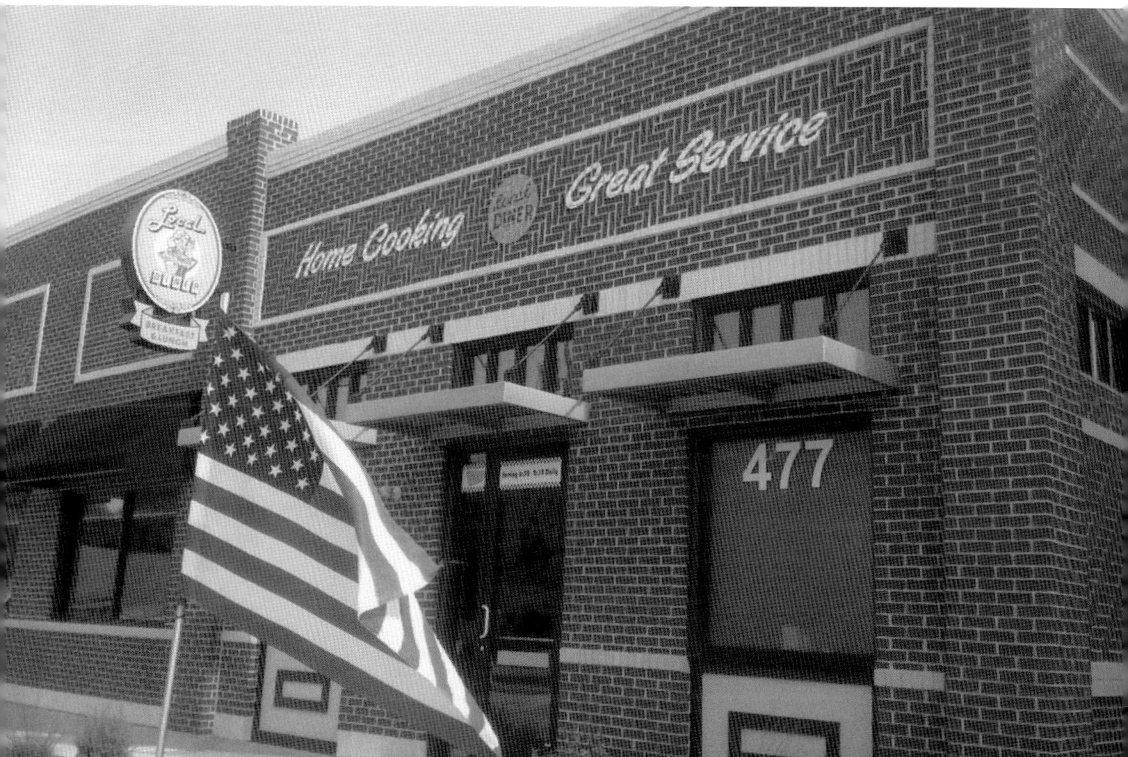

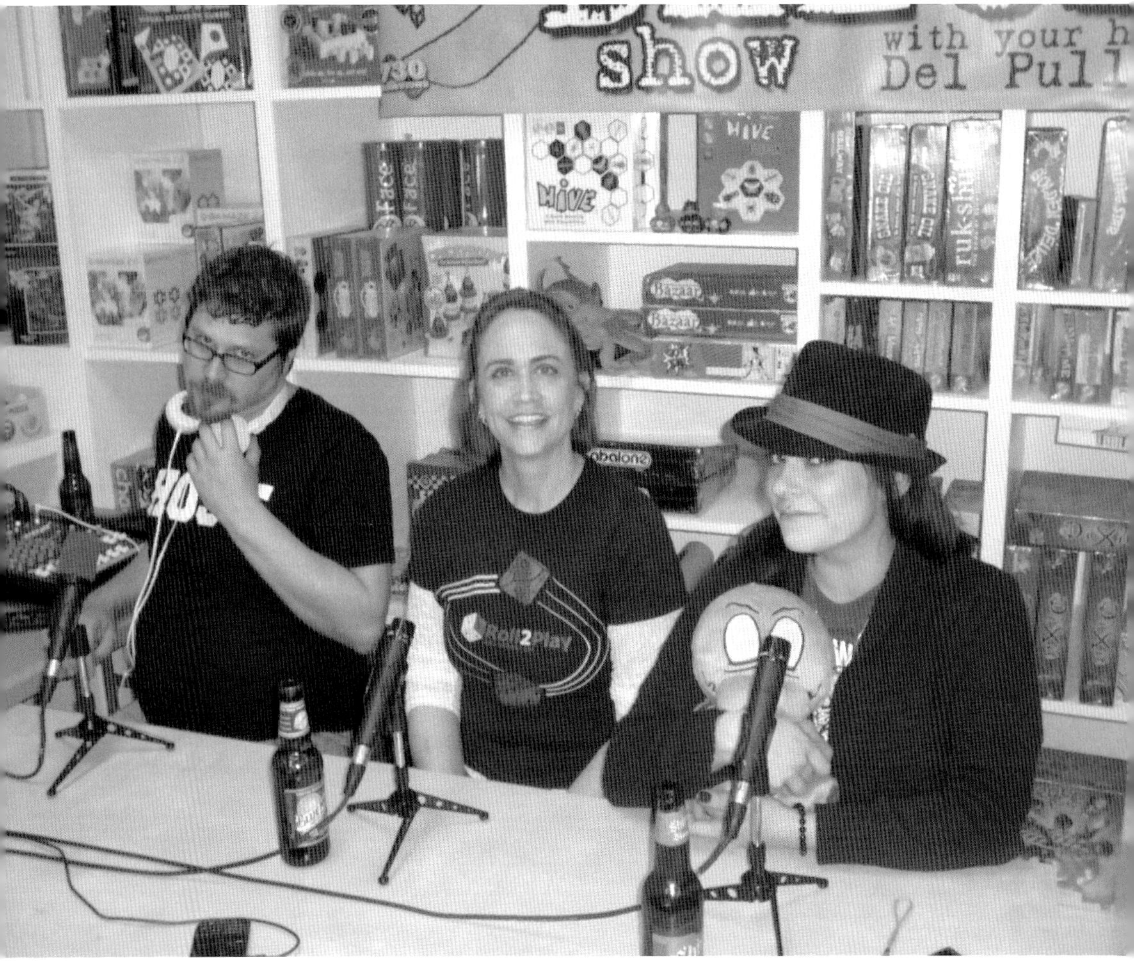

Tiffany Franzioni

Tiffany Franzioni is a self-described "viking or hobbit," in love with good food, story, and company. Since 2012, she has tried to bring this spirit to Coppell through her gaming store Roll2Play. Not content to simply sell games, Franzioni uses her store to build community through the art of game play. She spreads the word through podcasts and her newly launched TABLE gaming convention and promotes gaming innovation by providing a place for local and independent game makers to test their creations.

In addition, Franzioni regularly works at local schools and city events by teaching children how to play a variety of different games. (Courtesy of Tiffany Franzioni.)

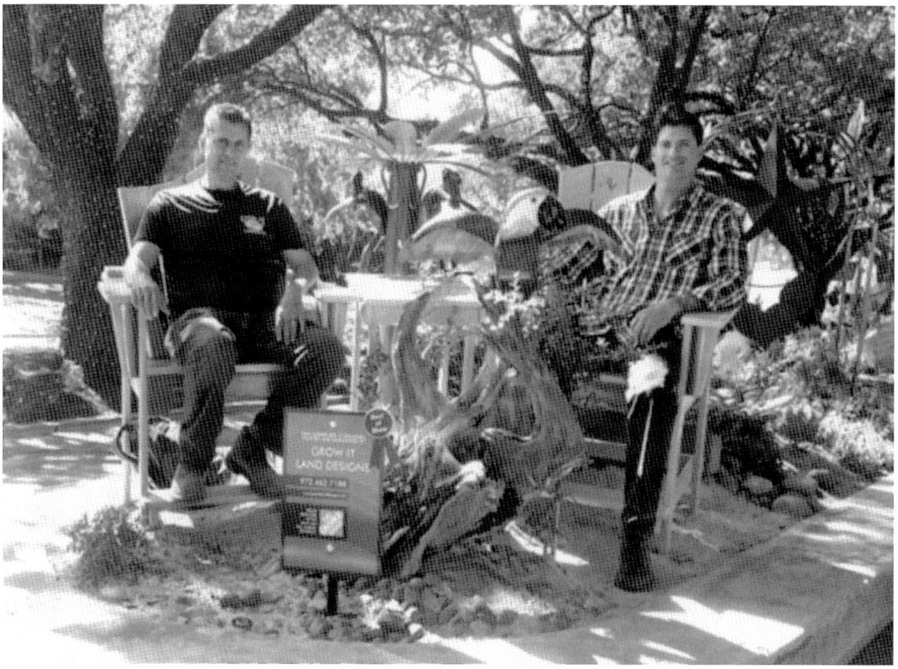

Don and David Flesher

Brothers Don and David Flesher grew up in the garden. Their father was the president of a gardening club, which led Don to study horticulture design at Kansas State University. In 1999, the brothers opened Grow It Landscape Designs and Garden Center, with a retail location opening in Coppell in 2009.

Over the years, the company has won numerous awards including Readers' Choice Awards for landscape services and multiple awards at the State Fair of Texas. These include Best of Show, Best Landscape Design, and the President's Award in 2010. (Both, courtesy of David Flesher.)

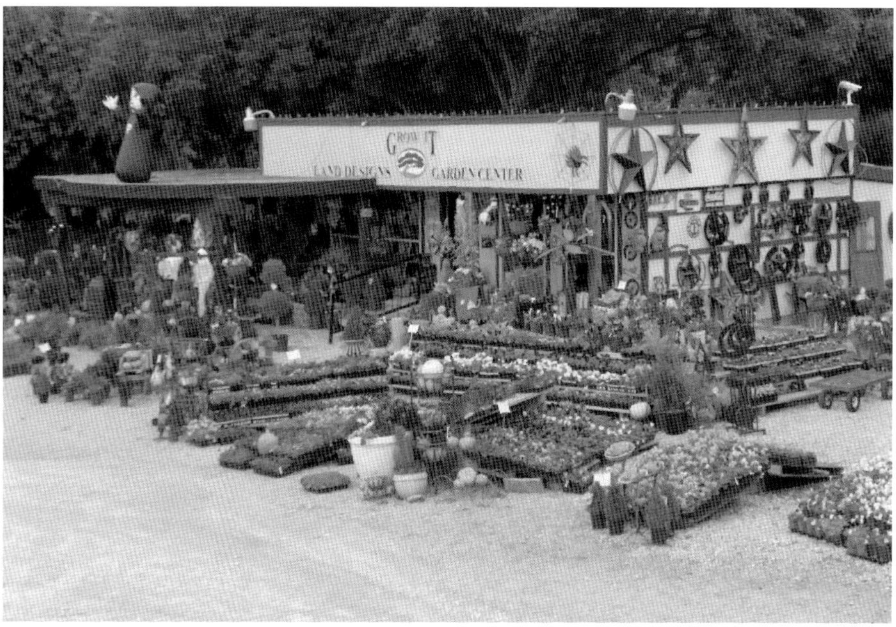

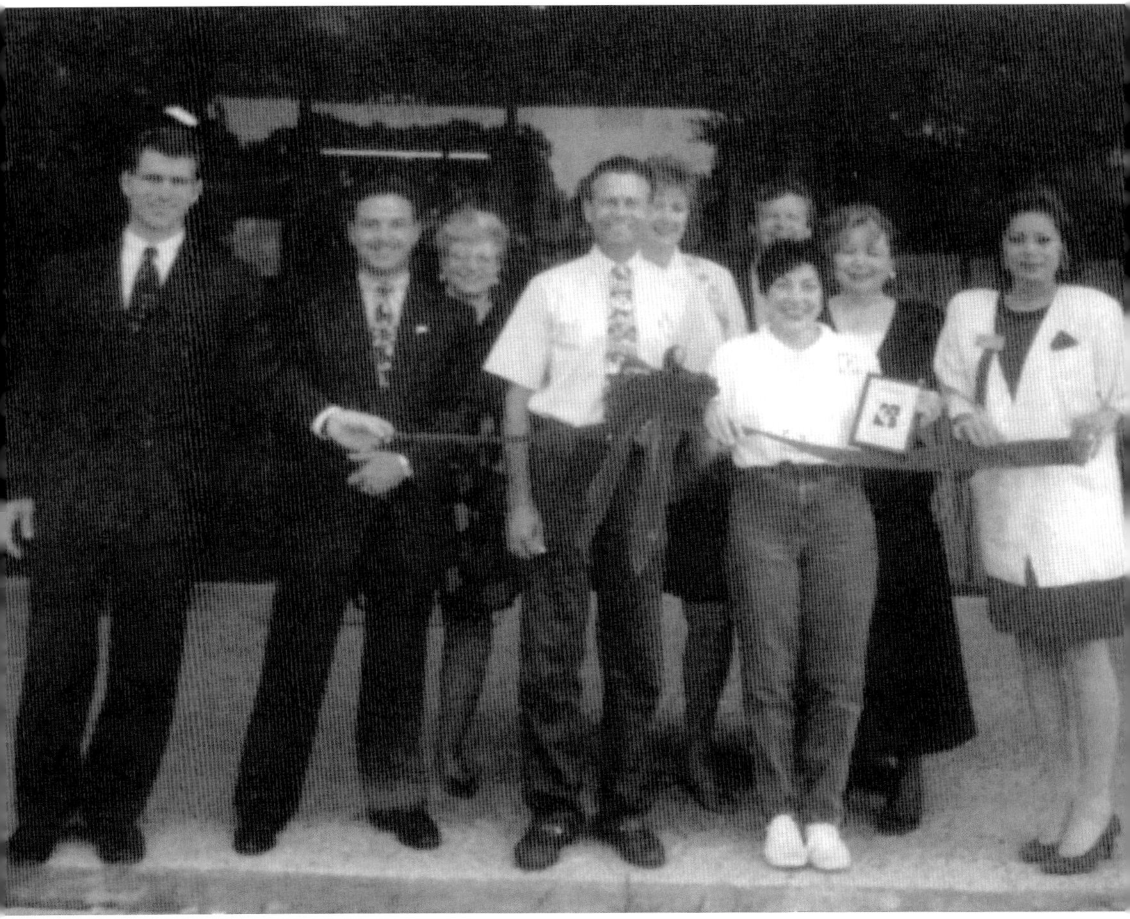

Gloria Salerno

Salerno's Pizza (later Gloria's) opened in 1984. At the time, it was the only Italian restaurant to serve the Coppell and Valley Ranch area. The restaurant was a family venture, founded by four generations of Salernos: Gloria; her mother-in-law, Betty; Betty's mother, Mela; and Gloria's six-month-old daughter, Nicole (credited as public relations). Gloria and Betty ran the day-to-day operations of the restaurant while Mela supplied the recipes.

For 27 years, Gloria's remained a staple in the Coppell community. It even became a regular eating spot for numerous Dallas Cowboys, including Troy Aikman and Roger Staubach. Gloria remembers receiving letters from local women who asked her to deliver their love notes to Aikman.

The restaurant closed its doors in March 2011. (Courtesy of Gloria Salerno.)

CHAPTER TWO

Art

As a child, Kent Darwin spent summers on his grandparents' farm in Arkansas. While there, he developed a deep love of nature that would remain with him his entire life. In 1972, Darwin began studying art in the form of pen drawings, and in 1974, he ventured into watercolors. For a time, he studied with respected American artist Jim Gray. The two shared a passion for land and seascapes, and Gray's influence is evident in Darwin's work.

Darwin moved to Coppell in 1986 and became involved in the Coppell Community Chorale as a singer. In the earliest years, the group was led by Tommy Fineout and had approximately 18 members. The programs tended to resemble variety shows, with the chorale serving as background for featured soloists. Darwin recalls that one early performance was a combination dinner and concert held at popular restaurant Gaspar's (owned by Gaspar Stanic).

Later chorale directors included Barbara Austin, Dr. Robert Chalwell, and current director Maestro Duillio Dobrin. Through it all, Darwin has remained a constant presence and is one of the longest tenured members of the group.

Darwin continued to develop his artistic talents, beginning a study of oil painting in 2005. As he continues to hone his craft, he makes regular retreats to a rural cabin that he owns near the Tennessee River. While there, he enjoys the splendor of nature and finds inspiration. He regularly donates his finished work to various community organizations for fundraisers and acts as a member of Coppell's Arts Council.

Darwin also spent over three decades with 3M's healthcare division, working with groups like Volunteer Hospitals of America and the Hospital Corporation of America. In 2001, he retired and now devotes his time solely to the growth of his artistic skills.

Coppell is home to a wide variety of artists, actors, authors, and musicians. Some, like Emily Elbert, have taken their talents around the globe. Others are content to use their gifts to build home and community.

Alice and Hilary Demske

Sisters Alice and Hilary Demske are two of the most accomplished musicians to come from the city of Coppell. Born to Gary and Davideen Demske, the sisters grew up in Coppell as early members of the city's Church of Jesus Christ of Latter-day Saints.

Alice (right), the older of the two, was born in 1978. She began playing piano at four years old and was teaching by the age of 14. She then went on to study at the Royal Academy of Music in London. While there, she studied under some of the world's great pianists before entering into international competition. She later became an adjunct professor at Utah Valley University and ran her own piano studio.

In May 2012, Alice gave birth to her third child with husband Kurt Hansen. During delivery, she contracted toxic shock syndrome and died several days later. Her obituary noted that for all her musical accomplishments, her greatest achievements came as a mother, wife, and church member. She was remembered for regularly leading her family in the singing of hymns around the piano.

Born in 1980, Hilary (left) also began playing music at a young age. She studied at the Juilliard School, the Peabody Conservatory of Music, and the Munich Conservatory. She also earned a doctorate in piano performance from the University of Michigan.

In 2010, Hilary released her debut album, *Henry Martin: Selected Piano Music*. The recording was met with critical acclaim. Hilary maintains an active touring schedule internationally and is also a music scholar. She has been named an honorary professor at Xi'an University in China and, like her sister did before, serves as a professor for Utah Valley University. (Courtesy of Gary and Davideen Demske.)

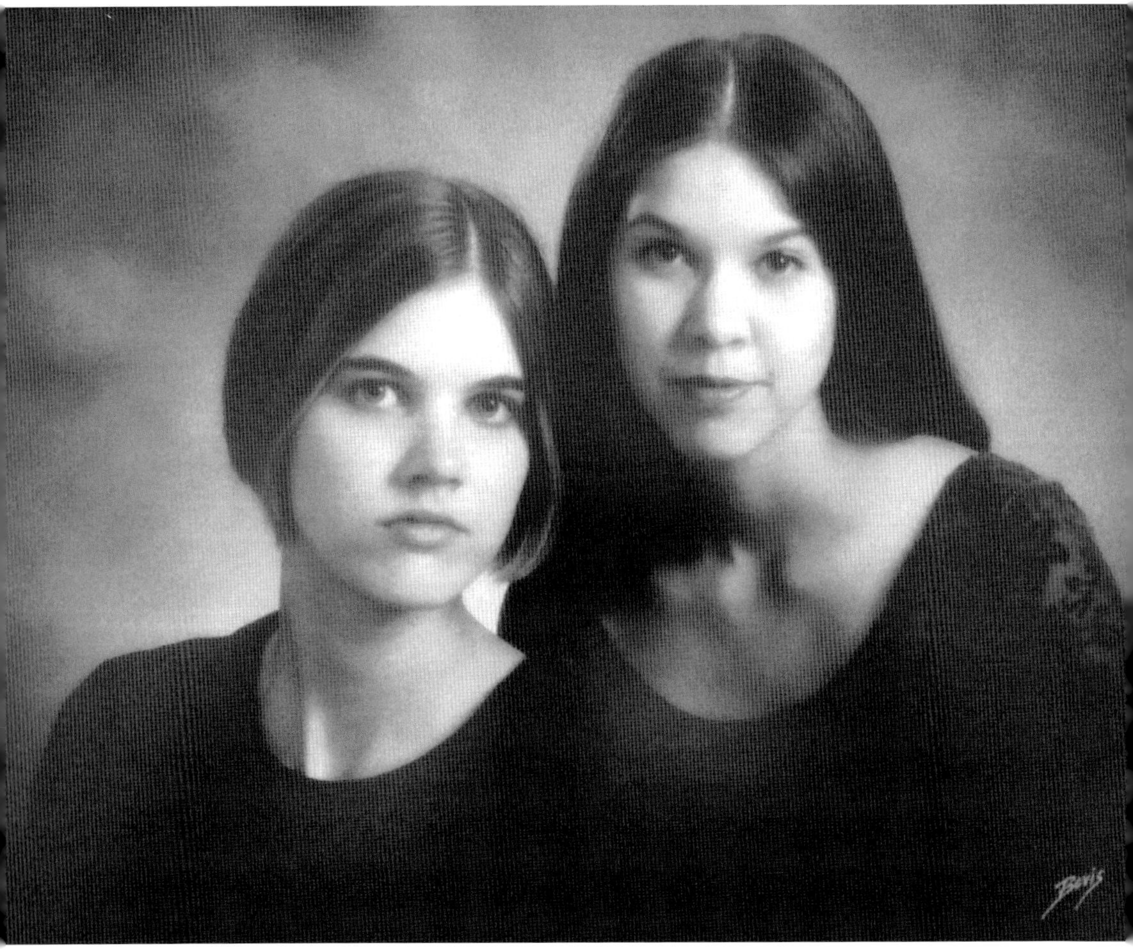

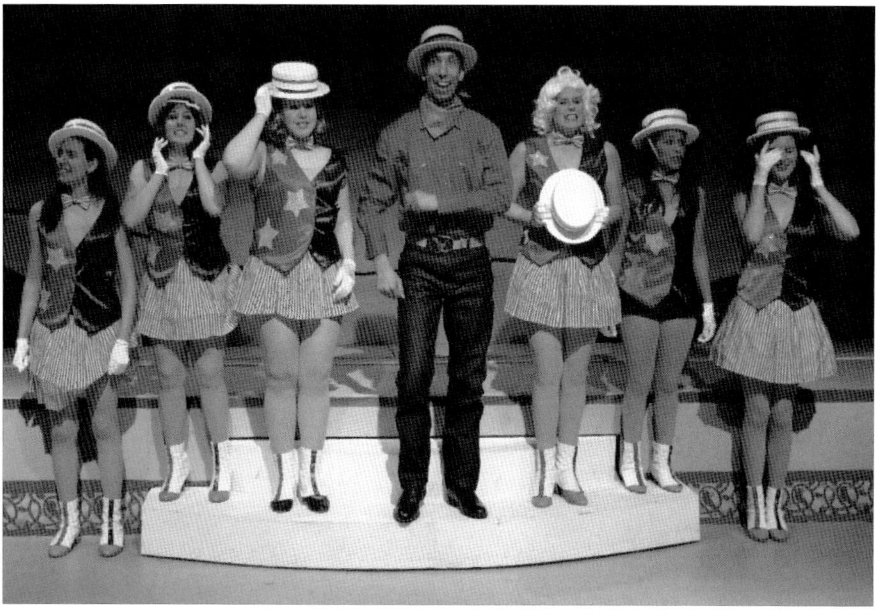

Una Williams and Theatre Coppell

In 1987, Una Williams began leading regular meetings in support of a community theater. The group named itself the Coppell Arts Theatrical Society, which was later changed to Coppell Community Theater. The first stage performance by the young group was a variety show titled *Mostly Music*, followed by a full production of *A Funny Thing Happened on the Way to the Forum*.

Variety shows, haunted houses, and New Year's Eve murder mysteries were staples of the early theater. The productions served as fund-raisers for the theater's more traditional work. Without a theater of its own, the company performed in schools around town. It was not until 1999 that the company moved into its own space. A renovated firehouse was transformed into the Coppell Center for the Arts, where the group continues to perform six shows a year. (Both, courtesy of Theatre Coppell.)

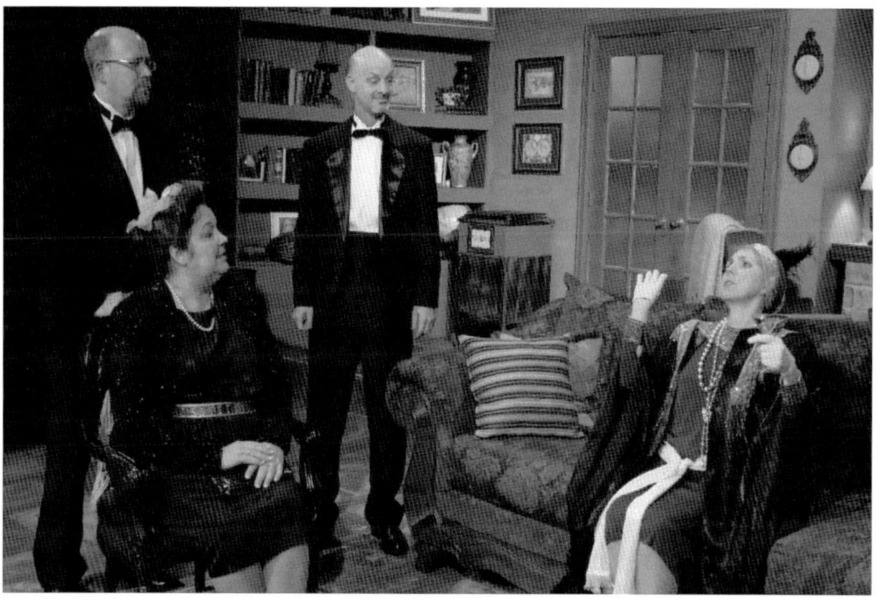

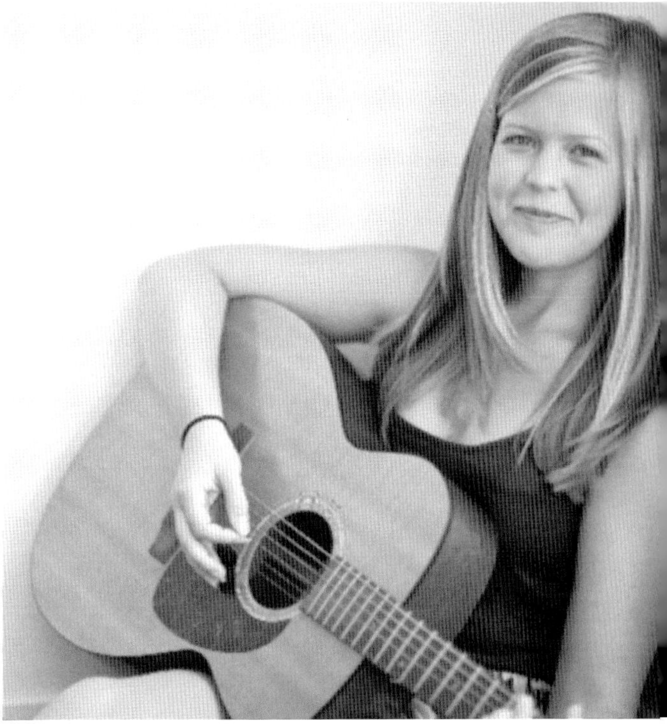

Emily Elbert
Emily Elbert is equal parts gypsy troubadour and jazz chanteuse. A graduate of Boston's prestigious Berklee College of Music, she has recorded four albums and performed in 15 countries ranging from Thailand to Saint Barthélemy. During her travels, she worked with the US Embassy, leading music workshops in places like Palestine, Israel, and Scotland.

Elbert grew up in Coppell and got an early start in music participating in the Methodist children's choir. Her first solo performance came at a middle school talent show where she performed The Mamas & The Papas classic "California Dreaming." (Both, courtesy of Emily Elbert.)

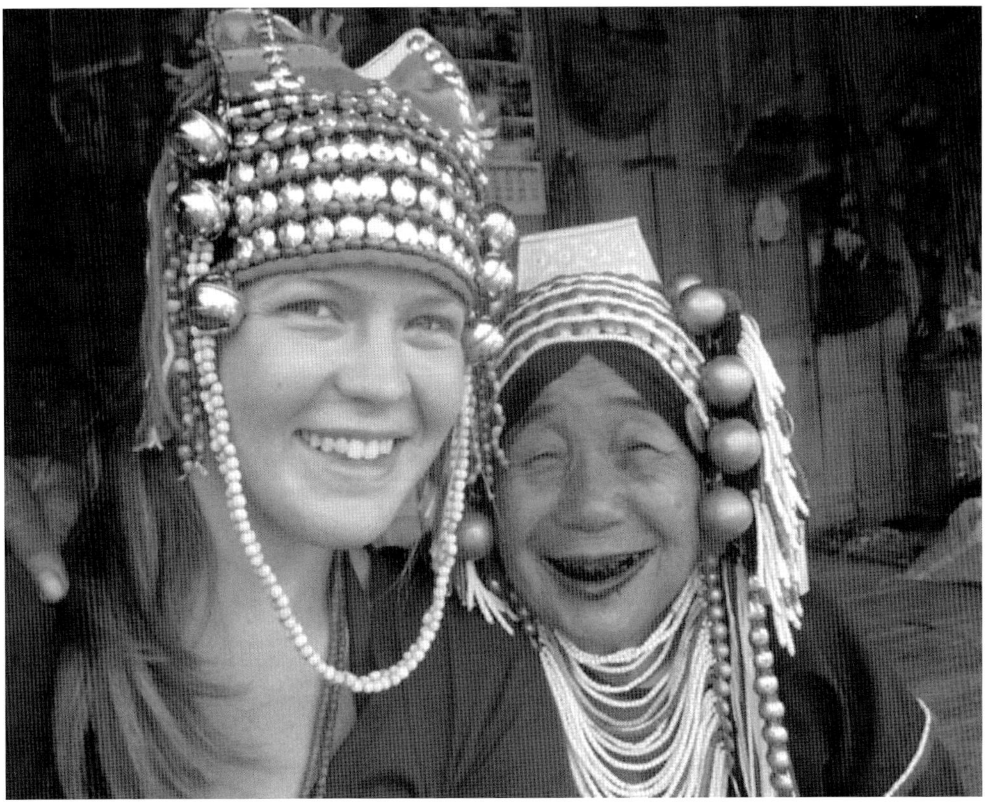

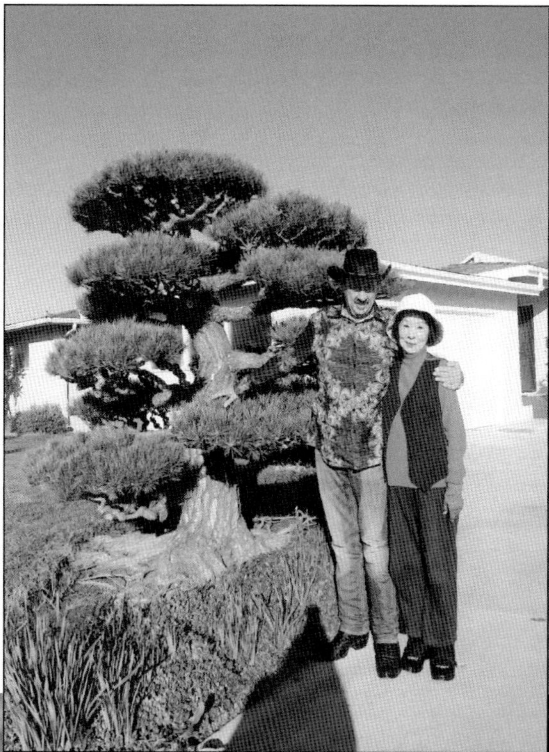

Larry Leone

Larry Leone grew up in Okinawa, Japan. While there, he soaked in the art and culture of Asia, which became profound influences on his later artwork. As an adult, he studied under bonsai master Masura Ishii. With this background, Leone developed living art—microscapes and perspective gardens, typically incorporating bonsai, sculpted stone, and water elements.

In January 2014, Leone reacquired a property he had owned in Coppell some 15 years prior. The building still retained many of the landscape elements that Leone originally built, and, at his son's suggestion, he decided to open it as an art gallery. The result is Deep Forest Gallery, an indoor and outdoor facility that features Leone's work as well as rotating displays of local artists. (Both, courtesy of Deep Forest Gallery.)

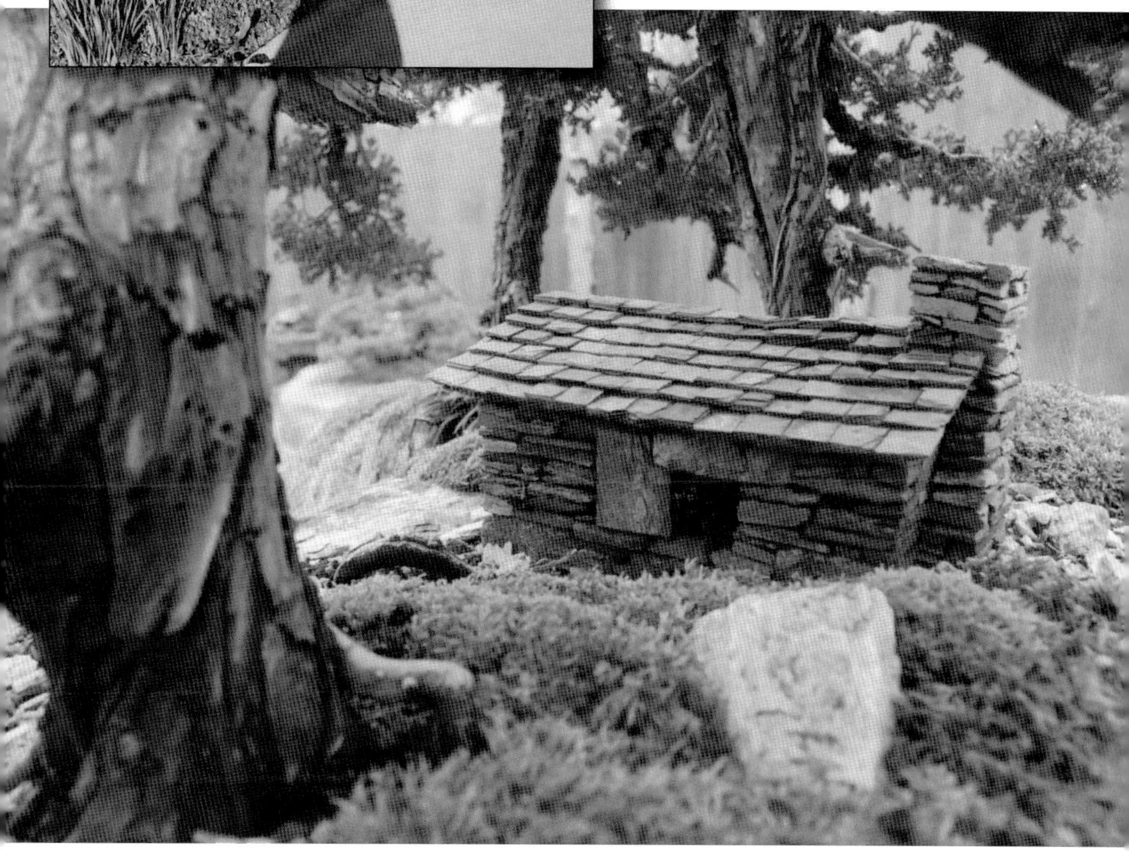

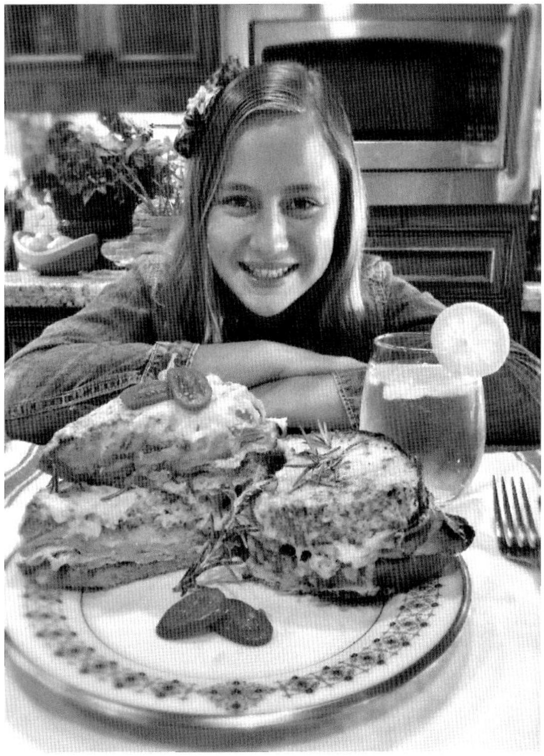

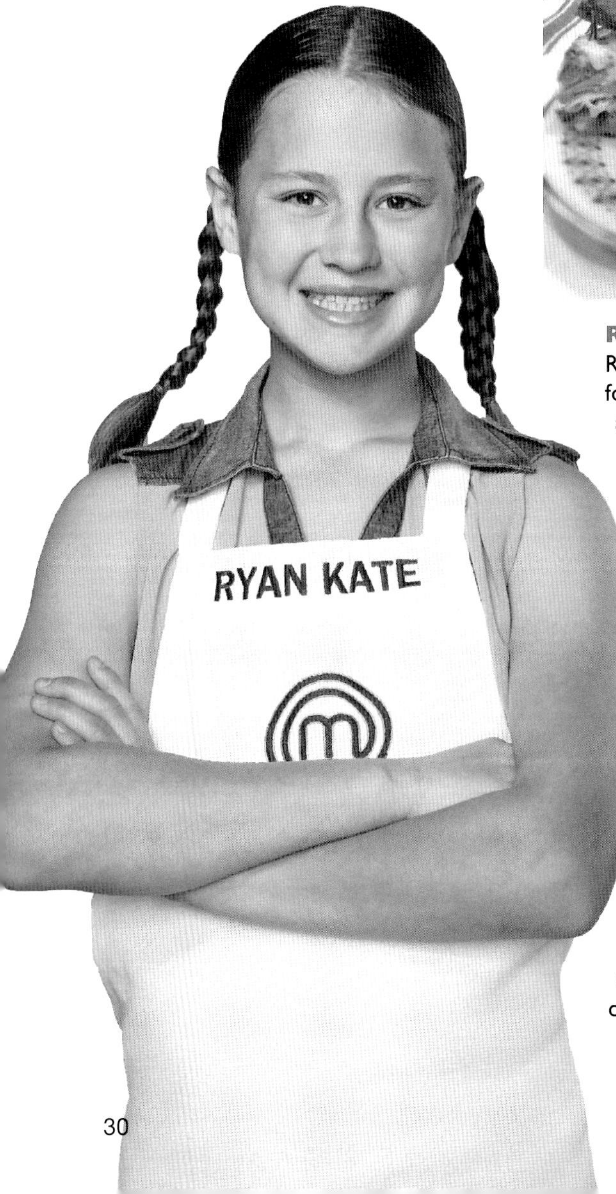

Ryan Kate Brandenburg

Ryan Kate Brandenburg has been in the kitchen for as long as she can remember. After cooking at home, she enrolled in cooking classes in first grade. When the environment proved too stifling for Brandenburg's ability, her mother Cristy found her personal instruction from Coppell resident Gabriella McCord.

Brandenburg appeared as a contestant on the Fox Searchlight series *MasterChef Junior*, where she progressed to the top eight before being sent home.

Brandenburg's life after the show remains busy. She teaches cooking lessons to children and performs catering jobs. She has also worked with Coppell Independent School District (CISD) chef Helen Duran and in community events such as the Farm to Market Diner and Healthy Kids Day. Going forward, she hopes to attend culinary school and potentially open her own restaurant or become a food critic. (Left, courtesy of Greg Gayne / FOX. © FOX Broadcasting Co.; above, courtesy of Cristy Brandenburg.)

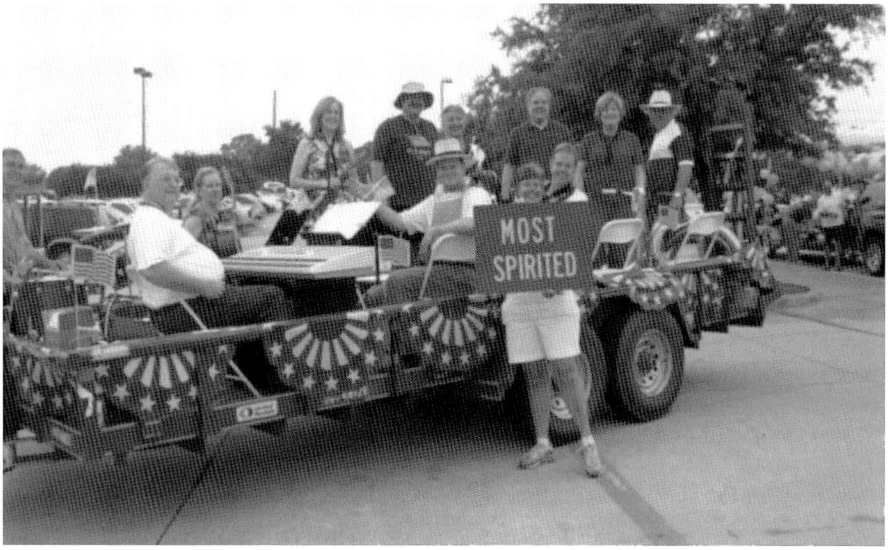

Lisa and Robert Rucker

Founded in 2001 by Lisa and Robert Rucker, the Dixie Disciples performed for over a decade as the "official" Dixie band for the First United Methodist Church of Coppell. The group performed regularly at city picnics, parades, and various church events like the annual Christmas Pops.

The original lineup consisted of Robert Rucker on trombone, Lisa Rucker on tenor saxophone, Holly Whiting on piano, Curtis and Collin Peele on bass and guitar, Haley Heffley on clarinet, Trey Smothermon on trumpet, and Scott Horton on drums. Over the years, the cast changed to include city figures like Councilman Wes Mays on clarinet and Methodist church music minister Ricky Mitchell on trumpet.

The group disbanded in 2013 when the Ruckers moved to Austin, but the Dixie Disciples are still remembered for their pitch perfect performances of jazz standards like Cab Calloway's "Minnie the Moocher" and Louis Armstrong's "What a Wonderful World."

Above, Lisa is fourth from left and Robert is third from right. Below, Robert is second from left in the first row. (Both, courtesy of Lisa Rucker.)

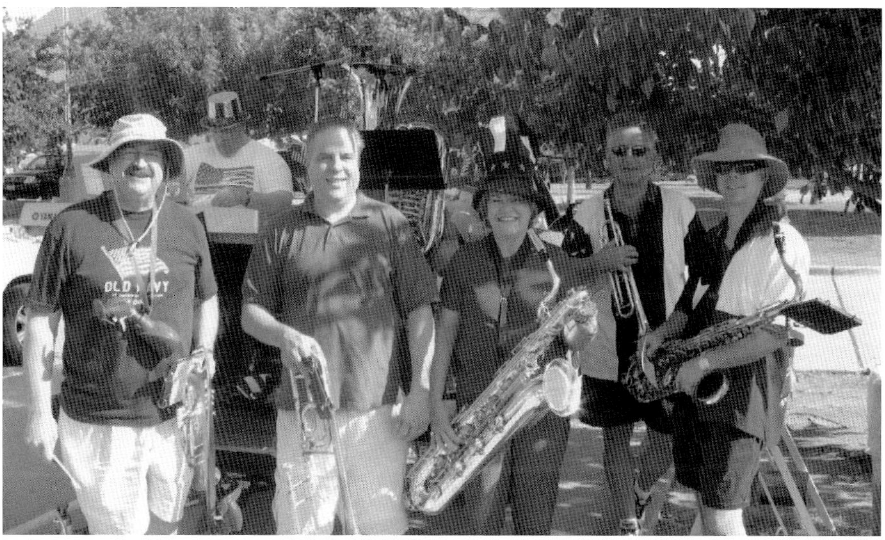

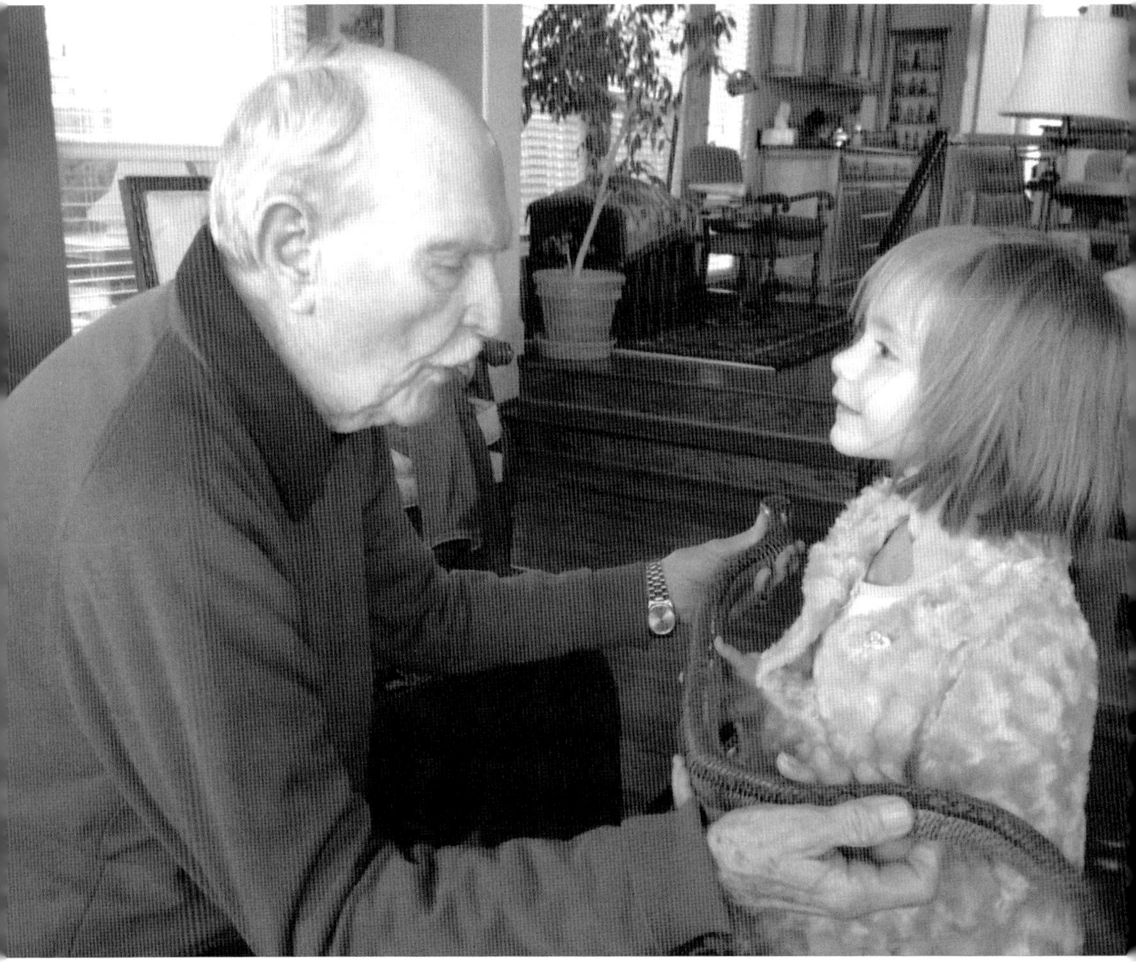

Jack Simmons

When Jack Simmons moved to Coppell in 2008, he had already blazed quite a trail in life. A successful businessman, he ran a large property tax company and worked for Six Flags Over Texas. He had a passion for assessing and buying land across the state. He took part in the founding of community theaters in Boerne and Bulverde, Texas. For a time in the 1960s, he owned an apartment complex in the Deep Ellum district of Dallas. He also assisted in the opening of the Early Learning Center of Saint Mark Presbyterian Church in Boerne.

A passionate actor, Simmons appeared in over 60 plays, including roles for Theatre Coppell and events at the Coppell Methodist church. He frequently reprised the role of Pontius Pilate, which he relished for the complexities inherent in the character.

At the time of his passing in 2015, he was working on a memoir titled *Folks I've Known*. (Courtesy of Jennifer Scott.)

CHAPTER THREE

Schools

Mary Jean Redden was born and raised in Coppell. In 1981, she graduated from Coppell High School (then located at present-day Middle School West) with a class of 38 students. The schools were a far cry from the mammoth institutions of today. In 2014, Coppell High School boasted a graduating class of 711 students.

In 1986, Redden joined the cafeteria staff at Coppell's newly opened Austin Elementary. In the 28 years that followed, she has worked in every school in the district. She helped open Cottonwood Elementary in 1996 and Richard J. Lee Elementary in 2014 (where she currently serves as cafeteria manager).

Redden, along with colleagues Robyn Anderson and Christine Elliot, has seen many changes in school cafeterias. In her earlier years, the majority of food was still cooked from scratch. Ground beef was used to make spaghetti sauce and tacos, and the cafeteria baked its own cornbread, rolls, and cookies. Desserts were offered with meals, and the elementary school still allowed deep fryers. Today, increased health awareness has led to whole grains, fruits, and the use of processed meats.

Over the years, Redden has taken inspiration from a poem titled "Hey Lady!" by Betty DeLozier, in which a student tells his lunch lady, "We don't get much food on our table," and asks, "Would you love me just a little today?" When reflecting on her years of service, Redden describes her work as a journey and a blessing, noting that, for some students, the meal she provides may be the only one they get to eat.

Coppell's school system has been described as the engine that drives the city, playing a significant role in the explosive growth from 1980 onward. Today, the district boasts 10 elementary schools, three middle schools, two high schools, and an alternative education facility. The school system is Coppell's single largest employer, with over 1,200 employees serving close to 10,000 students. The town is also home to a number of private and pre-K learning facilities. Maintaining such an enormous enterprise requires countless individuals who, like Mary Redden, view their work as a calling.

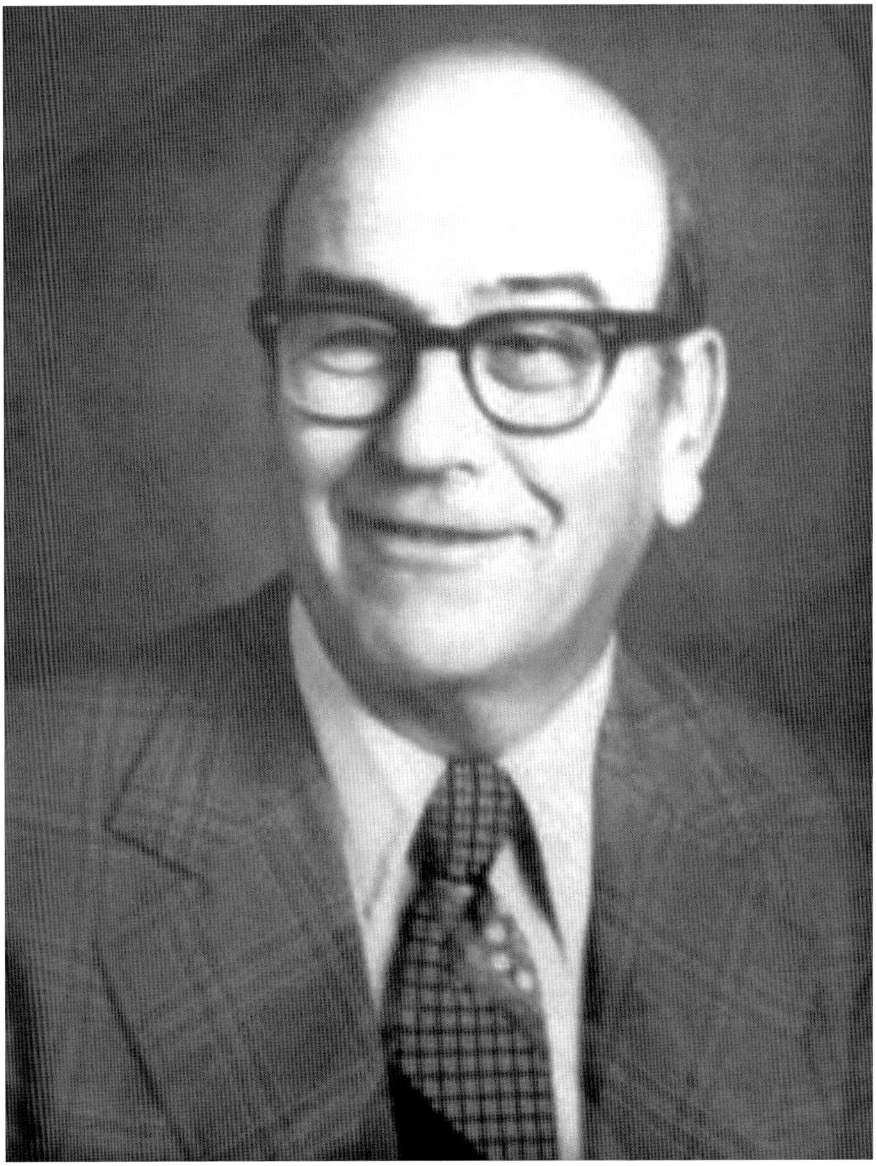

Woodrow Wilson Pinkerton

Woodrow Wilson Pinkerton was born on January 1, 1918, in Pike, Texas. He served in World War II as a member of the US Army.

Following the war, Pinkerton devoted his life to education. He served as superintendent of several schools in addition to holding the position of president at Clarendon Junior College.

In 1963, he became the first superintendent of the CISD, which was formed in 1959. During Pinkerton's time as superintendent, the school began transitioning to a full 12-grade system. The process was completed in 1965.

In 1967, Coppell's oldest school, originally established in 1928, was renamed Pinkerton Elementary.

Outside the realm of education, Pinkerton was an active member of Coppell's First Baptist Church, serving the church as an ordained deacon.

Pinkerton died in 1977 at the age of 59. (Courtesy of Pinkerton Elementary School.)

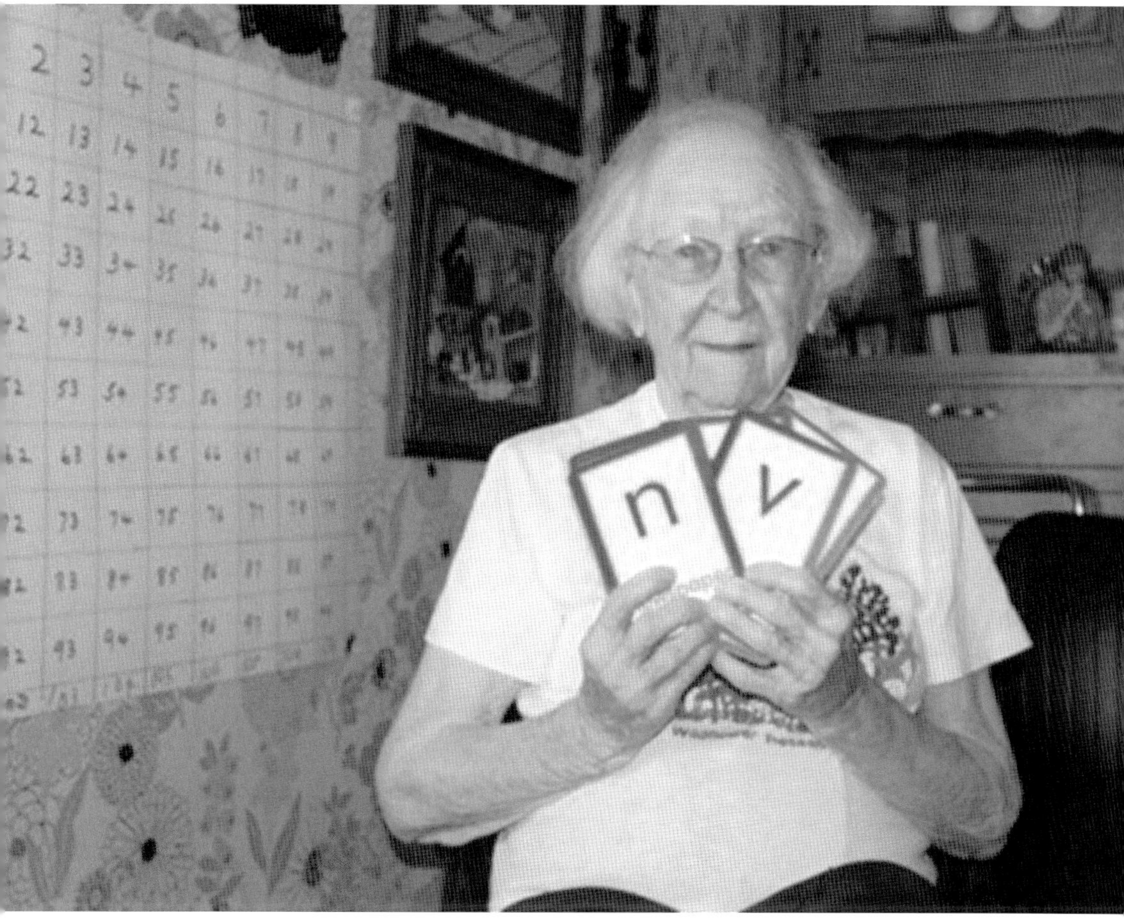

Ruby Handley
Ruby Handley spent close to three decades as a teacher before retiring in 1975. A resident of Denton, Handley taught in the Caddo area, temporarily leaving the profession at the end of World War II. For a time, she helped her husband run a dairy farm, but in 1957, decided to return to teaching.

In 1957, she was recruited to join the Coppell School staff. Though she remained a resident of Denton, she commuted to town every day, bringing along her young daughter (who eventually graduated from Coppell schools). During her time in Coppell, Handley taught first, third, and fifth grade.

In late 2014, her service to Coppell was remembered in a front-page article in the *Citizens' Advocate*. Handley died shortly after turning 101. (Courtesy of the Coppell Historical Society.)

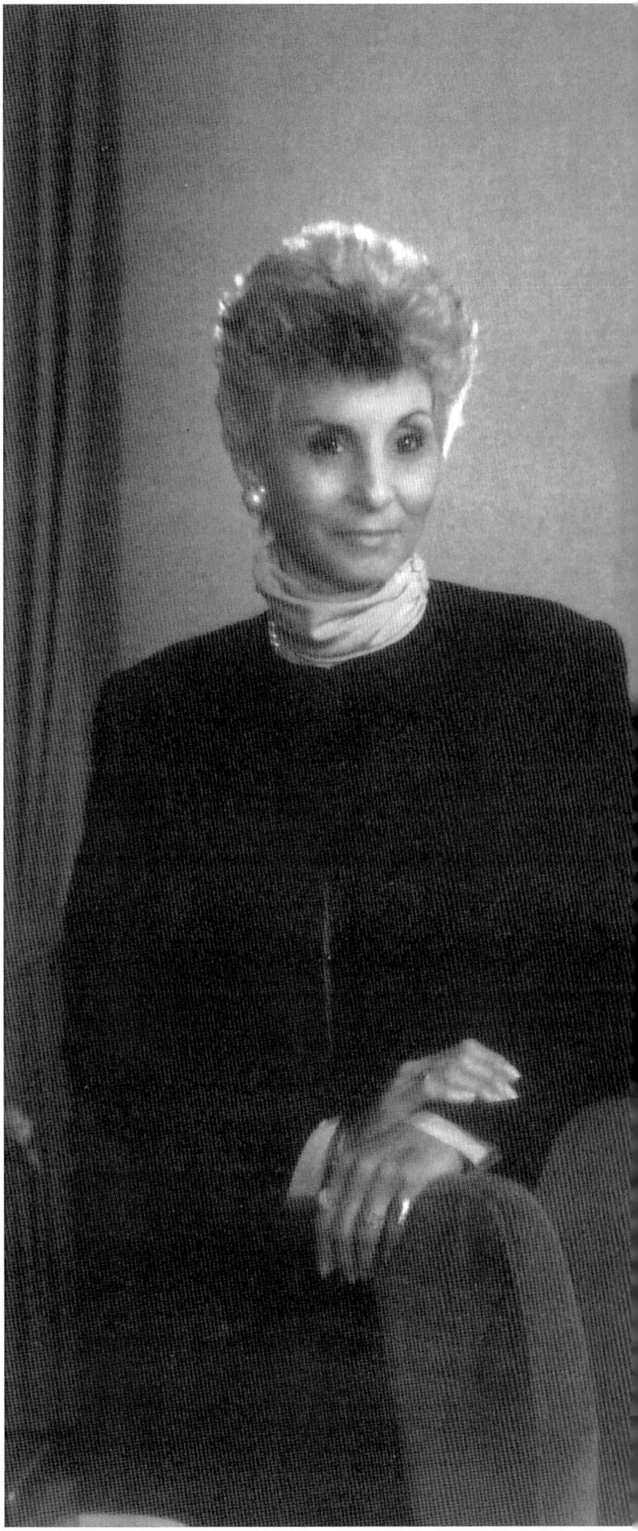

Barbara Austin

When Barbara Austin moved to Coppell, she was looking for a quiet, country home for her family and a place to stable her horses. She eventually settled into a large stone house built in 1936. The house was given the name Homewood by the builder.

Austin's children attended the Coppell School, where Austin played an active role in the PTA. As a former teacher, she was encouraged by Superintendent W.W. Pinkerton to run for the school board. She received a good deal of resistance as a woman running for the board. She still remembers one resident saying they "never had a woman on the school board—never would!" Despite this, Austin was elected and later became president.

She served the board during a time of considerable growth in Coppell. She worked to gain public approval for bonds to purchase land for future schools, including the high school. In 1976, she helped the city celebrate the country's bicentennial by directing a musical comedy called *Let George Do It*. The cast was composed of students, parents, teachers, and coaches.

In 1987, the school board decided to honor Austin's service to Coppell by naming a school after her. They worked to keep the naming a secret until the night of the announcement. The school, which sits on Moore Road, still bears the name Barbara S. Austin Elementary.

After leaving Homewood, Austin was given the chance to work with developers in building a new neighborhood on her old land. She designed the layout of the streets and named the roads. The development was given the name Austin Place. (Courtesy of Barbara Austin.)

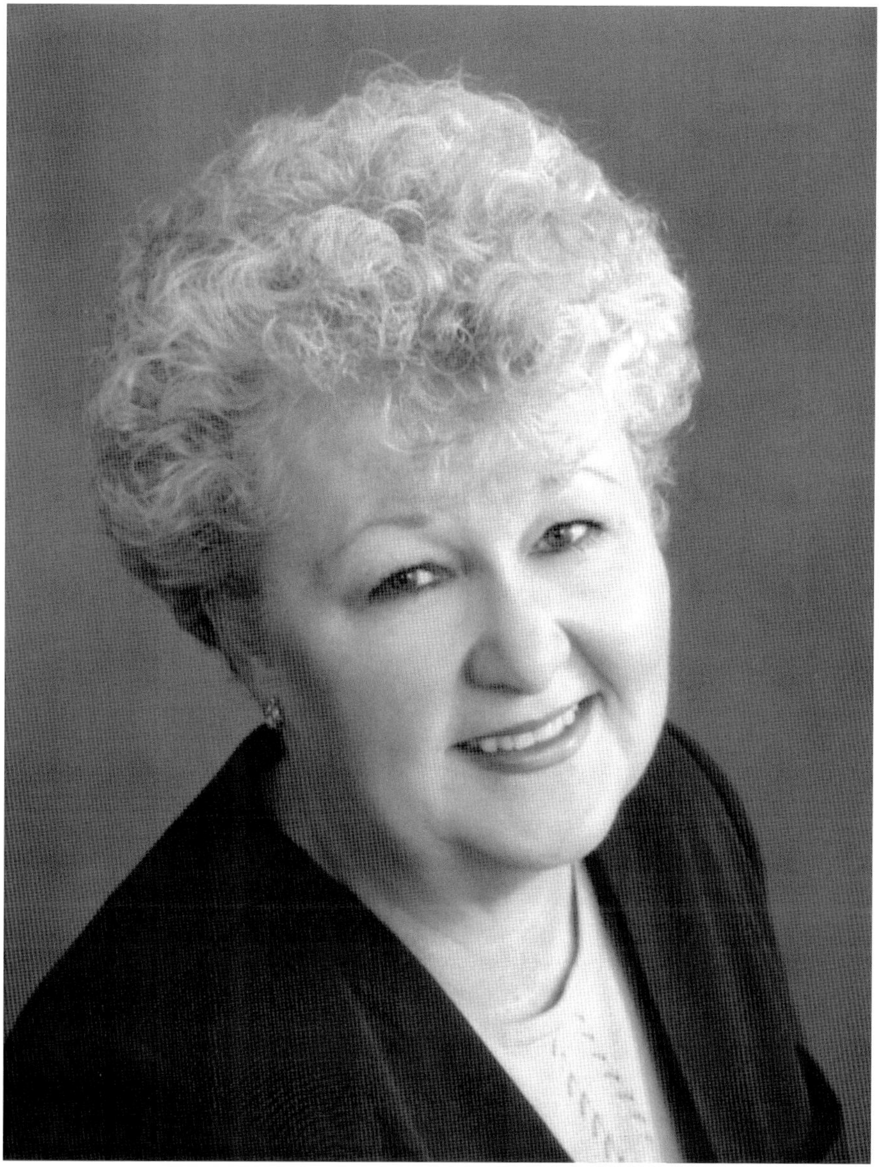

Vonita White
Vonita White moved to Coppell in 1971 and became a member of the town's Assembly of God congregation. She served as the children's church director as well as director of the adult choir program. Though the congregation has since merged with a church in Lewisville, Texas, White's singing is still remembered by former members of the church.

White also spent 32 years as a part of the CISD. During that time, she served as a teacher, middle school principal, assistant superintendent, and twice as interim superintendent.

White was awarded Outstanding Educator of the Year and was once named to a list of Coppell's 50 most influential women. In addition, she was honored by the Metrocrest Women's Charity as Woman of the Year.

White retired from Coppell education in 2003. Today, the CISD administrative building bears her name in recognition of her years of service. (Courtesy of Vonita White.)

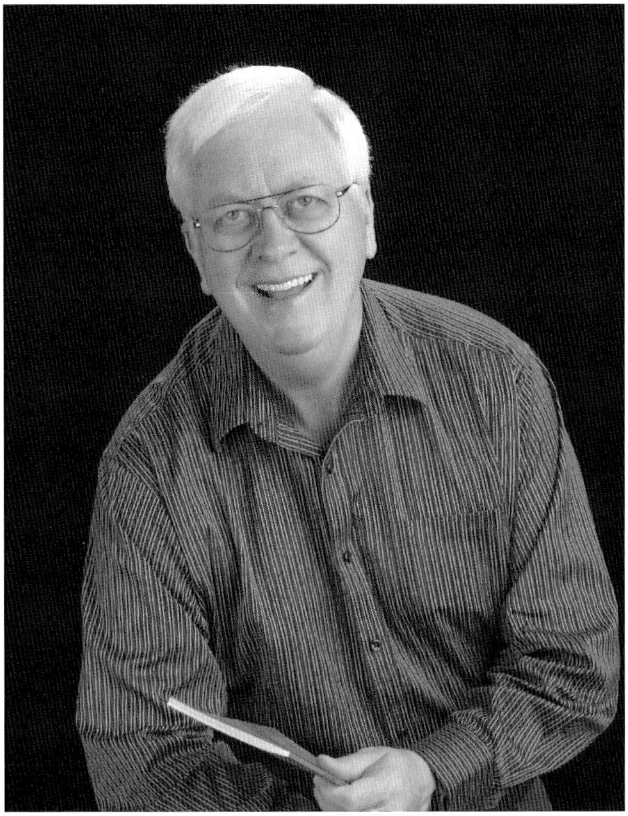

Wheelice "Pete" Wilson Jr.

Wheelice "Pete" Wilson Jr. was born and raised in Coppell. His parents, Wheelice and Ruby Nell Wilson, were always involved in the life of the community.

As a young man, Wilson ran a fireworks stand outside of his house. The project began as his father's attempt to teach his son how to conduct business. In the fall, the young Wilson would convert the stand into a haunted house, charging 5¢ a visitor (though, to his recollection, he may have only totaled five customers).

In high school, Wilson was involved in the drama program, which began his senior year. He took part in the production of a one-act play that was put on for competition. It was also during this time that he began looking for information on New York businessman George Coppell and his links to the city. Wilson graduated in the first class of students from Coppell High School in 1965 and was honored as the first Mr. CHS in recognition of his school involvement.

Wilson attended North Texas State University, beginning his studies as a physics major before gaining a degree in government and eventually earning a master's degree in speech and drama. He later went on to postgraduate doctorate work.

Wilson returned to Coppell as the drama teacher at Coppell High School, where he remained for 36 years until his retirement. During that time, he also acted as department head for the fine arts.

During the 1980s, Wilson was heavily involved in the theater at North Park before helping to found the company that would become Theatre Coppell. The troupe is comprised entirely of volunteers, and Wilson remains the artistic director to this day.

Wilson is active in the Coppell Historical Society. Over the years, he has gathered and archived thousands of pictures and written papers documenting town history. He recorded lengthy interviews with the town's oldest residents. He has also been instrumental in the protection of Old Town Coppell and the creation of Heritage Park. (Courtesy of Wheelice Wilson Jr.)

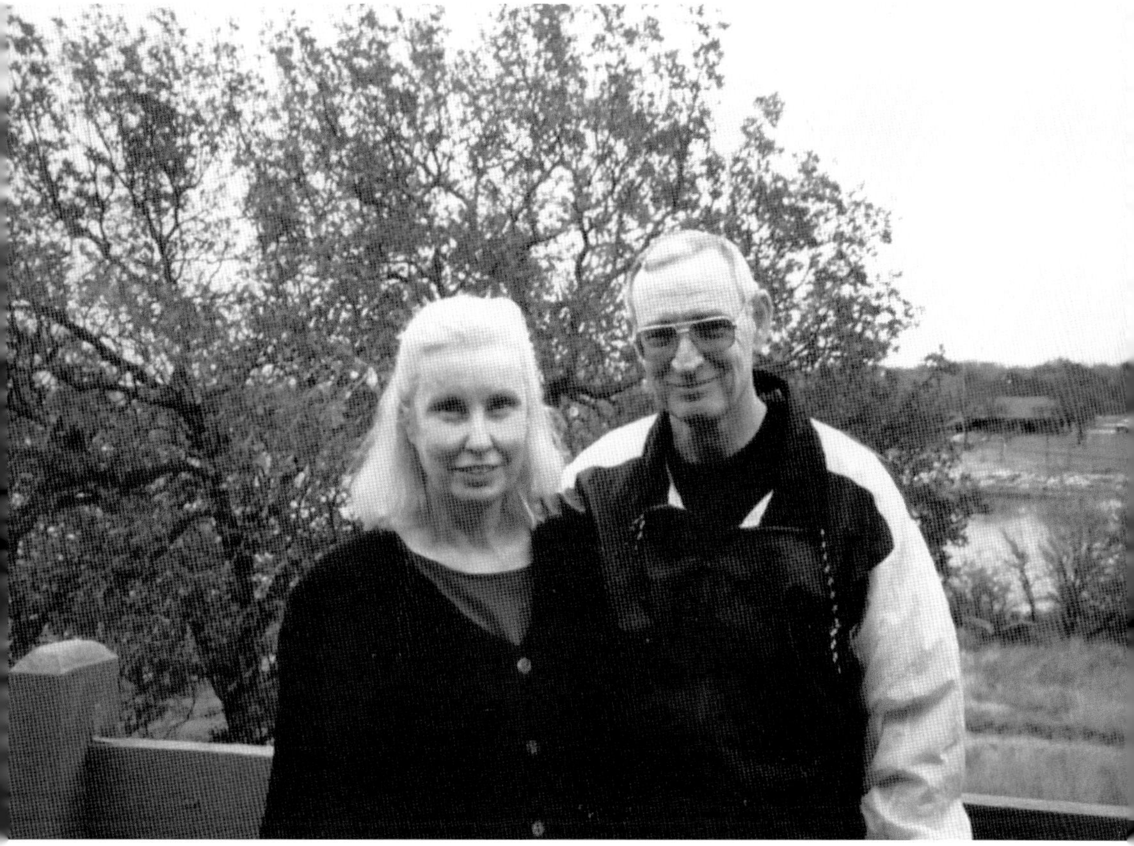

John and Anita Bowen
John and Anita Bowen were teachers in Coppell's schools for a combined 33 years. John was a student in Coppell from fifth to eighth grade before attending Grapevine High School (Coppell had yet to establish a high school). After serving in the US Air Force, he taught sixth grade for two years at Pinkerton Elementary. He then became the geography, world history, and driver's education teacher at Coppell High School.

Anita began her career as a reporter for the *Fort Worth Press*. She began teaching at Keller Middle School before going on to teach English as a second language, American history, journalism, yearbook, photography, and video at Coppell High School. Anita has also written for children's magazines and published several romance novels that have been translated into multiple languages.

The Bowens retired in 1999 and have spent the years since traveling in their RV. (Courtesy of Anita Bowen.)

Dena Nichols

For 17 years, Dena Nichols has served as the director of Coppell's Stringfellow School. Nichols received a degree in elementary education at Texas Tech University and a master's in educational diagnostics from East Texas State University. Prior to coming to Stringfellow, Nichols spent nine years as a kindergarten teacher and one year teaching preschool.

Nichols explains Stringfellow's teaching philosophy as one that believes that children learn best through developmentally appropriate play. The school provides chapel, music, science, and movement classes along with an outdoor learning environment. The result has been 30 years of education with an average of 200 students each year. In 2013, the school was chosen as the best preschool in Coppell in the *Star Local Media*'s Reader's Choice Awards. (Courtesy of Dena Nichols.)

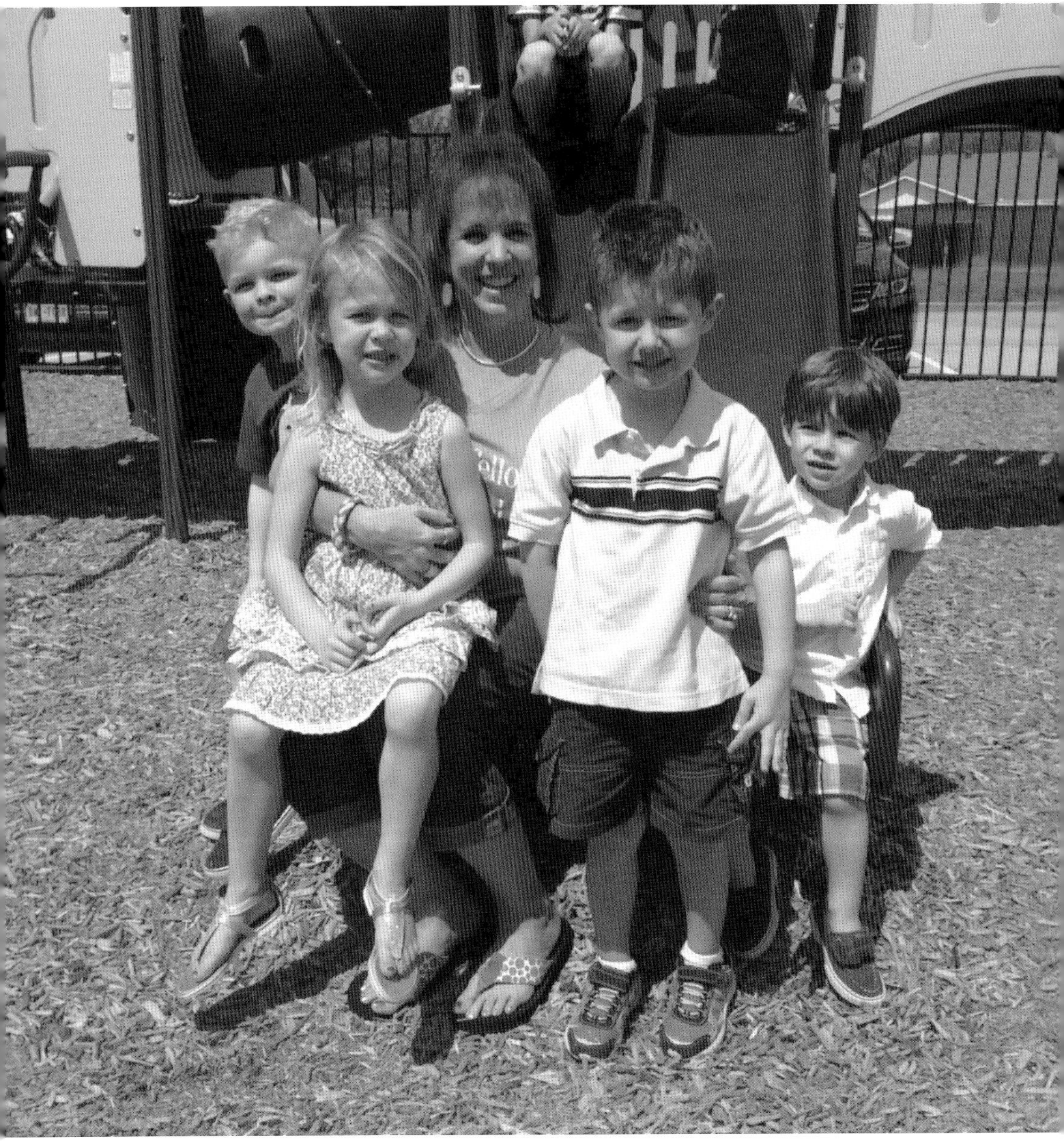

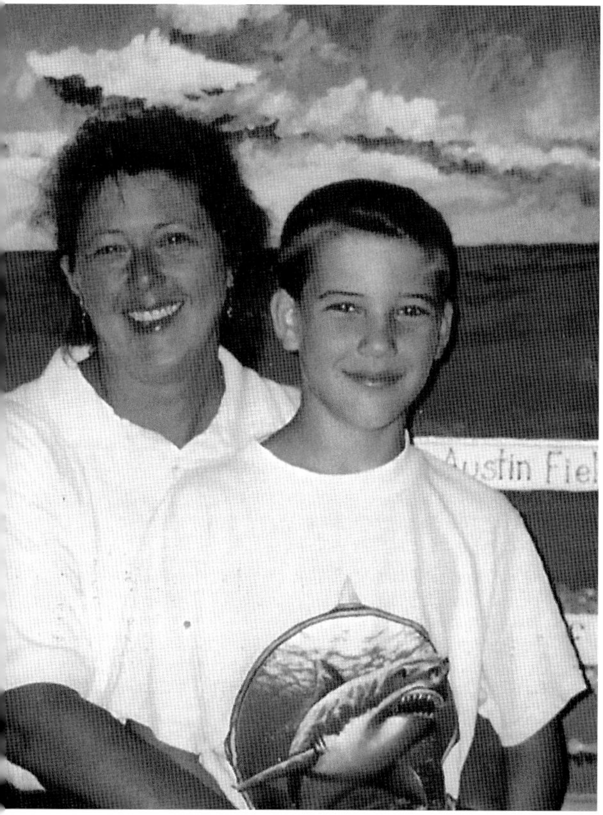

Gay Dobecka

Gay Dobecka is a lifelong resident of Coppell. Parents Richard and Barbara Lee have a long history of community and school involvement, making it no surprise that Dobecka has devoted her life to teaching.

Dobecka graduated from Coppell High School in 1978 with a senior class that totaled 28 students. She then went on to play basketball while attending Oklahoma Baptist University and Baylor University. During that time, she dreamed of coaching and never really considered a profession outside of education.

Dobecka taught at Coppell High School and Coppell Middle School until 1987, when she became the physical education teacher for the newly opened Barbara S. Austin Elementary. In 2015, Dobecka celebrated her 25th year with the school. She and Beth Cook are the only teachers to remain on staff since its opening.

Below, Gay is in front. (Both, courtesy of Gay Dobecka.)

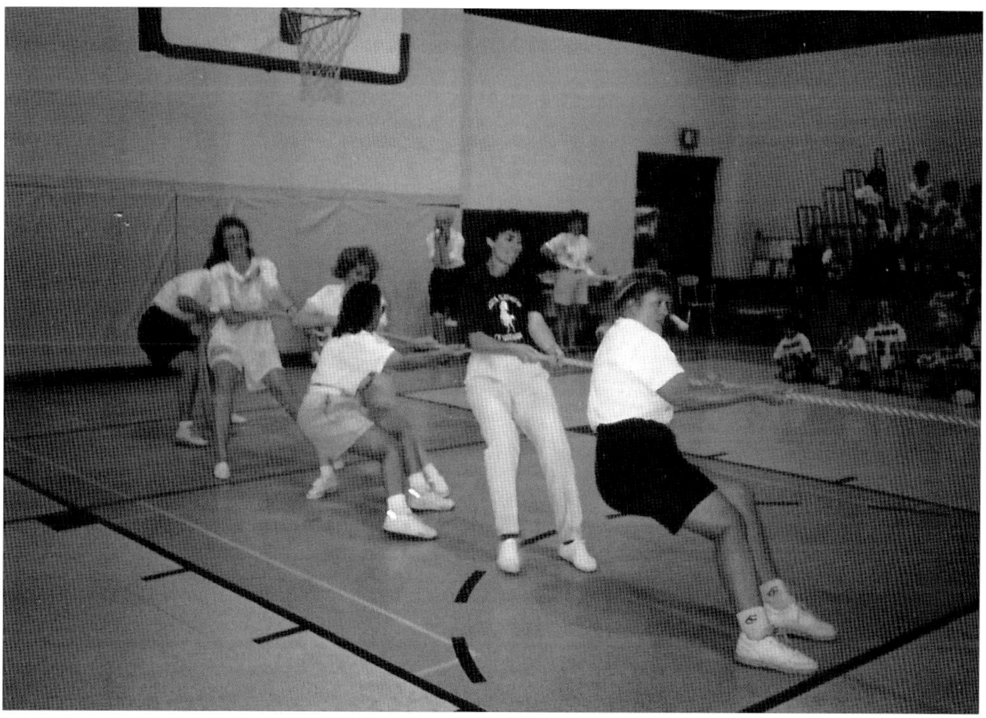

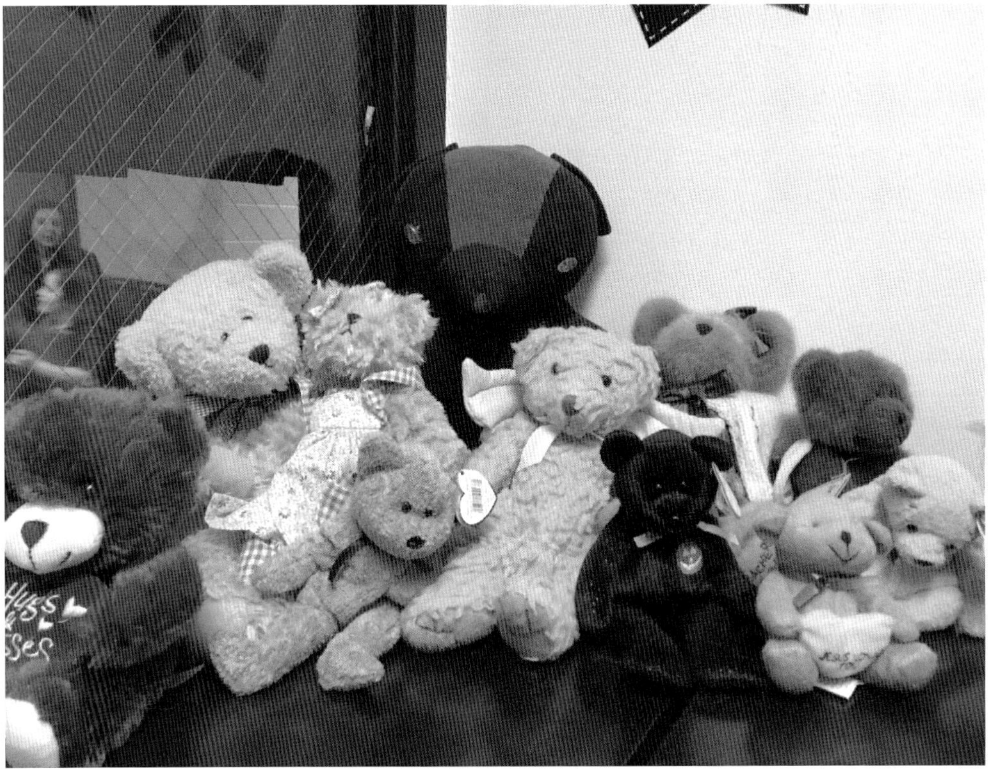

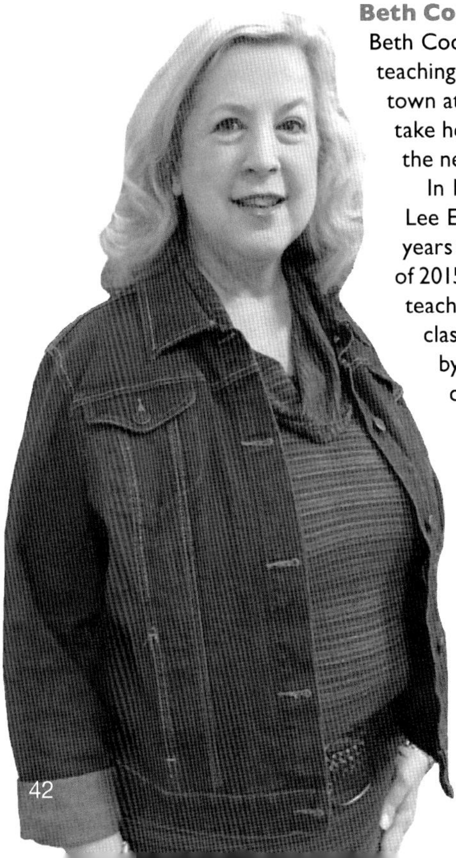

Beth Cook

Beth Cook has been a teacher in Coppell for 34 years. She began teaching at Pinkerton Elementary, which was the only school in town at the time. She remembers that, during recess, she would take her fifth grade students across the street to pick cotton in the neighboring fields.

In 1983, she became a fifth grade teacher at the newly opened Lee Elementary. She became a third grade teacher after three years and then, in 1987, began teaching at Austin Elementary. As of 2015, Cook continues to teach at the school as a second grade teacher with a focus on reading, writing, and social studies. Her classroom is filled with gifts of stuffed bears presented to her by students whom she affectionately refers to as "Cook's cubs." (Both, courtesy of Beth Cook.)

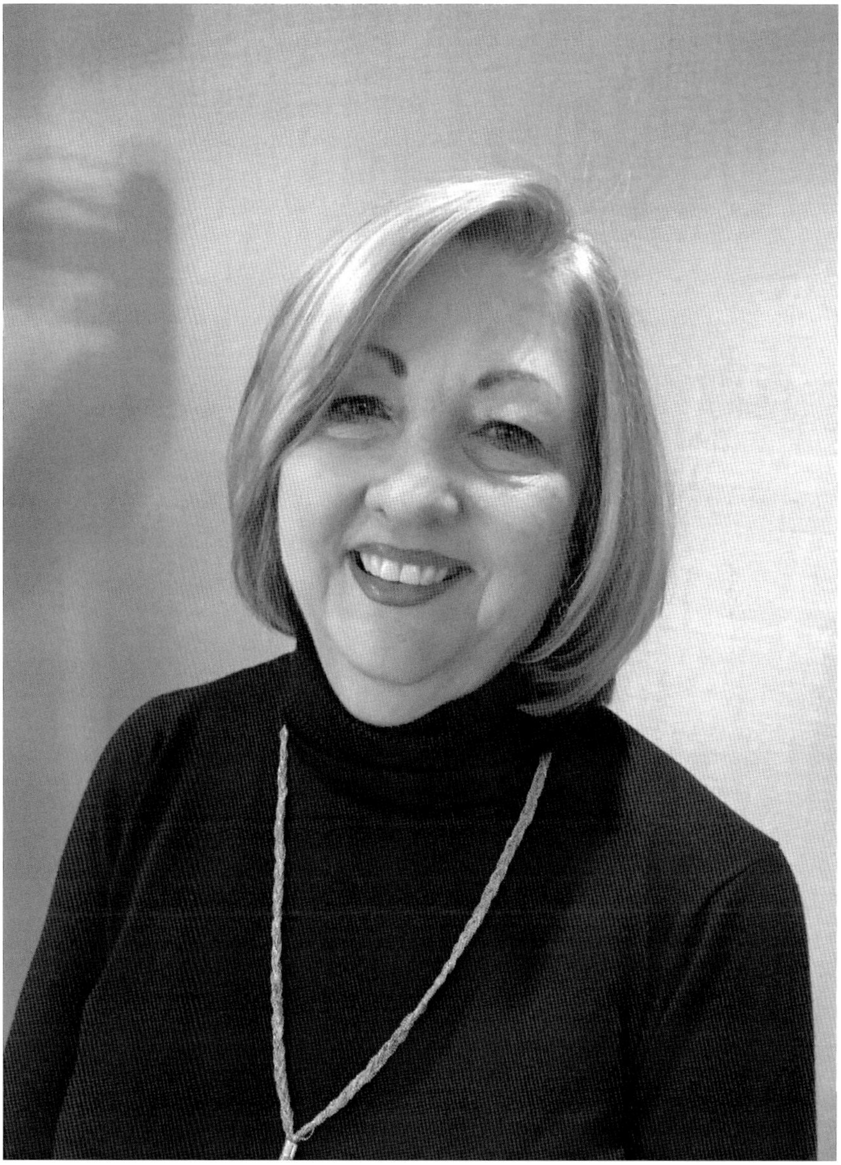

Joy Smartt
Joy Smartt was educated at Baylor University and began her teaching career in the city of Irving. During that time, she met her husband, William Terrell "B.J." Smartt, while living in the Village Apartments in Dallas.

Joy and B.J. moved to Coppell in 1984, and Joy eventually began working for the Coppell School District where she remained for almost 17 years. During that time, she taught at Austin Elementary, where she served as an elementary consultant and instructional specialist. In 1996, she became assistant principal at Lee Elementary. In 1998, she became principal of Coppell's oldest school, Pinkerton Elementary, where she remained for the next 10 years.

In 2008–2009, Joy joined the district's curriculum team as the director of mathematics for kindergarten through eighth grade. Joy also served on the board and was responsible for establishing the Stringfellow School, a private early education facility run through the Methodist church. (Courtesy of Joy Smartt.)

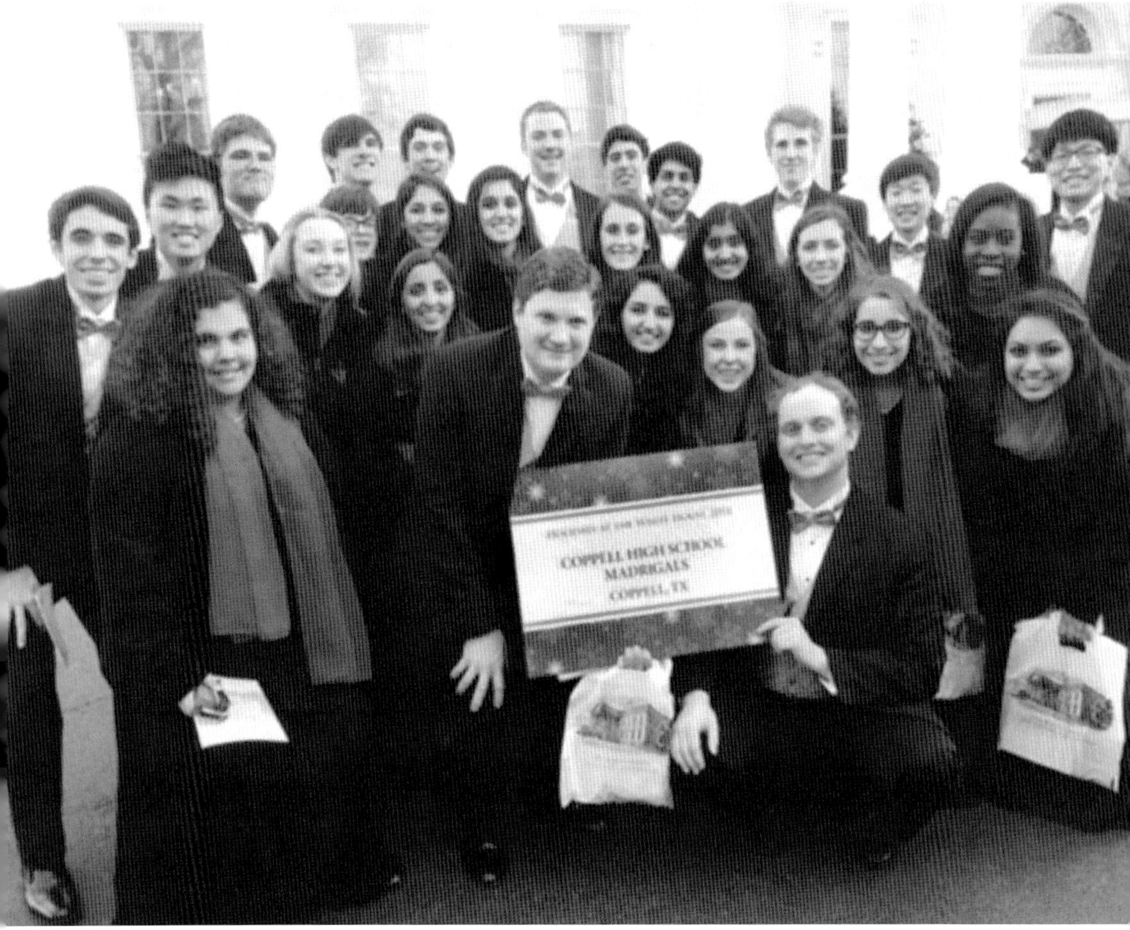

Josh Brown

In 2012, Josh Brown joined CISD as the director of choirs and instructor of music theory after spending three years teaching at Abilene High School.

An alumnus of Madisonville High School, Brown graduated magna cum laude from Dallas Baptist University before earning a master's in music from Baylor University. In addition to his work with schools, Brown served in the music ministry of numerous churches, including the First Baptist Church of Abilene, First United Methodist Church of Teague, and the First Baptist Church of Duncanville.

In December 2014, Brown led Coppell High School's madrigal choir in a two-hour performance at the White House in Washington, DC. (Courtesy of Josh Brown.)

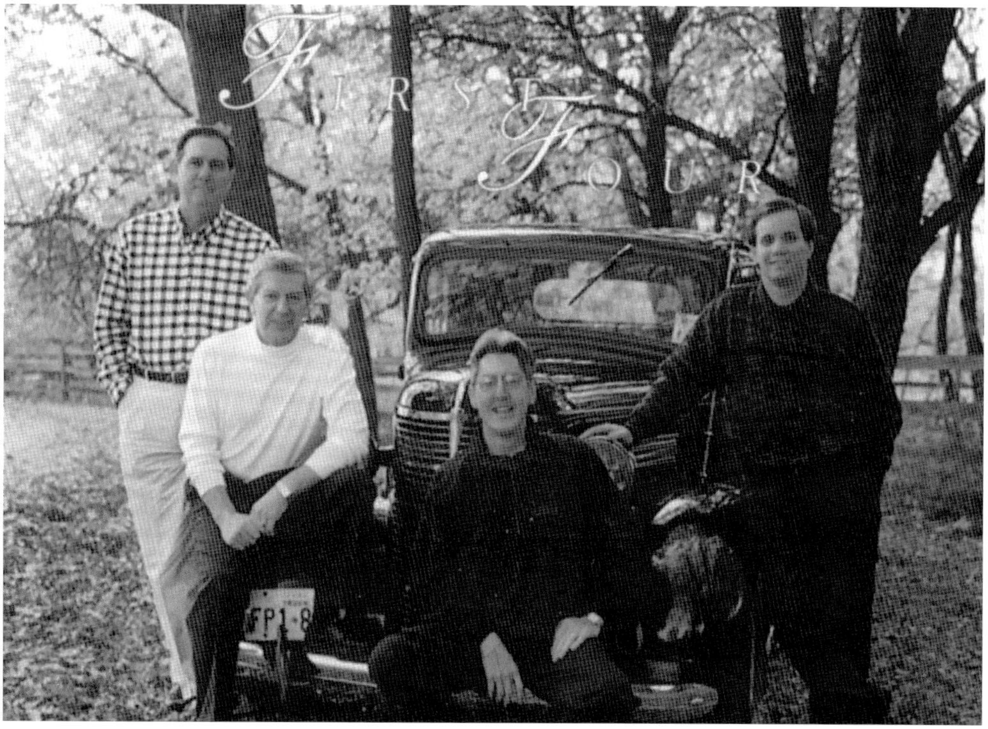

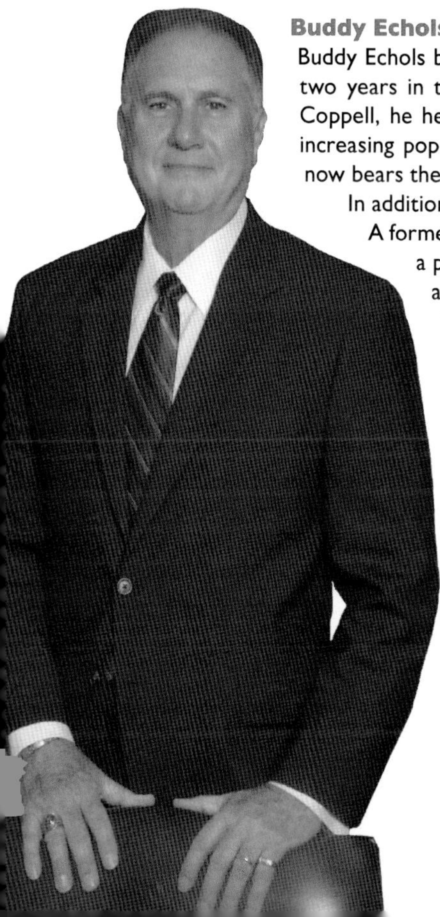

Buddy Echols

Buddy Echols became superintendent of the CISD in 1989 after serving for two years in the same position in New Carey, Texas. During his time in Coppell, he helped grow the school facilities to keep up with the rapidly increasing population of the town. The Coppell High School football field now bears the name Buddy Echols Field.

In addition to his work with the schools, Echols is a passionate vocalist. A former member of Coppell's First Baptist Church, he performed as a part of the gospel quartet known as the First Four. The group also included Tom Fineout, Clay Phillips, and Brian Tompkins. The quartet performed at numerous churches and made a number of recordings together. (Left, courtesy of Buddy Echols; Above, courtesy of Paul Douglas.)

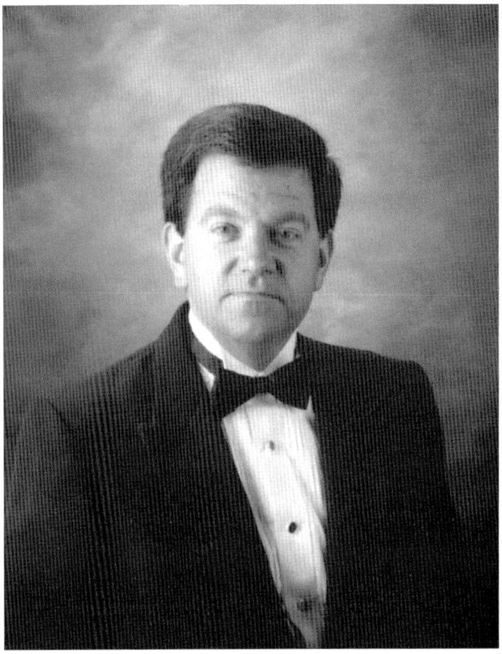

Scott Mason

Scott Mason began teaching at Coppell High School in 1990 as the head director of the school's band program.

In 1999, he led the Coppell program to a 4A state marching title. In 2001, the band appeared in the Tournament of Roses Parade, and in 2004, the band marched in the Dublin St. Patrick's Day Parade. In addition to the marching program, Mason led the band to numerous solo and ensemble accolades. A sign over Mason's office door speaks to his teaching philosophy. It reads, "Our Enemy Is Being Good." This determination has created one of the state's most successful high school music programs.

At the end of each school year, Mason honors graduating band students by leading the remaining members in a performance of the Rodgers and Hammerstein classic "You'll Never Walk Alone." (Left, courtesy of Scott Mason; below, courtesy of Jim Radcliffe.)

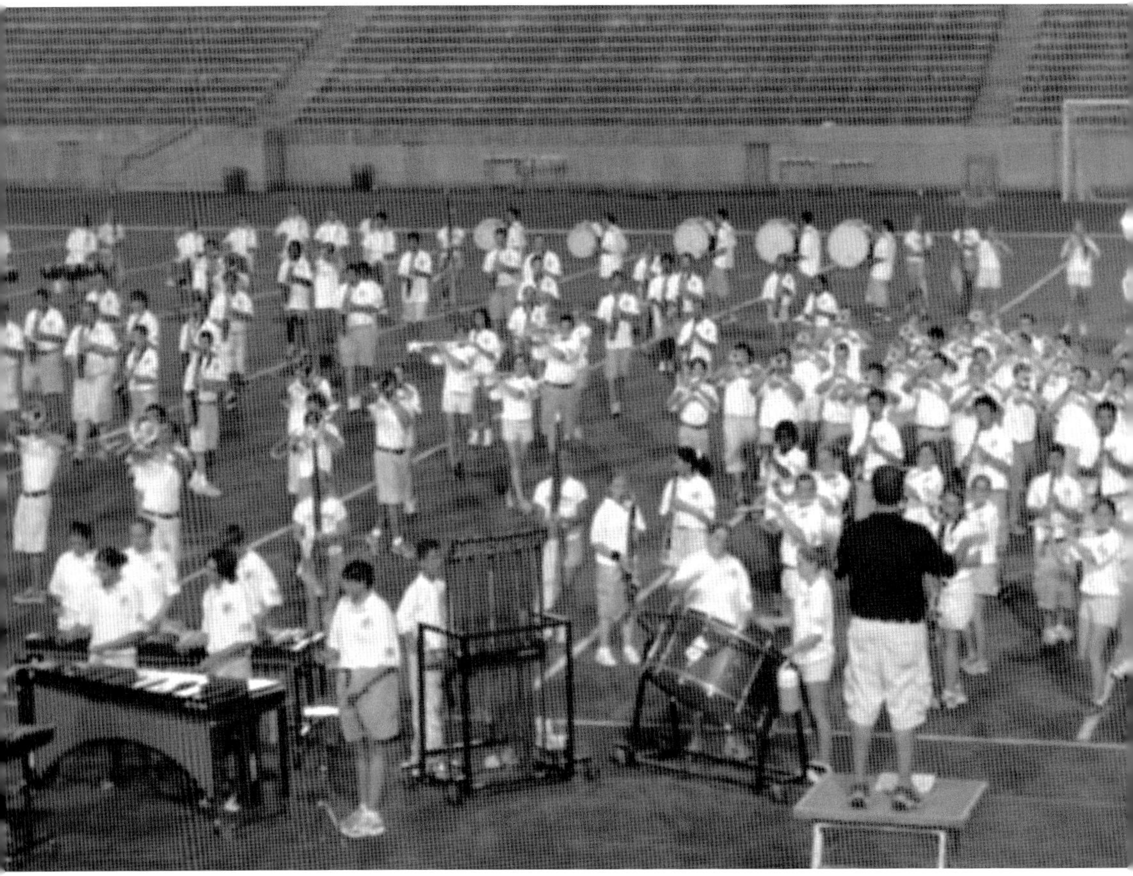

CHAPTER FOUR

Church

In the 1950s, Martha Thompson was a widow living in Coppell with her daughter. A devout member of the Assembly of God, Thompson attended services weekly with a congregation in Lewisville. Neither Thompson nor her daughter drove, and the two depended on others to bring them to the church. Without regular transportation, they could not attend services through the week.

Thompson and her daughter then began a campaign of prayer to bring an Assembly of God Church to Coppell. Less than one month later, Thompson was approached by Brother Noe from her Lewisville congregation. He was looking to start an Assembly of God meeting in town. With Thompson's help, he contacted the owner of an abandoned drugstore in present-day Old Town Coppell. Permission was granted to use the building free of charge, and Thompson's daughter donated an old pedal organ for the church to use in services.

In 1976, the church moved to a new building. The congregation celebrated with a parade of cars led by a police escort that brought them to the new building on Heartz Road. When they arrived at the new church, a ribbon cutting ceremony was held. Thompson was given the honors of cutting the ribbon before walking into the building with Pastor C.A. McBride. The congregation became one of the town's largest and continued to prosper until well after Thompson's passing in 1986.

The story of Thompson's faith and dedication is just one of many that illustrate the central role that the church has played in Coppell. In the town's earliest days, Baptists and Methodists shared one building, which also served as the town's only schoolhouse. Now it seems that churches dot every major road in town. It is impossible to tell Coppell's story without telling stories of faith.

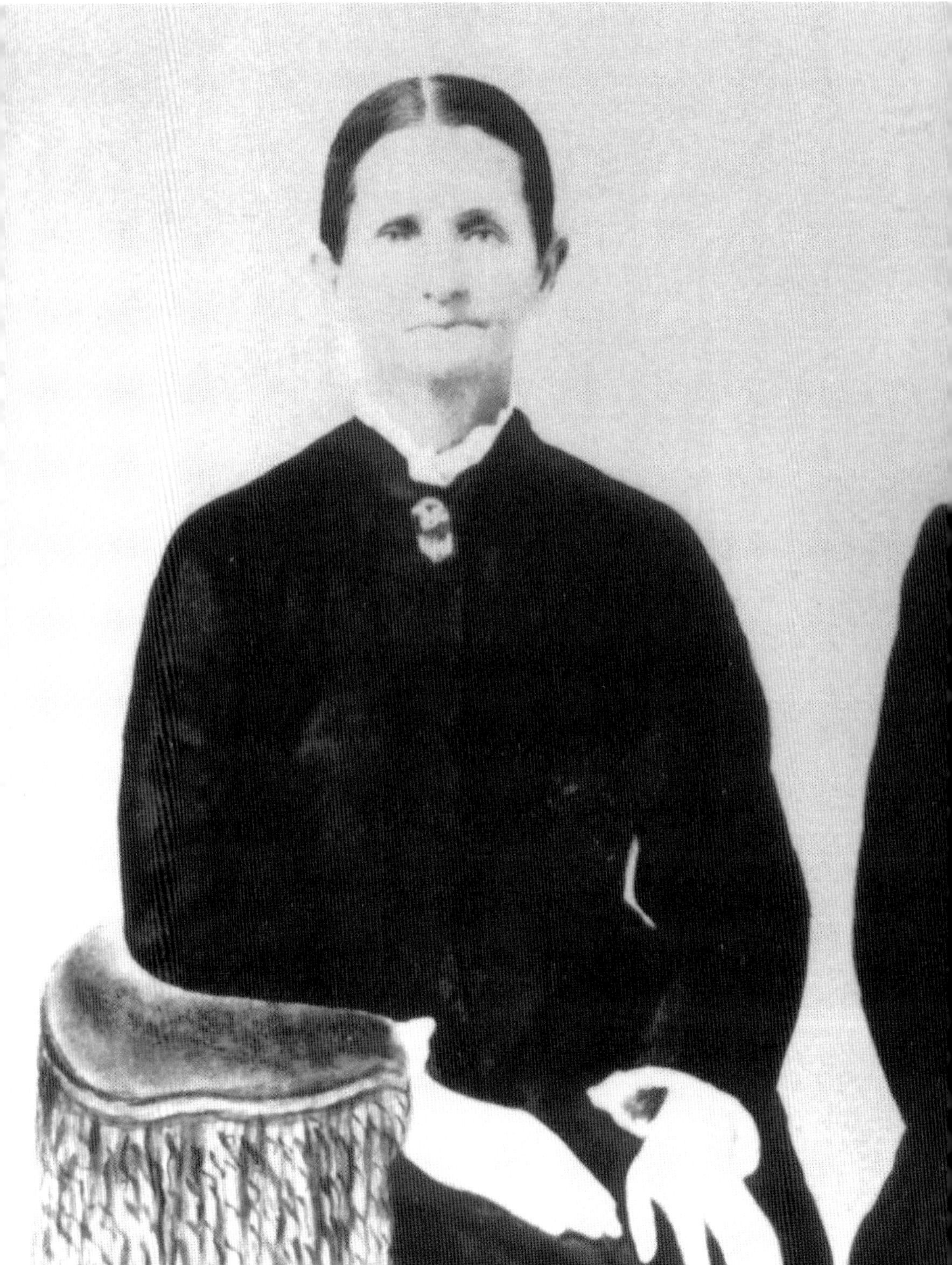

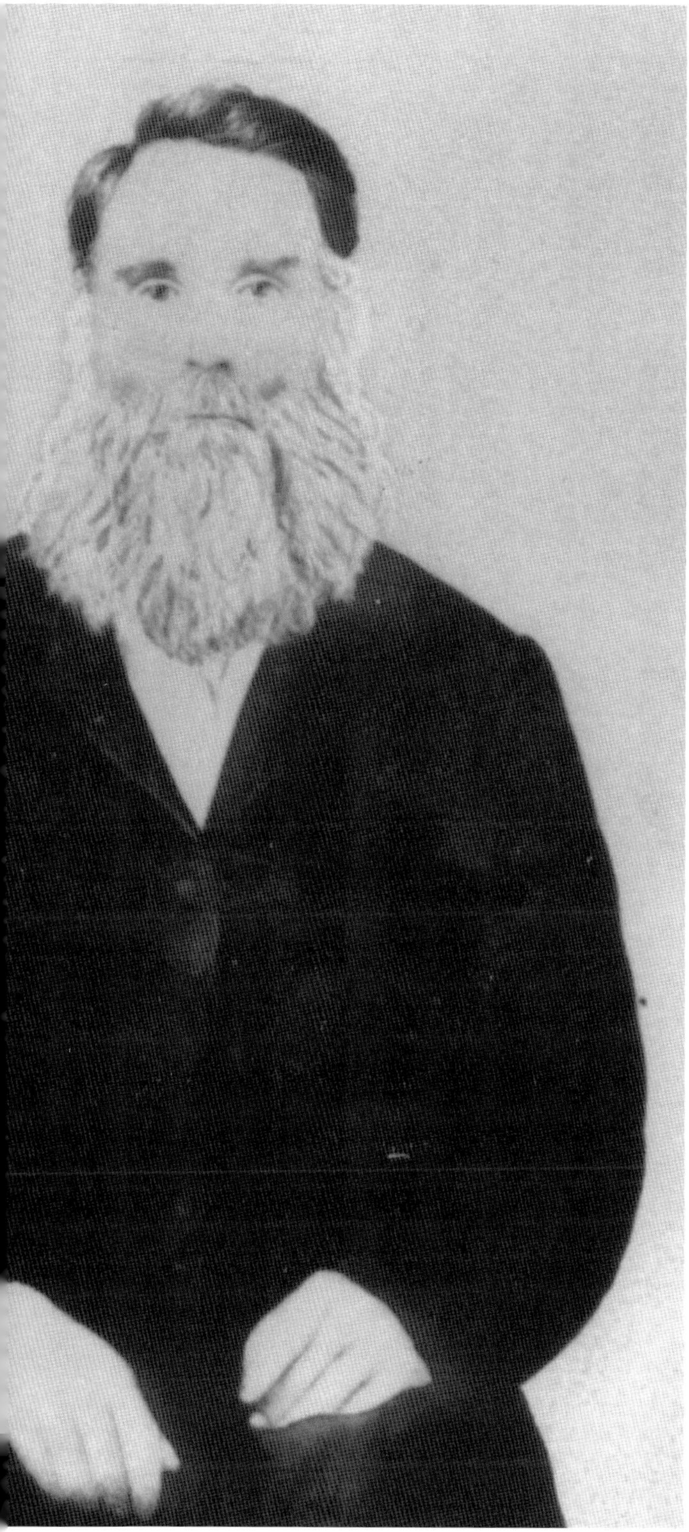

John and Sara Stringfellow
As early settlers in the Grapevine Springs area, the Stringfellows were instrumental in building the community that would become Coppell. In 1879, the couple donated an acre of land to help establish the town's first formal place of worship. At the time, it was known as the Grapevine Springs Methodist Chapel and has since become the First United Methodist Church of Coppell.

Prior to deeding the land, the local faithful met under tent tabernacles and brush arbors to hold services. Once the church was built, it also served as the meeting place for the local Baptist congregation and was the settlement's only school for approximately a decade.

The presence of the Stringfellow family is still strong in Coppell. A small private school attached to the church bears their name as does one of the town's historic cemeteries. (Courtesy of the Coppell Historical Society.)

REGISTER OF

No.	Names.	To Whom Married.	WHEN AND HOW RECEIVED. Baptism.	Vows.	Certificate	By order of Ch. Conf.
	Leon Thompson					
	Mary J. Corbin					
	John Cribbs					
	B. B. Howell					
	Elizabeth Howell					
	M E Henslee					
	L M Henslee					
	Kate P Henslee					
	W. T. Henslee					
	Mattie Harris					
	J T Howell Sr.					
	J. T. Howell Jr.					
	Jennie Kirkland					
	Jessie Naracs					
	J A Payne					
	Hannah Payne					
	Ella Harrison					
	W E Thomas					
	Minnie O Thweatt					
	Mallie A Thomas					
	Oscar Thomas					
	Edgar Thomas					
	Katie Beaton					
	Annie Harrison					
	Mattie Willingham					
	Gertrude Ward					
	Myrtle York					
28	~~Mrs Louise Howell~~	dropped		8-9-1909		
29	W. H York.		8-29-1909			
	Maggie Cribbs			8-29-1909		
	Cleatheus Thweatt		8-29-1909			
	Hubert Kirkland		8-29-1909			

J.E. Hightower

J.E. Hightower was Coppell's Methodist minister from 1909 through 1915. His first year with the congregation also marked the 30th anniversary of the Methodist church in Coppell. That year, he led the congregation in a two-week revival that came to be known as the Great Methodist Revival.

For two weeks in August, Hightower led services twice a day in a tent tabernacle near present-day Grapevine Springs Park. The services resulted in over 40 people being baptized into the Methodist faith. The name of each baptism was handwritten in a ledger that remains in the church's historical archives. Records also show that a number of other local denominations joined in the revival and also met with great success.

The revival was so successful that a local newspaper declared it "one of the greatest revivals ever known in this part of the country." (Courtesy of First United Methodist Church of Coppell.)

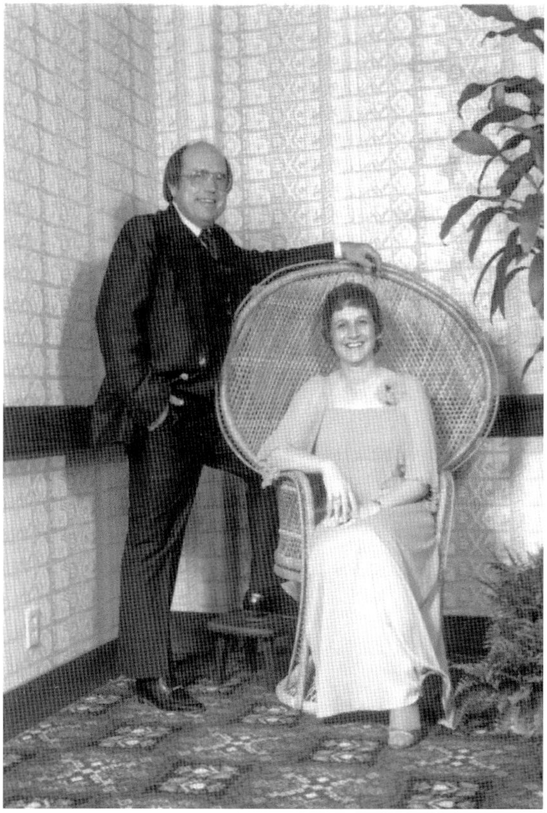

Foy Layton
Foy Layton wore many hats in his lifetime. He was the longtime minister for Coppell's Church of Christ congregation. He worked as a real estate agent and as a volunteer firefighter. He served as a trustee on Coppell's school board and founded a girls' softball league in town. He was also known as the voice of the Coppell Cowboys. He announced the team's games for 30 years, until his health compelled him to stop.

Layton served as a rural mail carrier for Coppell's post office. Beginning in 1978, he started working as a part-time carrier, which grew into a full-time position as the size of the town increased. In 1997, the City of Coppell honored Layton's years of community service by naming a street after him. (Both, courtesy of Sheri Moino.)

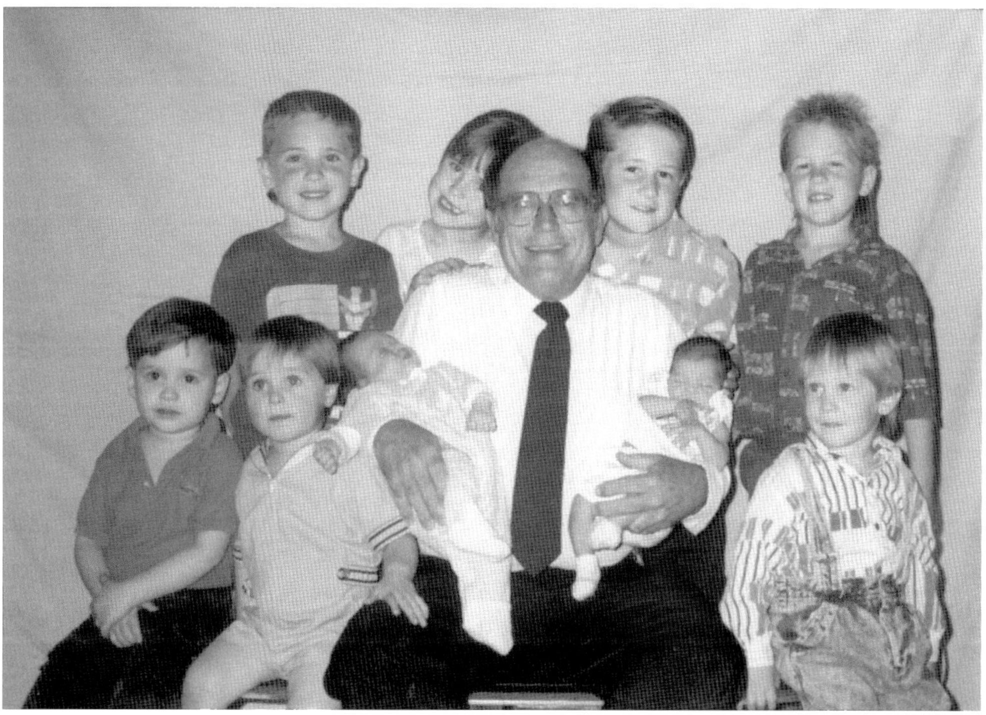

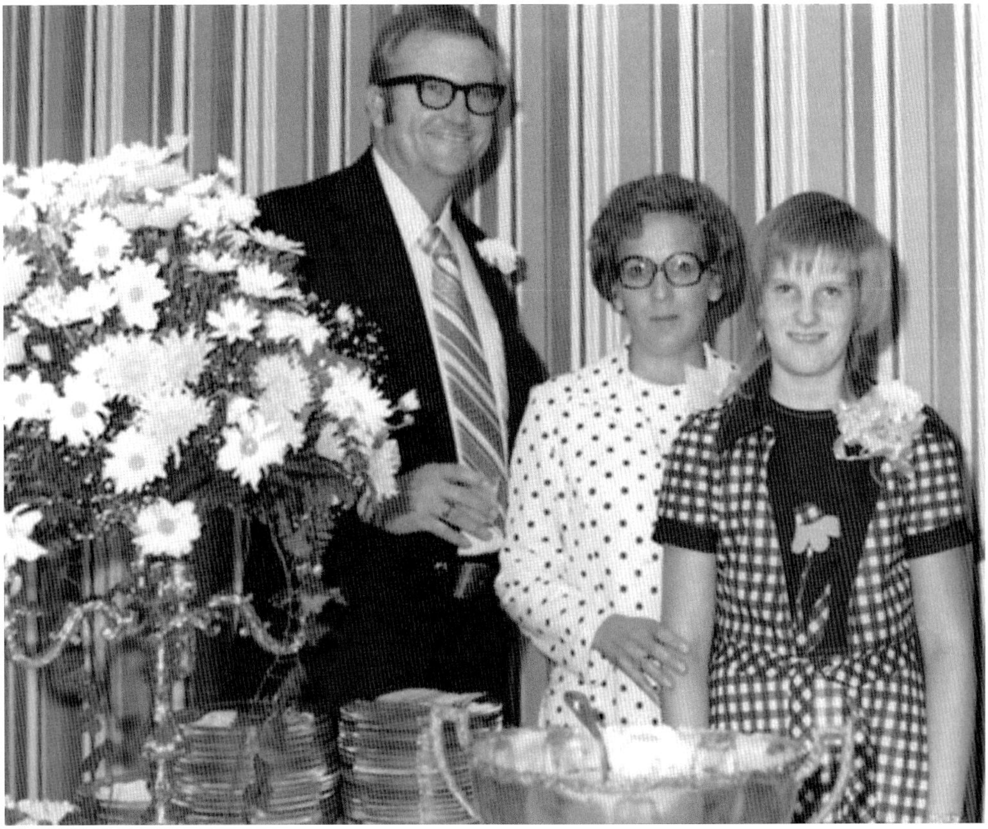

C.A. and Carol McBride

Reverend C.A. McBride was the pastor of Coppell's Assembly of God congregation from 1964 to 2000. McBride and his wife, Carol, came to Coppell after residing in Carlsbad, New Mexico. The two were chosen to lead the church after previous pastor A.L. Perry stepped down. They were contacted about the position while preaching a revival in East Texas. The congregation voted him in unanimously.

The congregation was small at the time, averaging about 30 people. However, under McBride's leadership, the church began to grow. It was an uphill battle, as the church was met with suspicion and ridicule by much of the community. The church's focus on the Holy Spirit meant that their meetings could be raucous affairs, heard from outside the church building.

After outgrowing the old building 12 years into his pastorship, McBride led the congregation to a new location.

Carol played an equally vital role in the congregation. Married since 1954, Carol helped her husband begin his ministry in New Mexico. Over the years, she served as church secretary, Sunday school teacher, and organist for the church. In addition to his work with the church, C.A. served the city for many years on the school board.

Carol was known for her avid horse riding. The hobby earned her the nickname of "The Rodeo Queen." She passed away in February 2014 after a protracted illness, and C.A. currently lives in Oasis Care Home in Lewisville, where he continues to receive regular visits from his former parishioners. (Courtesy of Mary Ann Marcantel.)

Fr. Killian Broderick

When Monsignor Killian J. Broderick died in July 2004, he had been serving St. Ann Catholic Parish for close to three decades.

Ordained in 1967, Broderick was a student of civil rights law and later became the director of the Dallas branch of Catholic Charities. In 1978, he worked on a large program aimed at aiding Ethiopian refugees.

By far Coppell's largest church, St. Ann began in 1984, holding its first mass in October. The mass was led by Father Leo Duessman. In the early years, Duessman and Broderick rotated preaching duties. The congregation met in the former Methodist chapel located in the Old Town area of Coppell. As attendance numbers rose, the congregation began temporarily meeting in the cafeteria of a local middle school.

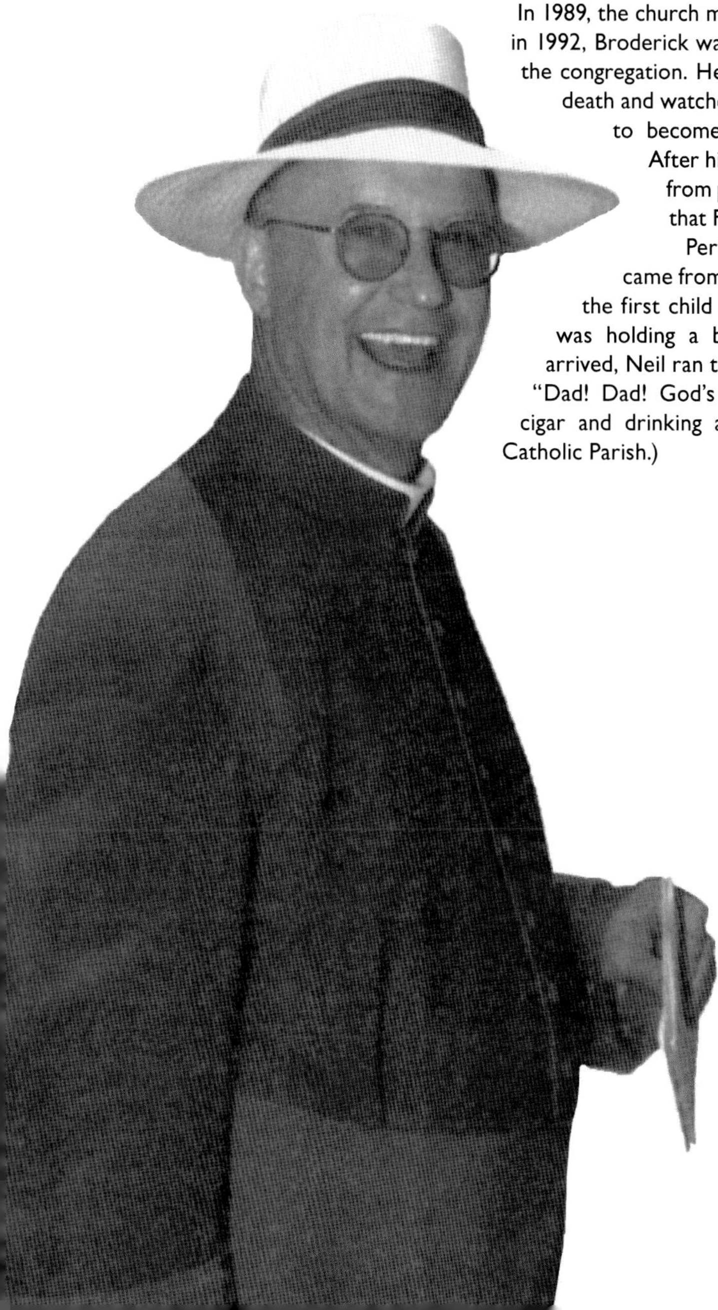

In 1989, the church moved to its current location, and in 1992, Broderick was named the full-time pastor for the congregation. He served in this capacity until his death and watched as the once small church grew to become the largest diocese in Dallas. After his passing, a flood of stories came from parishioners regarding the impact that Father Killian had on their lives.

Perhaps the most amusing story came from Jay Turner (whose son Neil was the first child baptized at St. Ann). The family was holding a barbeque, and when Broderick arrived, Neil ran to his father, proudly announcing, "Dad! Dad! God's here . . . and he's smoking a cigar and drinking a beer!" (Courtesy of St. Ann Catholic Parish.)

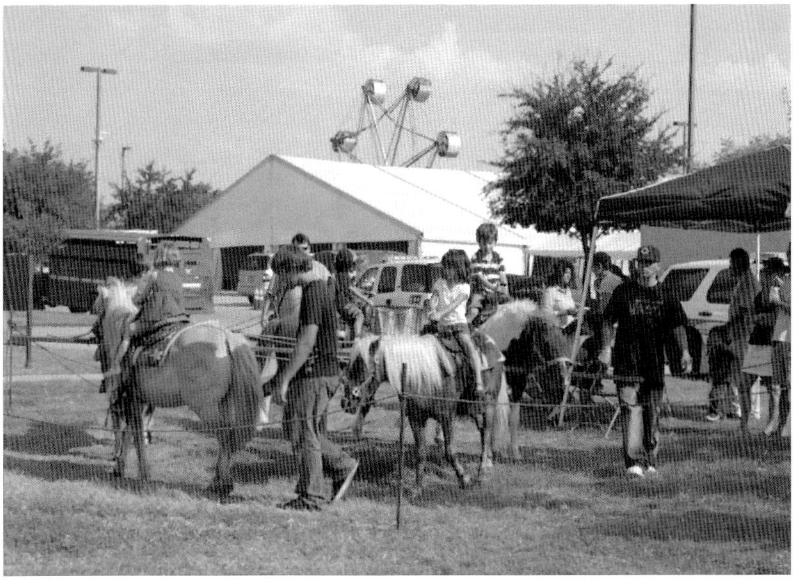

St. Ann Carnival

The St. Ann Carnival began as a project of the church's men's ministry. The first carnival was held in October 1993 and had three tents and roughly 700 volunteers. Today, the carnival is chaired by Tim Barr with a crew of 1,700 volunteers. Barr estimates that 20,000 people attend the carnival each year, and his goal is to expand and improve the event even more.

The St. Ann Carnival also maintains a long-standing relationship with Triple T Amusements. The company, owned by the Shaffer family, began its association with St. Ann through the friendship of Monsignor Killian Broderick and Helen Shaffer. Though both have since passed, the Shaffer family continues to supply the rides and games for the carnival every year. (Both, courtesy of St. Ann Catholic Parish.)

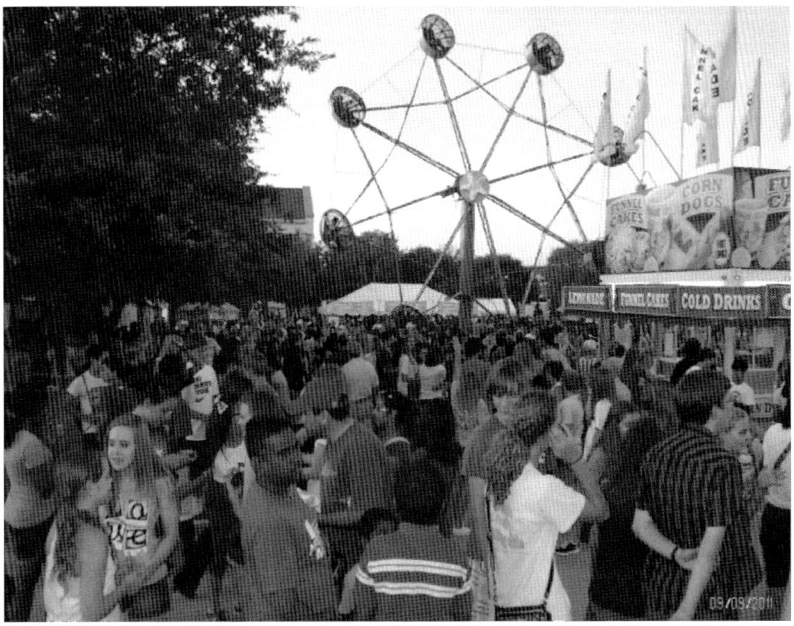

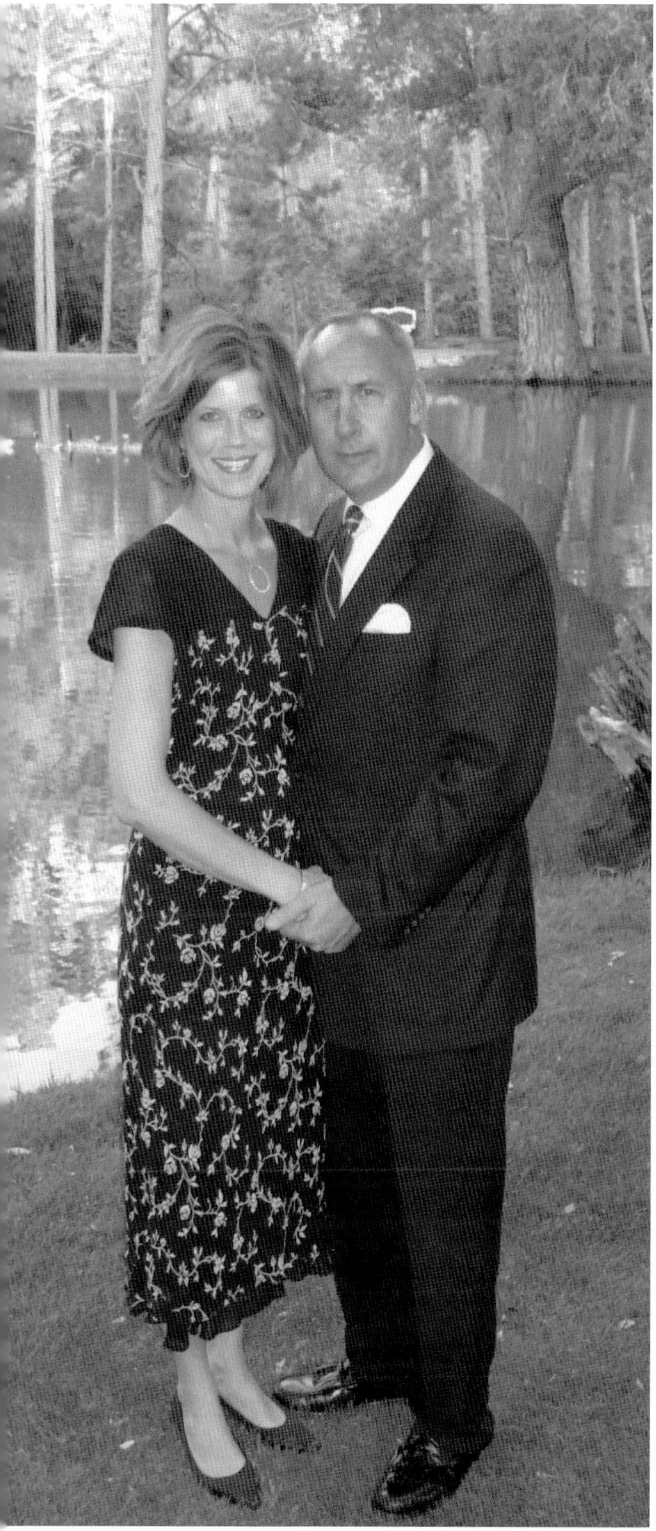

Kathy Braem
In 2006, Ann Sisk started a ministry through Coppell's Methodist church aimed at serving children with special needs. The ministry adopted the name Loving HANDS, an acronym for Hope, Acceptance, iNclusion, Dignity, and Support. The ministry was envisioned as a night of rest for parents and a chance for the children to find a warm and welcoming environment. Though a function of the church, it was created to serve the community at large and regularly has children attending from surrounding towns.

Leadership changed in 2008 to Kathy Braem, who also serves as the assistant to children's ministries. A resident of Coppell since 2000, Bream leads the group once a month with the help of certified and trained student and adult volunteers. In addition, she keeps a registered nurse on hand in case of emergency.

Over the years, Braem has established numerous friendships with the children, their parents, and the volunteers. The work done is often used as a service requirement for students in confirmation, but the experience keeps them coming back well after their requirement is filled. In addition, Braem leads a smaller Loving HANDS Sunday school class that serves the church on Sunday mornings. (Courtesy of Kathy Braem.)

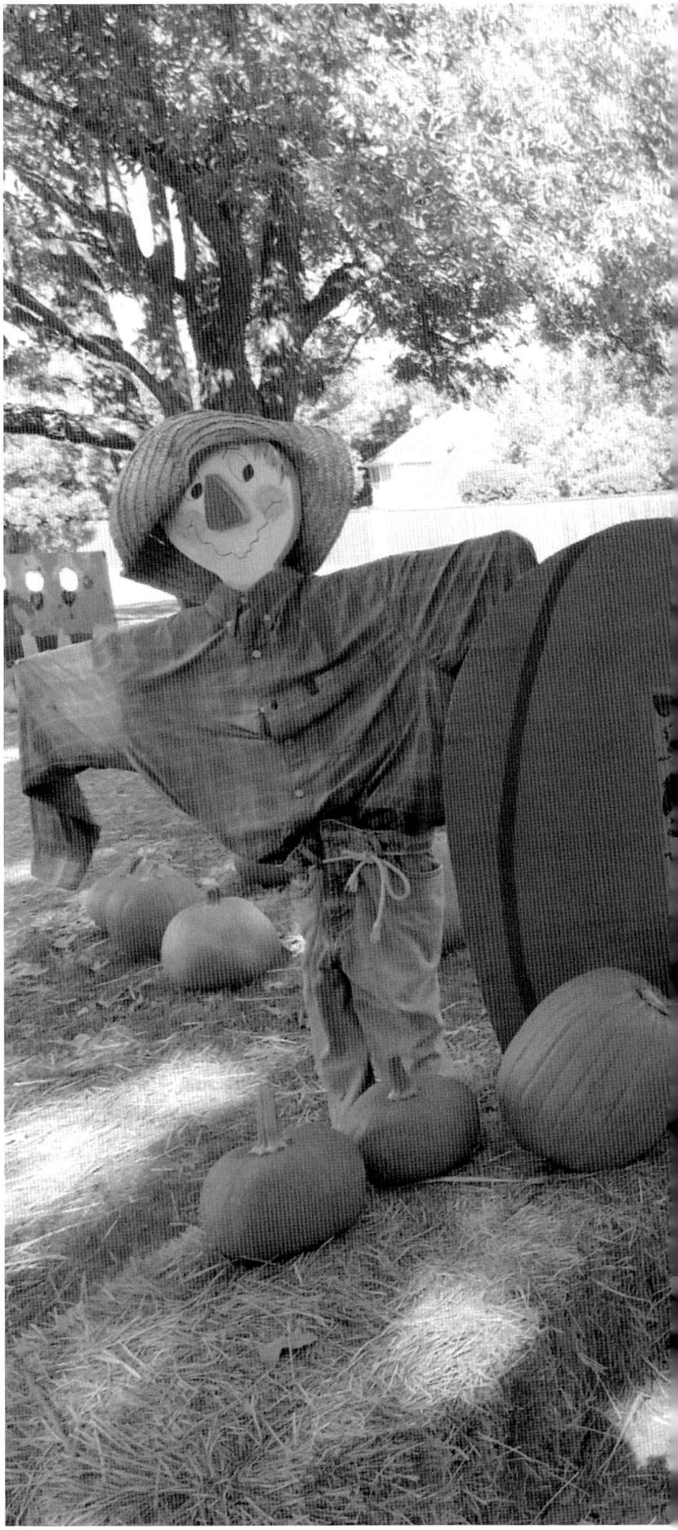

Rejoice Lutheran Pumpkin Patch

In 1994, the fledgling community of Rejoice Lutheran Church was looking for ways to raise money. They were in the process of building a sanctuary and owned a small plot of land on Sandy Lake Road. Charter members Marcy Hempel and Sandy Roberts, along with Angela Tieberg, began developing an idea to host a pumpkin patch. The plan was to run the event as a one-time fundraiser.

Twenty years have passed, and the pumpkin patch has become a staple of the fall experience in Coppell. Three days a week, local preschools come to the patch for story time. Along with pumpkins, the patch sells a variety of gourds, decorative hay bales, and a cookbook. For $1, a visitor to the patch can also purchase a ticket for the quilt raffle.

With the funds raised from the pumpkin patch, the church has funded its ministry work and donated to charities such as Christian Community Action, the Family Place, and the Assistance League of Coppell. (Courtesy of Rejoice Lutheran Church.)

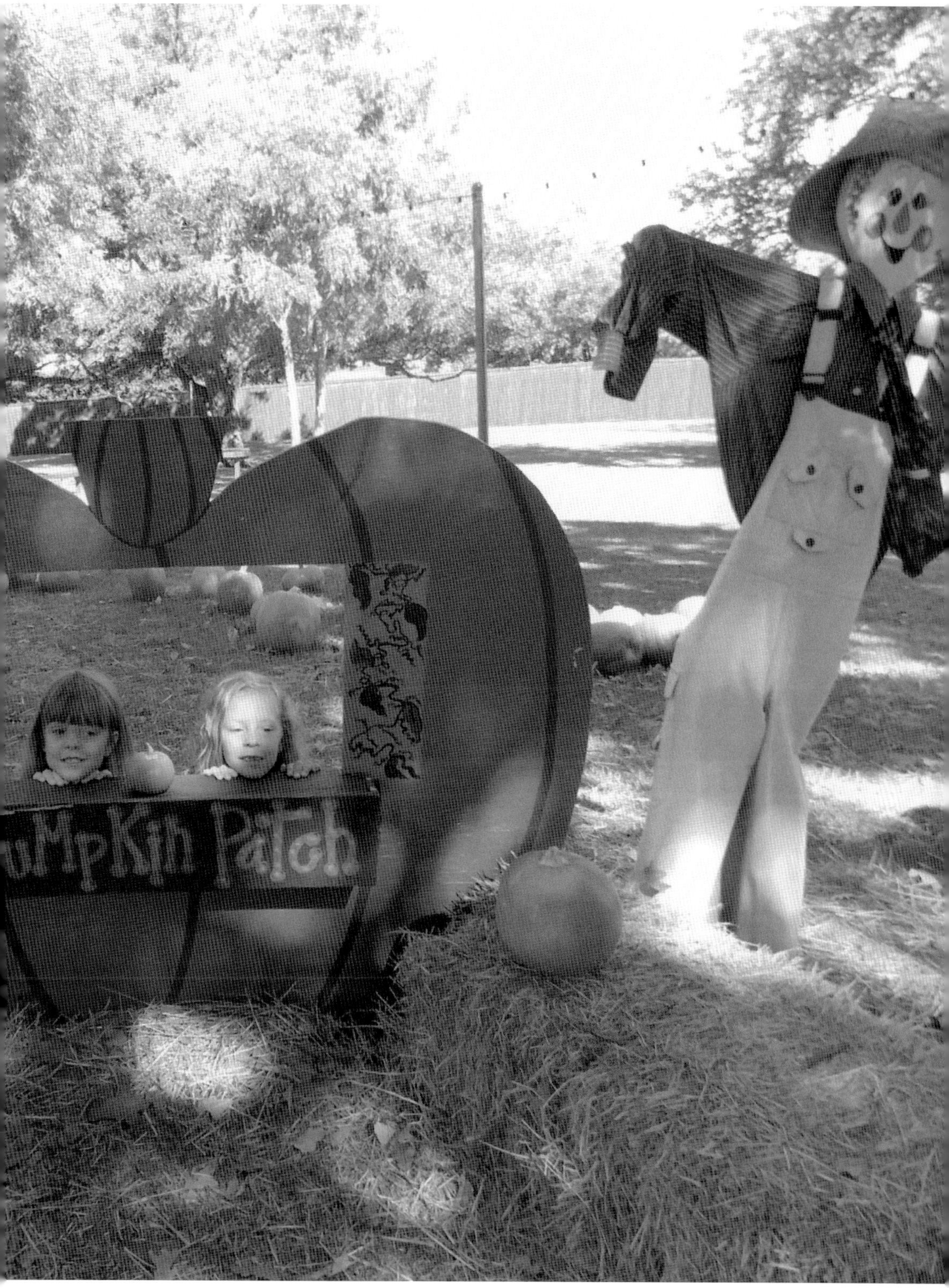
Patch

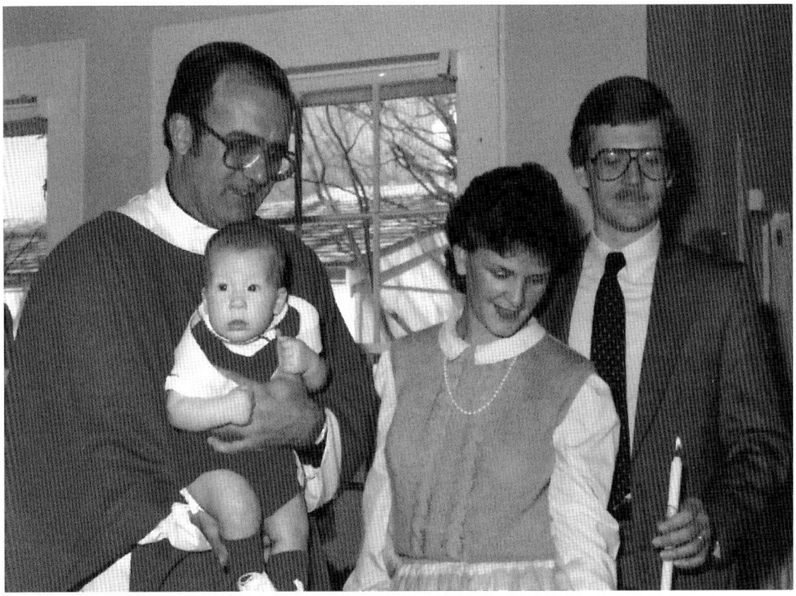

Jay and Elaine Turner

The Turners were one of the charter families for St. Ann Catholic Parish. Neil Turner was the first baptism at the church, and Jay Turner was instrumental in raising the money for the church's land acquisitions. Jay worked as a member of the parish council for 20 years, and Elaine Turner served the church by teaching religious education.

Jay helped found the Coppell Business Association (a forerunner to the chamber of commerce) and served on the board of directors for First Coppell Bank.

In the 1980s, a competition was held to name one of the city's parks. Elaine offered the simple moniker of the Duck Pond, which is the name the park bears to this day.

Above, Jay and Elaine are at right. Below, Elaine is at far left and Jay is at far right. (Both, courtesy of Jay Turner.)

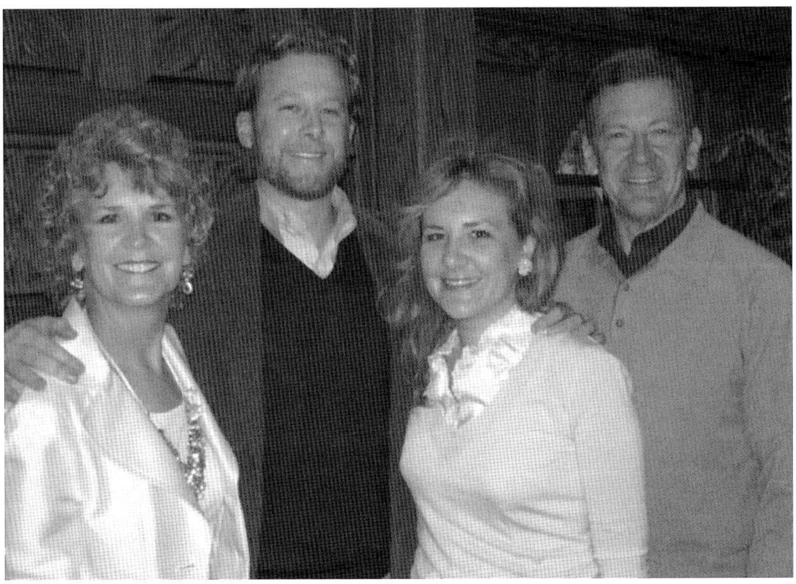

CHAPTER FIVE

Neighborhood

On October 31, 2014, Jim Hall dressed in a pair of bloodstained overalls and clutched a long machete. He stalked the streets of Lakeview Terrace, startling the multitude of visitors at his annual "Halloween Spooktacular."

The show, which was in its ninth year, is known as the "Mystery of Lakeview Terrace." The sprawling combination of music, lightshow, and animatronics tells the legend of a gruesome murder that allegedly occurred on the property. A fake historical marker sits in the front yard, offering a summary of the story. Visitors are invited to listen to the full performance through their car radios or the speakers set in the lawn. Pumpkins sing and light up to the beat of music, while a knife-wielding skeleton narrates. A silhouette of a man murdering a woman appears in the upstairs window, and a giant spider in an expansive web is highlighted halfway through the show. Observers may also spot Hall's son peeking from his bedroom window at the guests.

Furthermore, Hall employs a number of pneumatic props, such as a monster that pops up from a trash can. He manually operates these effects, using them to startle trick-or-treaters as they retrieve their candy. As the show prepares for its tenth year, Hall's plans are even more elaborate. His passion for lights and moving objects might come from his childhood fandom of carnival dark rides. This passion led to a media appearance in May 2015, when he appeared in news and print, reviewing the newest dark ride attraction of Six Flags Over Texas in Arlington.

Hall, whose day job is the director of corporate finance for American Airlines, joins the list of Coppell personalities. Though these residents belong to no distinct category, they help give the community its unique character.

The Houston Campsite Oak

One of Coppell's oldest and arguably most historically significant residents is the Houston Campsite Oak. Located on the grounds of Grapevine Springs Park, the post oak is forever tied to Texas history. It grows in the place where Sam Houston camped in 1842 while attempting to negotiate a treaty between Texas and a grand council of Indian tribes. For many years, it was believed that the treaty was signed at the location. However, it has since been determined that the treaty was signed later in 1843 at Bird's Fort near present-day Six Flags Over Texas in Arlington.

In 1936, the tree bore witness to history again as the park lands were donated to Dallas County and developed with bridges, rock walls, and picnic facilities. A stone retaining wall was also built around the tree. The project was performed by the Works Progress Administration.

On April 22, 2014, the oak was dedicated as a Famous Tree of Texas by Coppell mayor Karen Hunt and the Coppell Historical Society. It was marked with a plaque and will appear in the *Famous Trees of Texas* book. (Courtesy of Kara Jex.)

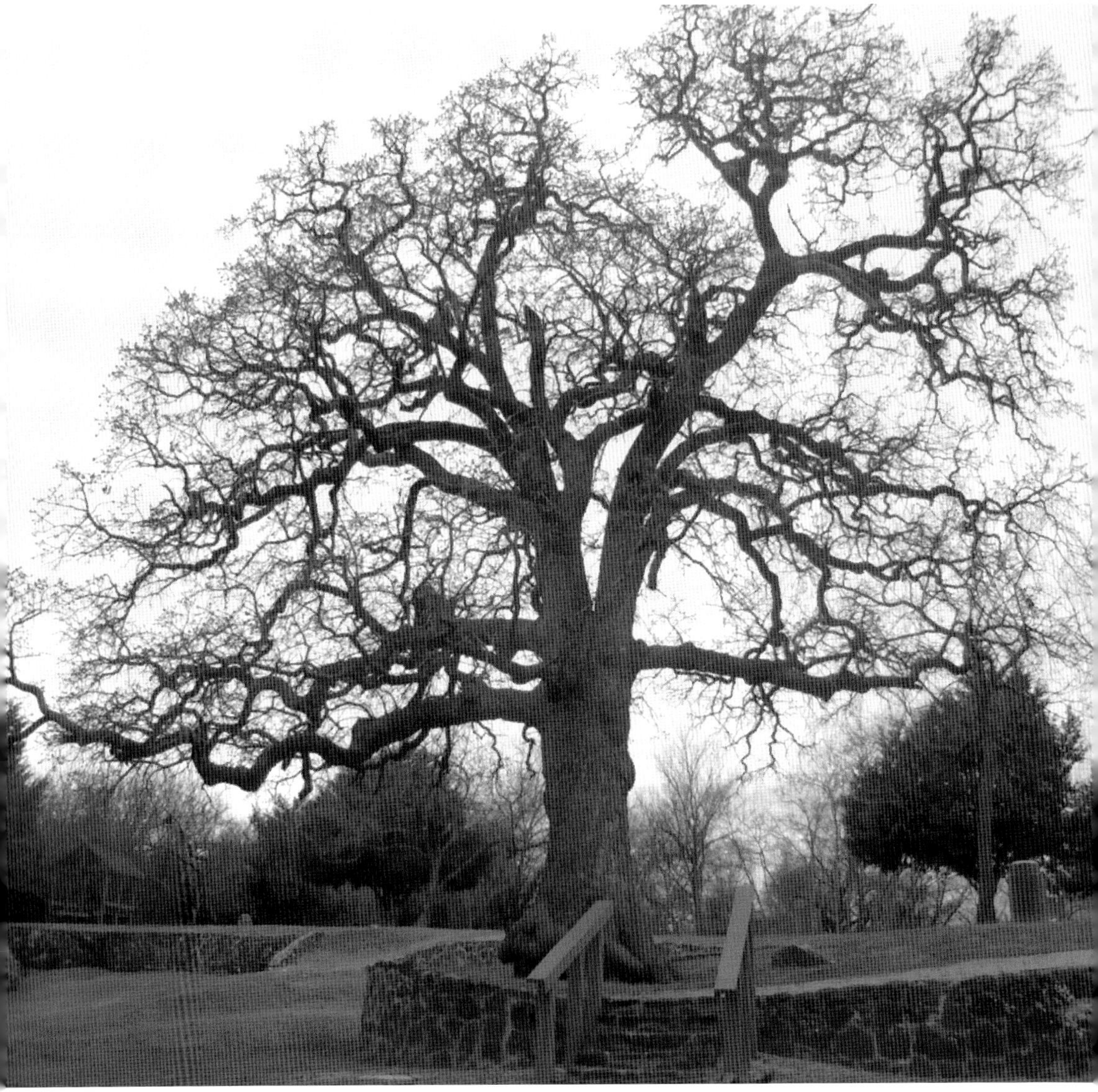

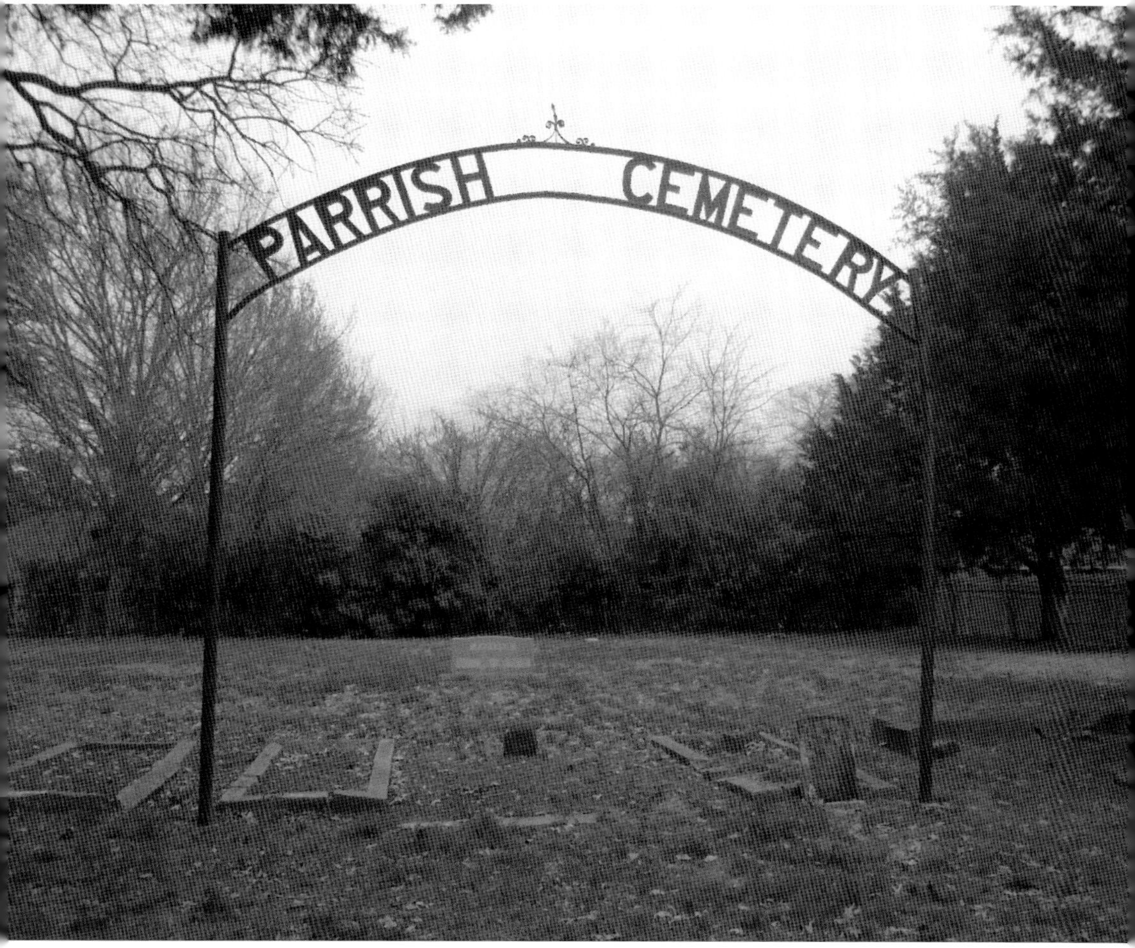

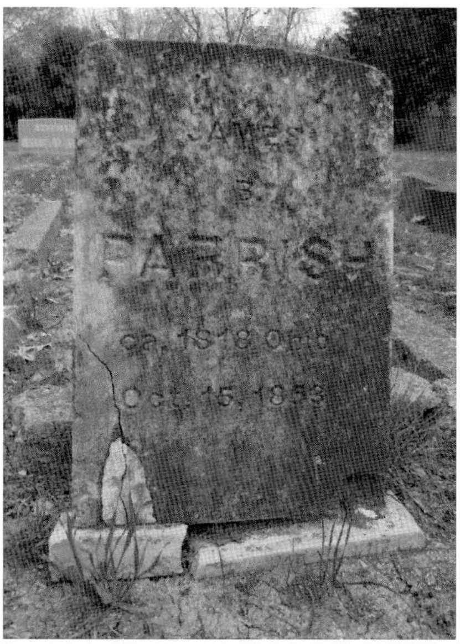

James Parrish

Born in Ohio on October 10, 1820, James Parrish settled in the Coppell area with his wife, Eliza Record, in 1848. Parrish came to Texas as a member of the Peters Colony, receiving a land grant of 640 acres. The Parrish land ran from present-day Moore and Bethel Roads to Denton and Denton Creek.

Today, the family legacy in Coppell is primarily seen in the two cemeteries they established. Both are preserved as Coppell historical sites. The first, set aside on the Parrish farm to be a community cemetery, was known as Sands Cemetery and later became Bethel Cemetery. The second, known as the Parrish Family Cemetery, was created by Eliza shortly after her husband's death in 1853. More than 35 other members of the Parrish family are buried on the grounds. (Both, courtesy of Kara Jex.)

William Ewing Thomas

William Ewing Thomas was a veteran of the Civil War who served the Confederacy in Company D in the 29th Regiment of the Tennessee Infantry. He was wounded in the Battle of Chickamauga on September 19, 1863. Nine months later, he was captured by federal forces and sent to a military prison in Louisville, Kentucky. He remained in the facility for a year before signing an oath of allegiance and gaining his freedom on June 16,1865.

Approximately seven years after the war, Thomas moved to the Grapevine Springs area. He was a charter member of Coppell's Methodist church and remained in the community until around 1920, when he moved to Grapevine. He remained in the neighboring town until the time of his death in 1930. (Courtesy of the Coppell Historical Society.)

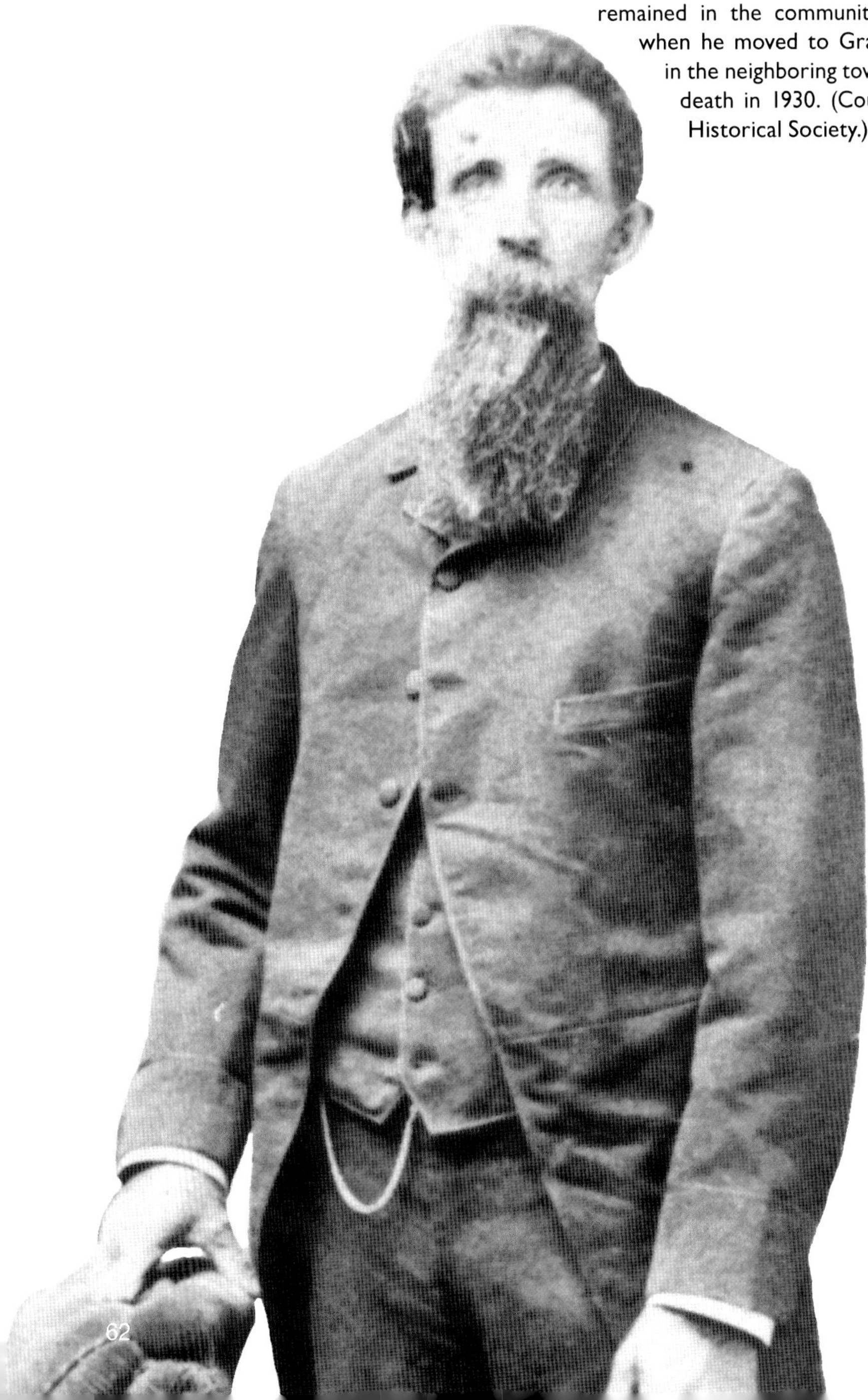

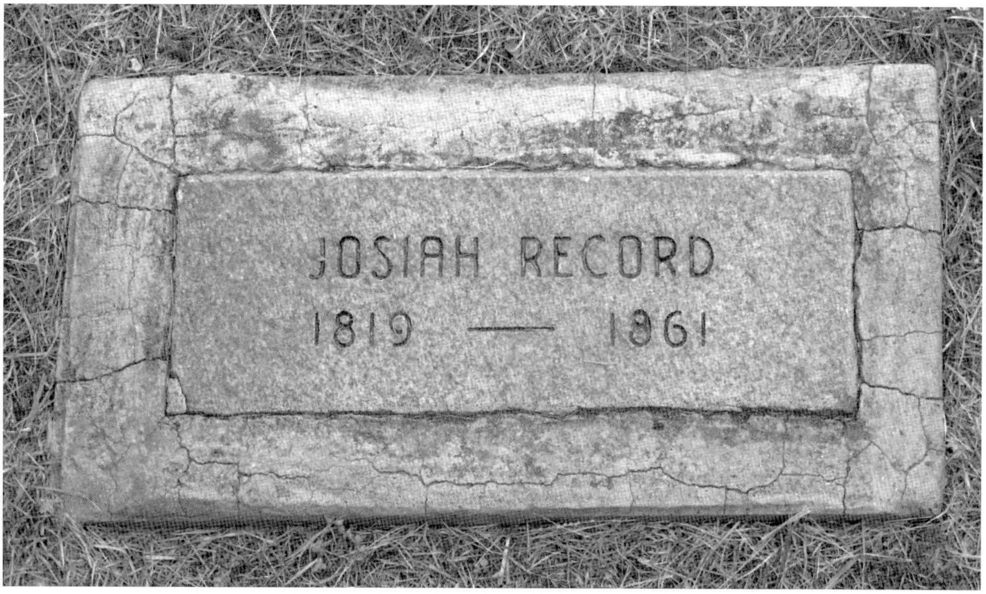

Josiah and John Record

The saga of the Record family reads like an old-fashioned Western. Having moved to the Grapevine Springs area from Indiana, Josiah Record quickly drew the ire of locals by insisting in the early days of the Civil War that the Confederacy did not have the men or resources to win. The statement led to his lynching and a declaration of vengeance sworn by his son John.

John went on to fight in the Civil War for the Confederate cause, but he did not forget his father's murder. He eventually found and killed a man named Mr. Copeland, who is presumed to have participated in his father's lynching. Many prominent locals had turned toward the Union cause, and John was never prosecuted for the killing.

The incident seemed over, but in 1869, while working near Hackberry Creek, John, his 12-year-old brother, and three others were accosted by vigilantes (possibly in the Ku Klux Klan). All five were lynched, though one escaped the noose. When the bodies were found, they were described as being hung "like you were going to hang a hog." (Both, courtesy of Kara Jex.)

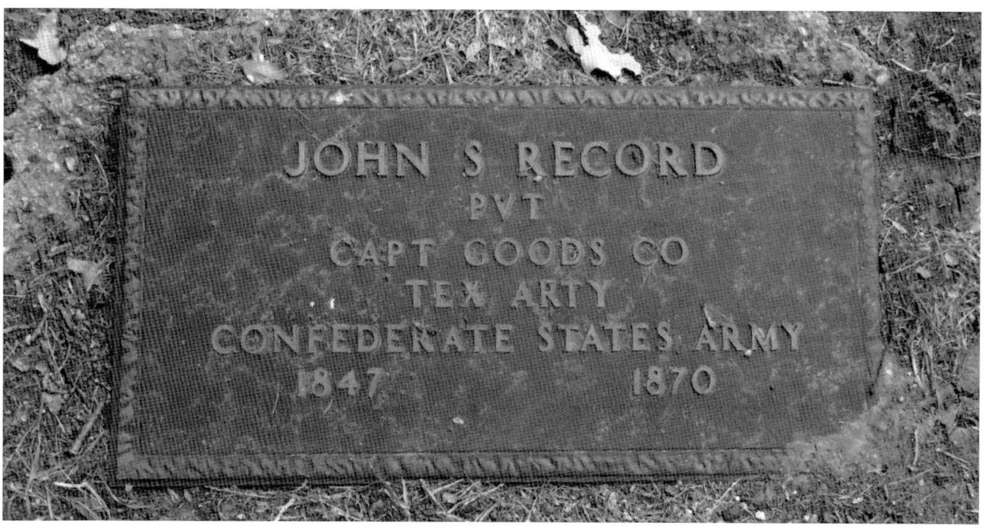

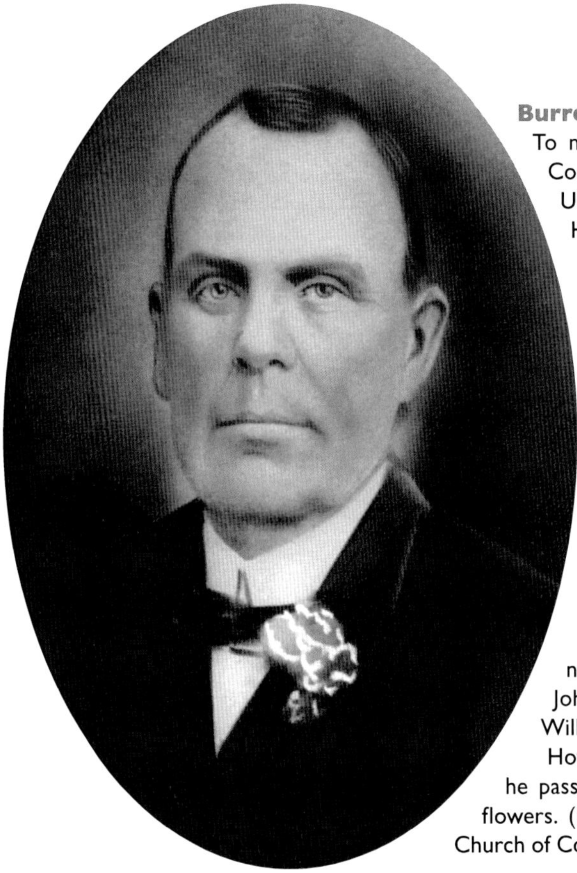

Burrell B. Howell

To most citizens of Grapevine Springs (later Coppell), Burrell Howell was known simply as Uncle Burrell. Born in Blue Springs, Kentucky, Howell's grandfather served as a soldier under George Washington. Howell later continued the family tradition of military service by fighting in the Civil War for the Confederate army in Captain Witt's company.

A tall, slender man, Howell made his living as a farmer. In 1879, he became one of the founding trustees of Grapevine Springs Methodist Chapel (below, with Howell in front). He was a dearly loved member who was known for bringing flowers for the chapel as well as gifts for the congregation's children.

Howell was married four times, most notably to Susan Bullock, the widow of John Record. He was also the grandfather of William T. Cozby, an early mayor of Coppell.

Howell lived until November 1929, when he passed away on a bus, holding a bouquet of flowers. (Both, courtesy of First United Methodist Church of Coppell.)

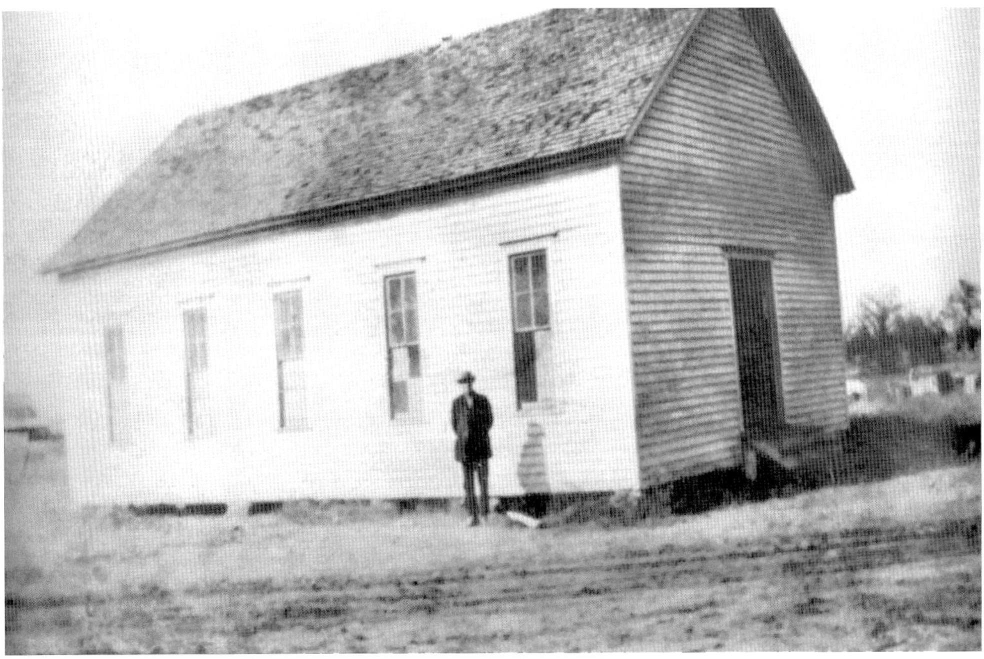

W.C. Bullock

Washington Curtis Bullock was born in 1821. He moved to the Coppell area in 1855 with his wife, Carroll, and their four children. After settling in the area, Bullock constructed a brick house (pictured, with Ruby Pruitt in front). Popular history refers to the home as the first two-story brick house in Dallas County, though evidence does not seem to support this claim.

Bullock served as a justice of the peace and built a small schoolhouse that his children and neighboring children attended.

In 1869, Bullock's youngest child, Julia, died at the age of three. Bullock created a small cemetery for his daughter. Over the years, the cemetery continued to serve the Bullock family. It is also the resting place of Coppell notables such as Burrell B. Howell and William T. Cozby.

Bullock died on October 6, 1889, and was buried on the family plot. (Courtesy of the Coppell Historical Society.)

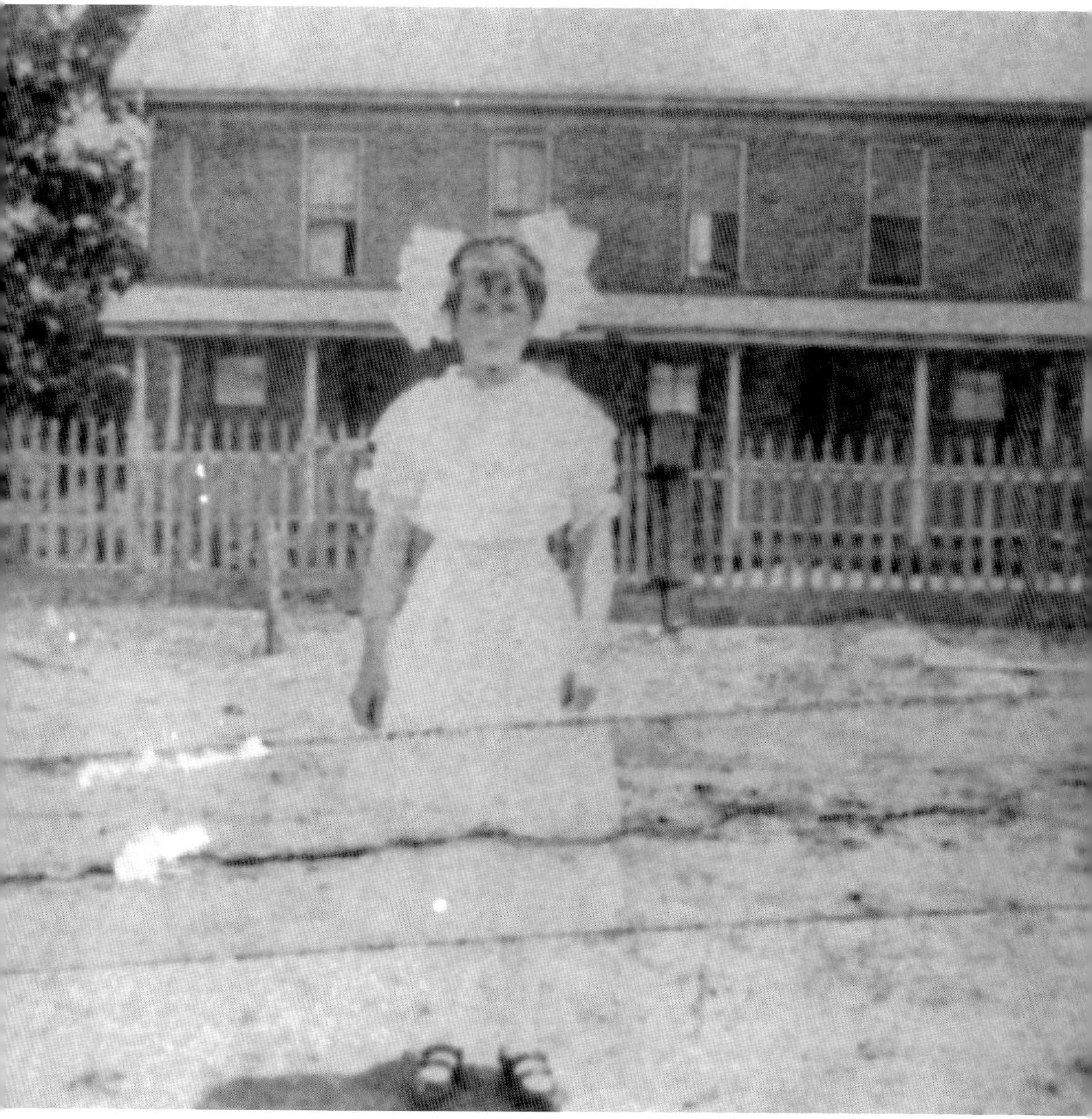

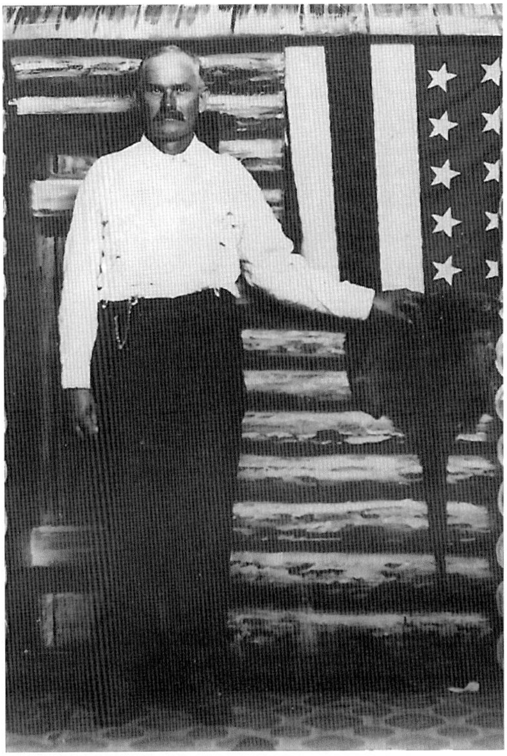

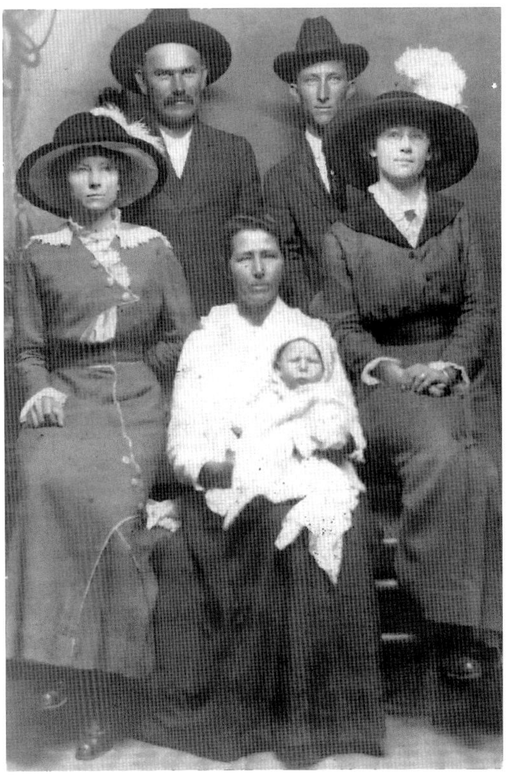

Frank Dobecka

Frank P. Dobecka was born in 1876 in Fayette County, Texas. Dobecka was a first-generation American of Moravian descent. Both parents had emigrated as young children from what is now the Czech Republic.

In May 1900, Dobecka married Mary Nazier in Granger, Texas. The couple had 11 children, nine of which survived into adulthood. In 1912, the family moved to a 286-acre tract of land along the Trinity River, situated between Carrollton and Coppell.

The family farmed the land, growing cotton and other crops. The family also raised hogs and horses on the land. Among the difficulties they faced were floods. Dobecka's first crop was destroyed twice when the Trinity River overflowed.

Dobecka passed in April 1944 after a lengthy illness. Mary lived with their children until her death in 1967. The family land was later transformed into a dairy.

In the bottom image, Dobecka is standing in the rear at left. (Both, courtesy of Cecil Dobecka Jr.)

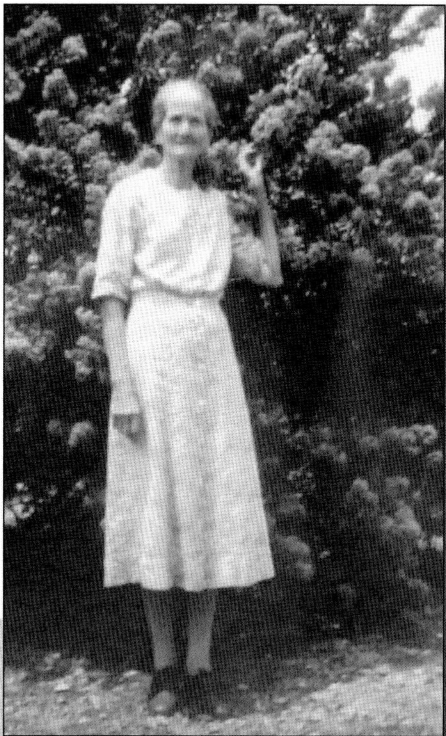

Edna Kirkland

Edna Jeanette Kirkland was the daughter of early Coppell resident John Stringfellow. After marrying, Edna and husband John Kirkland continued living at the Stringfellow home until moving into their own house in 1904.

Edna served as a teacher and was a devoted Methodist. In later years, she often spoke of the camp meetings that the church would hold in nearby Grapevine Springs Park.

Today, the Kirklands' home is the centerpiece of the Coppell Heritage Park. In 2011, the house was moved from its original location and fully restored. It is the meeting place of the Coppell Historical Society and is used for public events such as A Vintage Christmas. Residents can also take tours of the house, which has been designed to resemble the original structure that Edna Kirkland called home. (Left, courtesy of the Coppell Historical Society; below, courtesy of Kara Jex.)

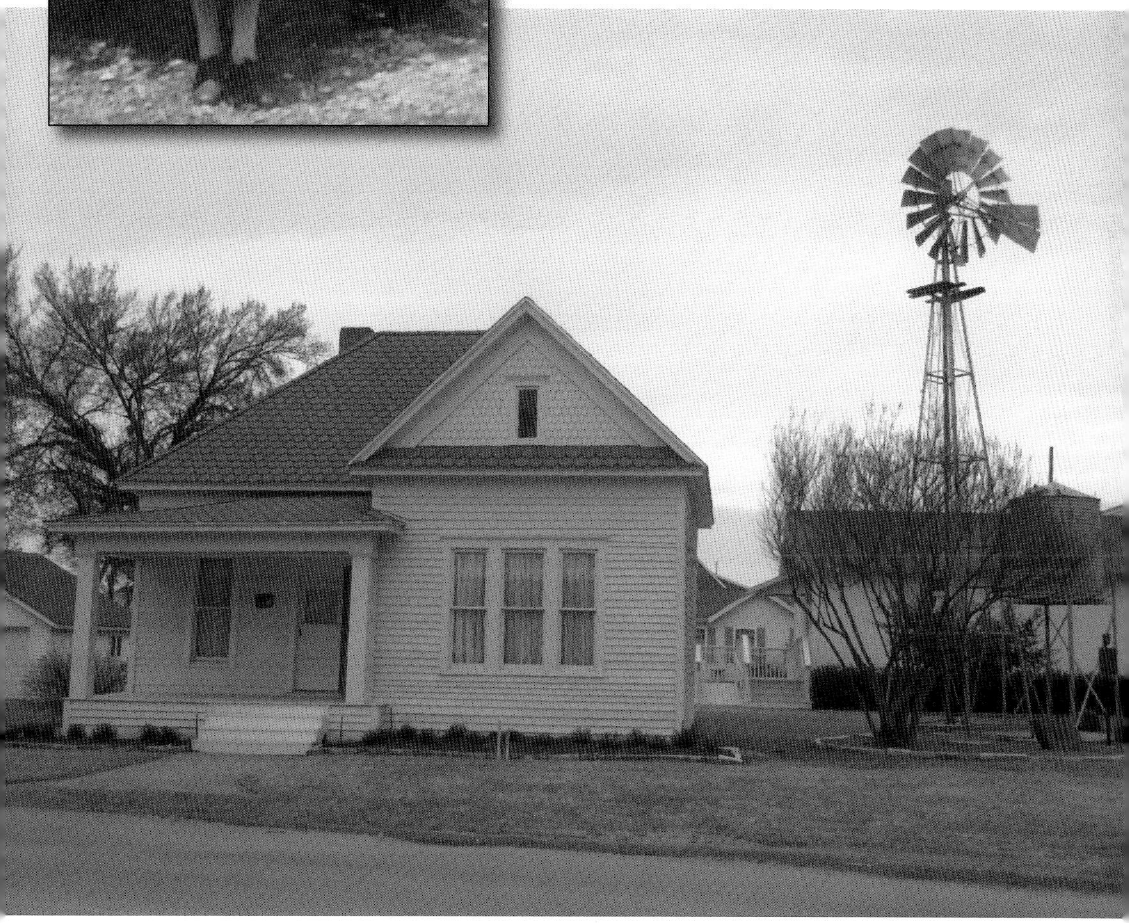

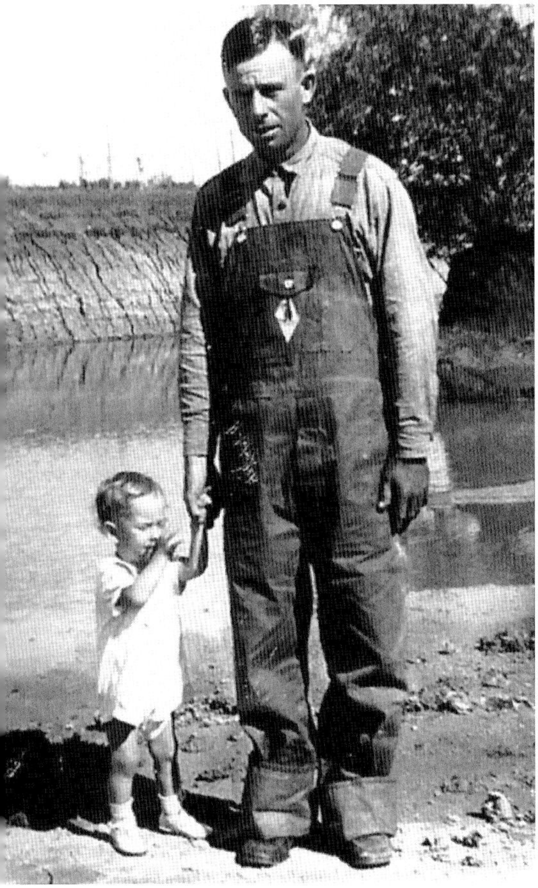

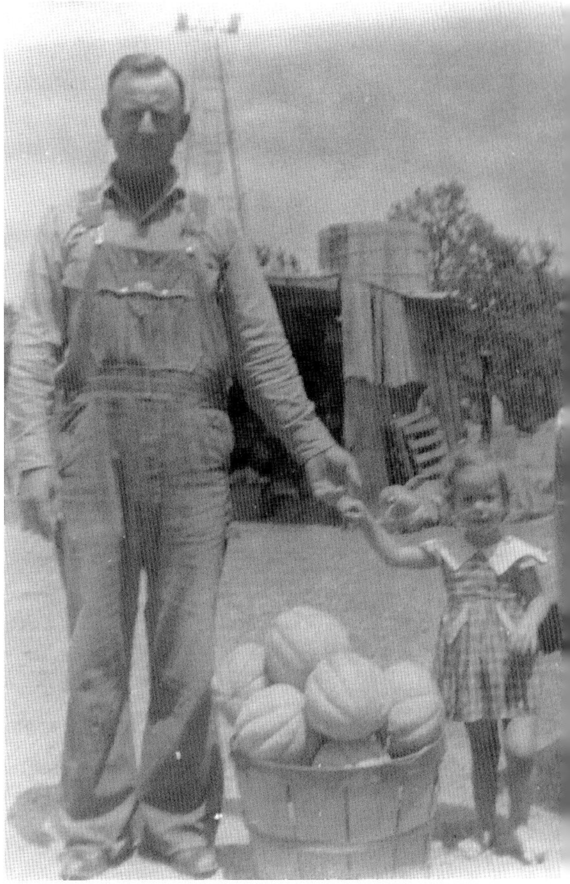

W.A. Ottinger

W.A. "Mike" Ottinger moved to the Coppell area in 1914. His bride, Eula, arrived three years later. Together with their children, they would spend almost five decades farming in Coppell.

In the early years, the family grew cotton, hay, corn, and vegetables. They worked as tenant farmers, giving as much as one-third of their crop to a landlord.

In 1939, the family entered into hog and cattle farming. Ottinger's son Bobby recalls that the farm typically held around 1,500 hogs and 100 head of cattle. The family also sold gravel culled from the property.

In 1968, ill health forced Ottinger to leave the farming business. In 1975, he passed away after an extended illness.

Ottinger is pictured in both images with unidentified children. (Both, courtesy of the Coppell Historical Society.)

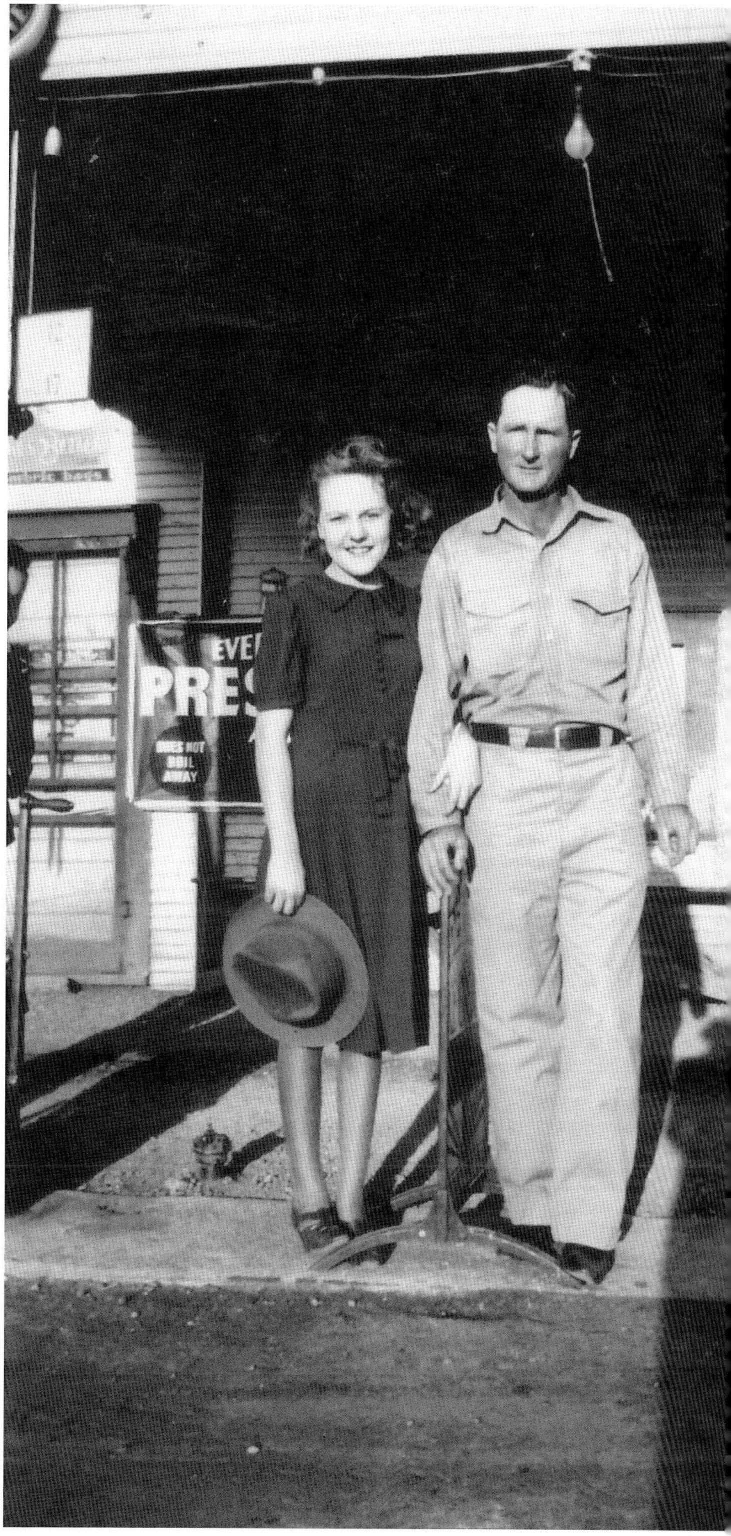

Ernest Gentry
In 1932, Ernest Gentry purchased a small service station in the heart of Coppell and converted it into a service station and grocery store. He previously ran a grocery with his brother Emmett but entered into the new venture alone.

Prior to owning the store, Ernest spent time farming. He also worked for Dallas County as a truck driver. The family struggled during this time, and his daughter Lorene records that one summer they worked with local farmers, helping can black-eyed peas, corn, and tomatoes, and then splitting the finished product. The entire family, down to the youngest children, participated.

In 1937, during the heart of the Depression, men would gather in front of Gentry's store, waiting to perform day labor for the Works Progress Administration. During these years, Ernest's children Lorene and Elzworth helped run the store.

In 1942, the store was sold. Elzworth entered the Air Force, and Ernest went to work for a defense plant.

Family history records that Ernest was baptized in 1915 in Denton Creek before joining the First Baptist Church of Coppell and being ordained a deacon in 1918. In 1969, under the direction of Rev. Lou Brown, the church honored Ernest for 50 years of service to the congregation. The event was patterned after the popular *This Is Your Life* television program.

In 1977, Ernest was taken with an illness that claimed his life on January 21, 1978. (Courtesy of the Coppell Historical Society.)

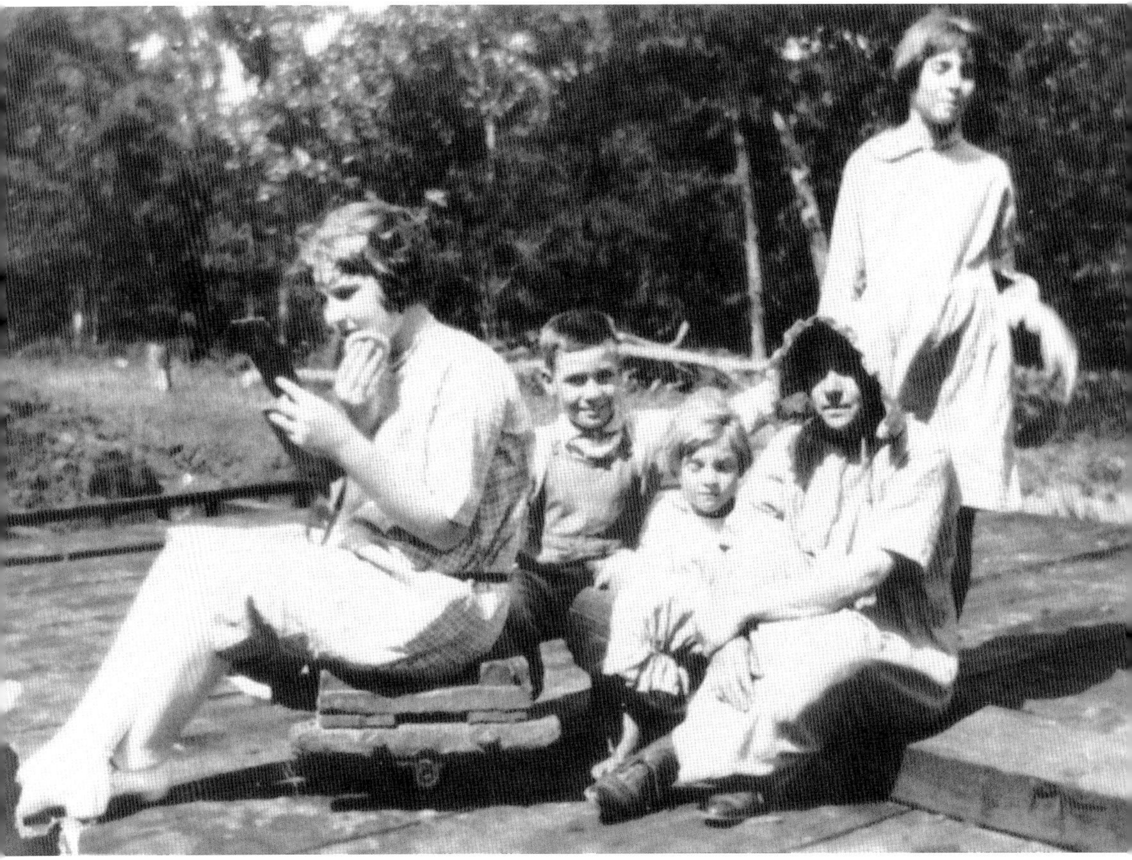

Ruby McDowell

Ruby McDowell was born in 1904 and remained a lifelong resident of Coppell until her death in 2001. McDowell married her husband, Rufus, in 1923. In 1930, the couple moved to a house on Heartz Road where they raised cotton and corn. They then took their cotton crop to a local gin that was later destroyed by a tornado.

The couple moved again, this time to a home on present-day Sandy Lake Road. The land was owned by Walter Thweatt and doubled as a gas and grocery store that the McDowells operated.

The store suffered in the Great Depression, and McDowell later reflected that there was a week when they did not have so much as a dime in the cash register. When Prohibition was repealed in 1933, Thweatt prompted the couple to begin selling liquor. The McDowells refused, and Thweatt raised their rent, forcing them to move again.

McDowell also recalled that the first election she ever voted in was concerning the sale of liquor in the Coppell area. In a story again involving the Thweatt family, J.C. Thweatt's grandfather was serving as election judge and tried to trick McDowell into voting "Yes" to allow liquor sales.

McDowell was a lifelong Baptist and, as a child, attended Bethel Baptist Church until it burned in 1915. Members of her family were buried in the church's cemetery now known as Historic Bethel Cemetery. In later years, McDowell visited the cemetery to straighten the stones that marked her siblings' graves.

In 1992, McDowell and family hosted a family reunion in Coppell, marking the first time they had all been together since 1930.

McDowell is among those pictured here. (Courtesy of the Coppell Historical Society.)

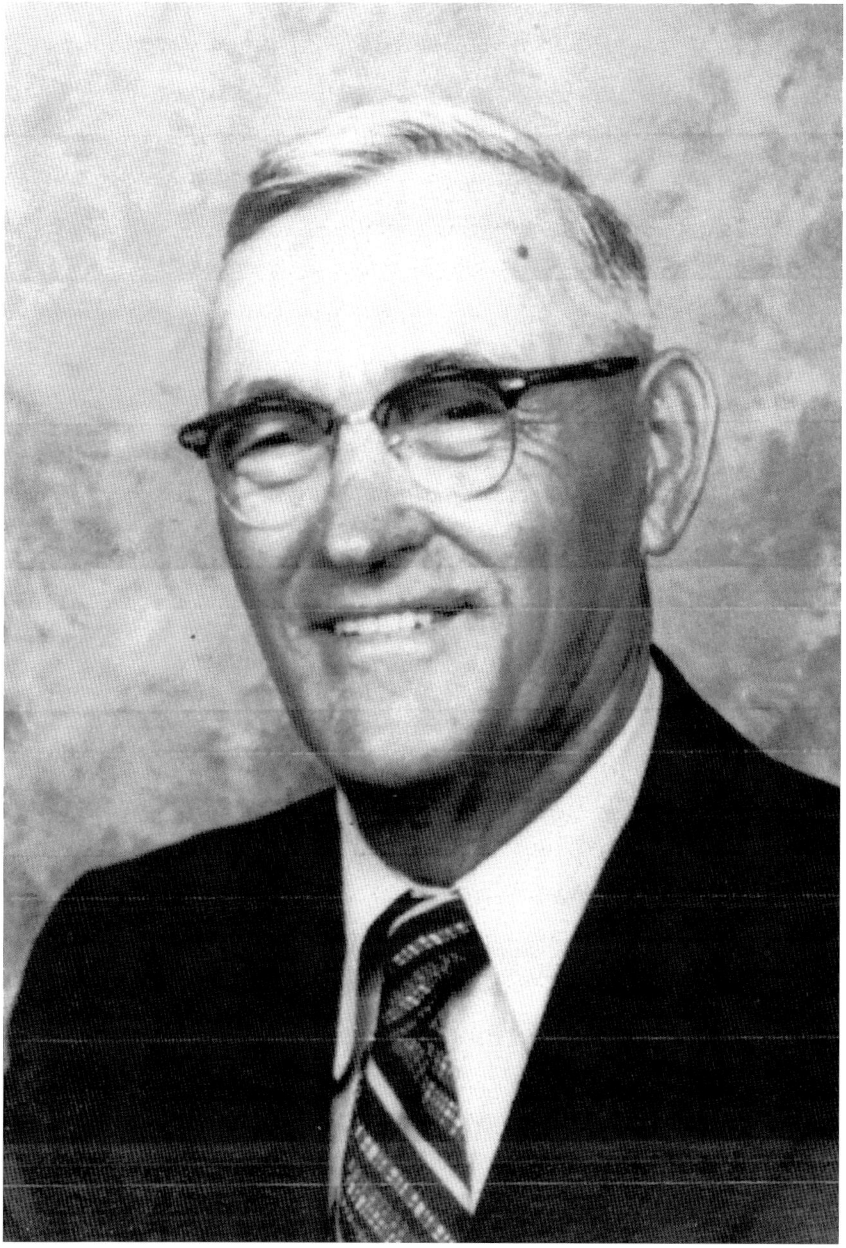

Buren Ledbetter
Buren Ledbetter was born in 1908 in Ferris, Texas, to Elector Ledbetter and Eugenia Bryant. In 1916, the family moved to a plot of land in the country between Carrolton and Coppell. They built a farm on the land, growing cotton, corn, and maize for silage. In addition, the family raised pigs, cows, turkey, chickens, guineas, and ducks.

As an adult, Buren continued to farm the land. He brought his cotton crop to the gin located in Coppell and regularly played dominoes with men in town. Buren's daughter Joyce recalls that he would often walk from the family farm all the way into town to spend hours playing the game. (Courtesy of Joyce Webb.)

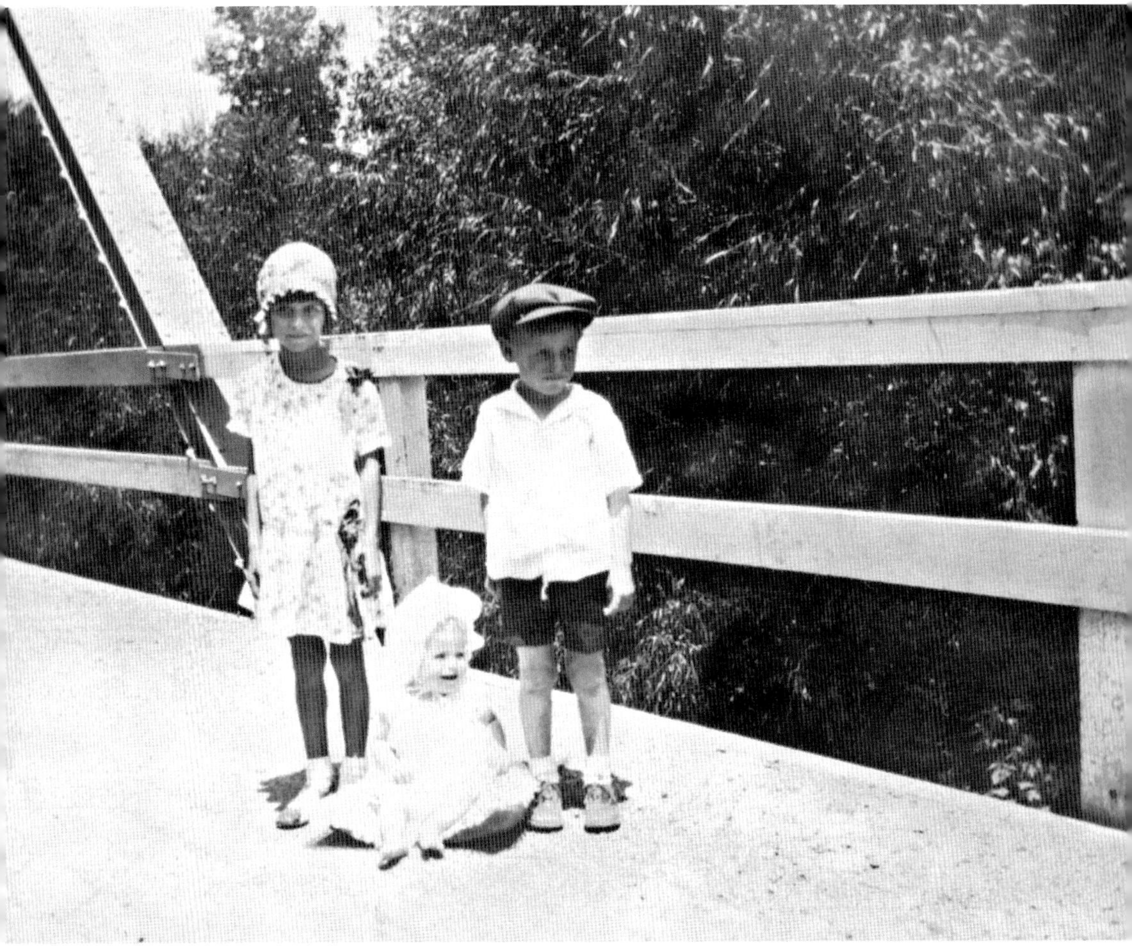

Juanita Strong

Juanita Strong (center) was born in Coppell in 1927 to William and Anna Barfknecht. Her family is considered one of the town's pioneer families.

The Barfknechts were devout members of the United Church of Christ, attending Round Grove United Church of Christ in Lewisville. The congregation was originally known as the German Evangelical Friedens Congregation, and Strong's father was a charter member. Today, the church has been transformed into the Special Moments Wedding Chapel.

Strong was also a member of Coppell's historical society and contributed a number of the items now on display at the historic Kirkland House. (Courtesy of the Coppell Historical Society.)

J.C. Thweatt

Though J.C. Thweatt was born in Oakcliff, his story has always been rooted in Coppell. He was the great-grandson of James Parrish, one of Coppell's first residents.

Thweatt frequented Coppell as a child, going on hunting trips with his father and working on his grandfather's farm. At 13 years old, his family moved to Highland Park, where he attended high school.

Thweatt later worked for an electric company. He also worked with his father at a Dallas publication called *The Pink Sheet*, which served auto finance and insurance companies.

In 1965, Thweatt moved to Coppell with his wife, Jean, who was known to most as "Shorty." They developed a mobile home park, which was open until Jean's passing in 1972. Thweatt was openly against the town's expansion and is remembered wryly (and with a good deal of affection) as something of a curmudgeon. Stories still circulate about a fistfight that Thweatt was involved in during a school board meeting, though some of the details may be apocryphal. People also remember Shorty chasing school buses off the family property with a broom.

Evidence of the Thweatt family dots Coppell. For many years, Sandy Lake Road was known as Thweatt Road. After it was changed, the city dedicated a park as Thweatt Park. In 2004, Thweatt donated the windmill from the family farm to the City of Coppell. The windmill now sits in Heritage Park near the Kirkland House and is one of the centerpieces of the Old Town Revitalization efforts.

Thweatt passed away in 2005 at the age of 89. (Courtesy of the Coppell Historical Society.)

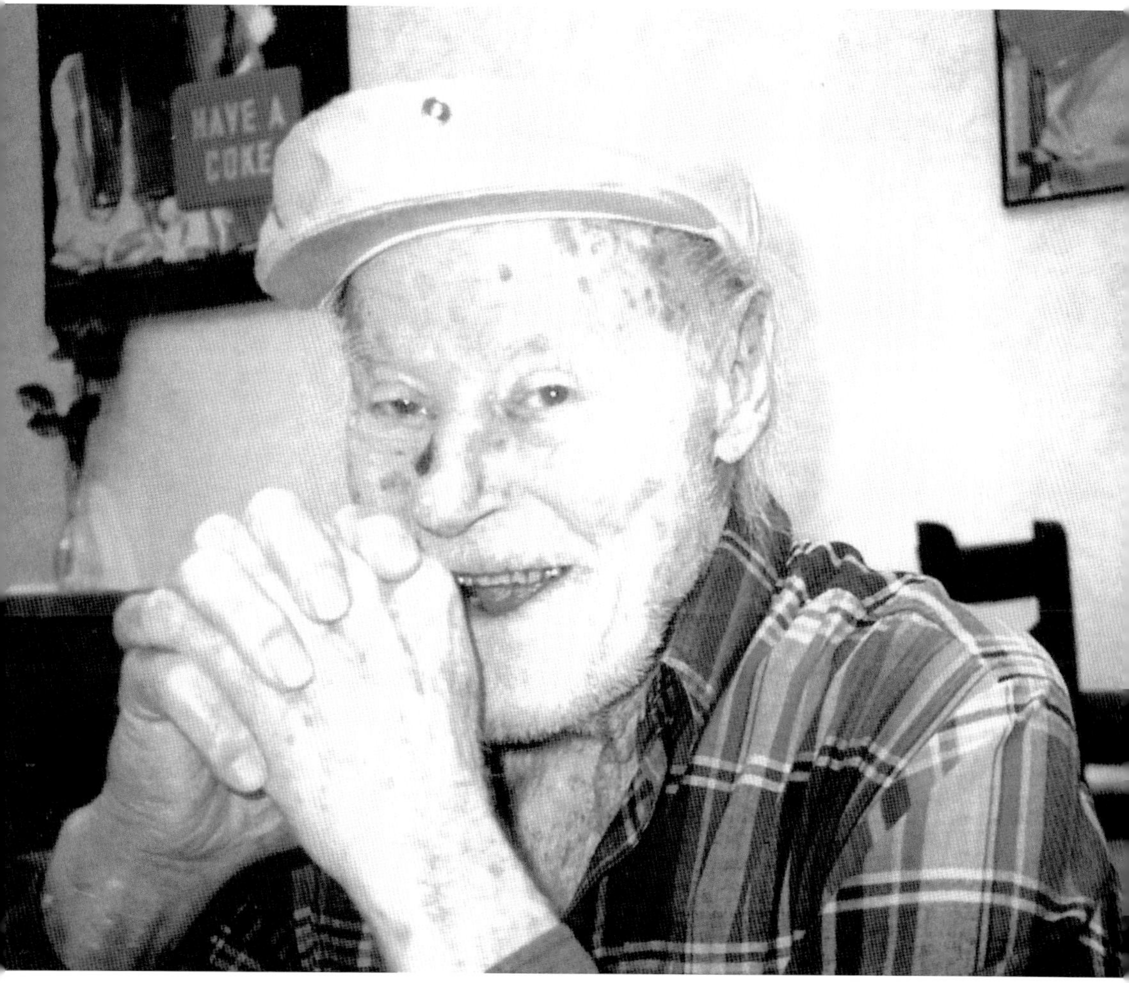

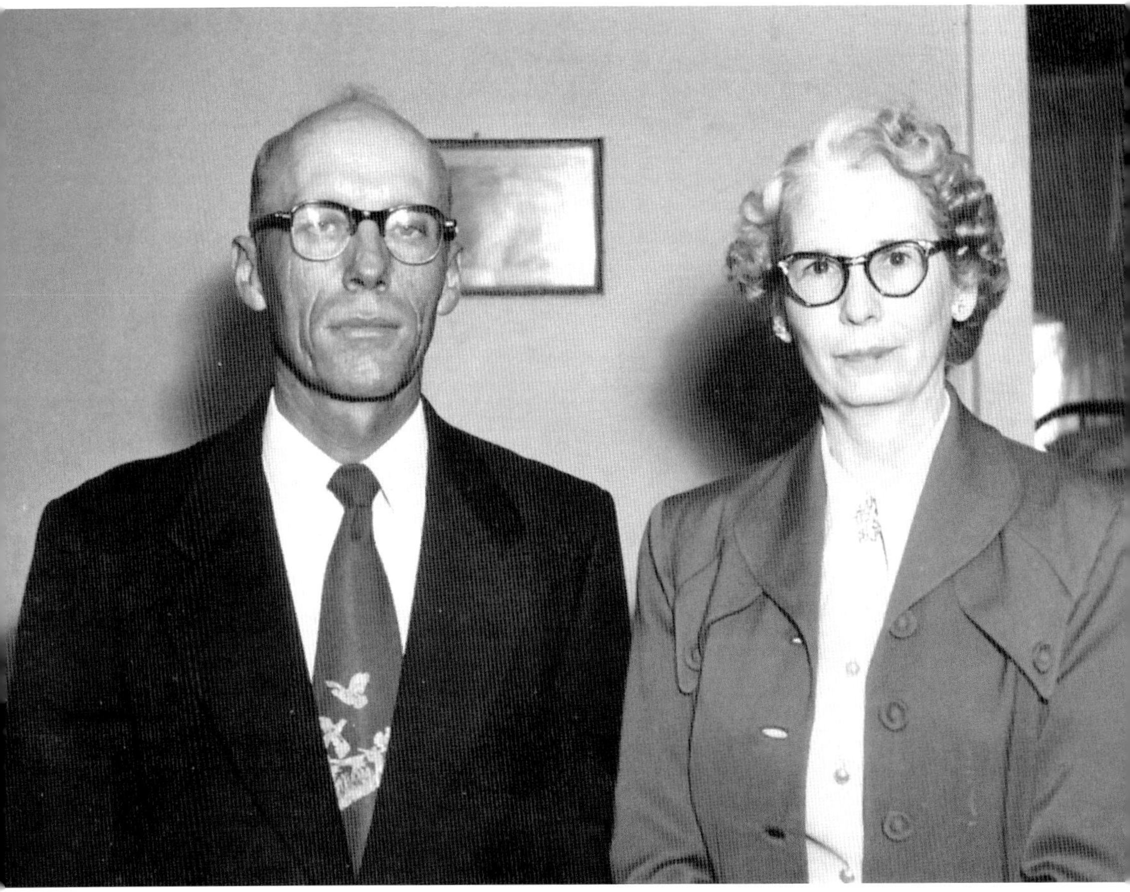

Clayta Harwell

Clayta Plumblee Harwell was born in Coppell in June 1908. Her father, Claude, sharecropped on the land of "Grandpa Harrison," growing numerous crops that included watermelon, cantaloupe, and peanuts. After harvest, the crops were taken to Market Street in Dallas to be sold.

In 1927, Clayta married Floyd Harwell, the owner of a barbershop on Bethel Road. In 1931, Clayta gave birth to the couple's only child, Bill.

In 1941, Clayta began working for the railroad as an express agent, shipping and handling items delivered by train to the town. For a brief period, her duties included handling cotton. At the time, the rail through town rarely carried passengers. Two trains a day stopped in town to make deliveries or pick up items. Clayta would inventory any arrivals and arrange for their pickup. She remained a railroad employee until 1955.

While working for the railroad, Clayta also worked as a cook for the Coppell School. Residents would frequently interrupt her work at the school when they needed items picked up from the depot. Clayta later recalled that, in her first years at the school, there was no running water in the building. It had to be retrieved from outdoor faucets. The water was boiled in a kettle and then poured into tubs that were used for both cooking and washing the dishes. (Courtesy of the Coppell Historical Society.)

Jewel "Jack" Kirkland

When Coppell held its first Founders' Day Celebration, special recognition was given to lifelong resident Jewel Kirkland. Known to most as "Jack," she was brought to the event in a horse-drawn carriage and honored as Coppell's oldest continuous resident. She was also presented with a special commemorative pin.

Born to John and Edna Kirkland in 1902, Jewel grew up in Coppell and lived most of her life in what is now the Historic Kirkland House. As a young girl, Jewel recalled that the school in Coppell had no playground equipment and that the children would spend recess picking wildflowers from a nearby field. She also recalled that, as a young girl, she would pretend to smoke and dip snuff by burning reeds and dipping cinnamon.

Jewel was an active Methodist and recalled a brush arbor built behind the original church where outdoor services were held in the summer.

She was on the first basketball team in the Coppell School. She joined knowing virtually nothing about the sport and stated that the team was terrible in its first year.

In 1988 and 1992, Jewel met with Pete Wilson to give detailed histories of Coppell, providing key information about the location of early businesses, residences, and other major landmarks like old bridges and the town's cotton gin. Jewel also contributed to the preservation of the town's history through numerous photographs she took over the years, many of which are now permanently archived by the Coppell Historical Society. (Courtesy of the Coppell Historical Society.)

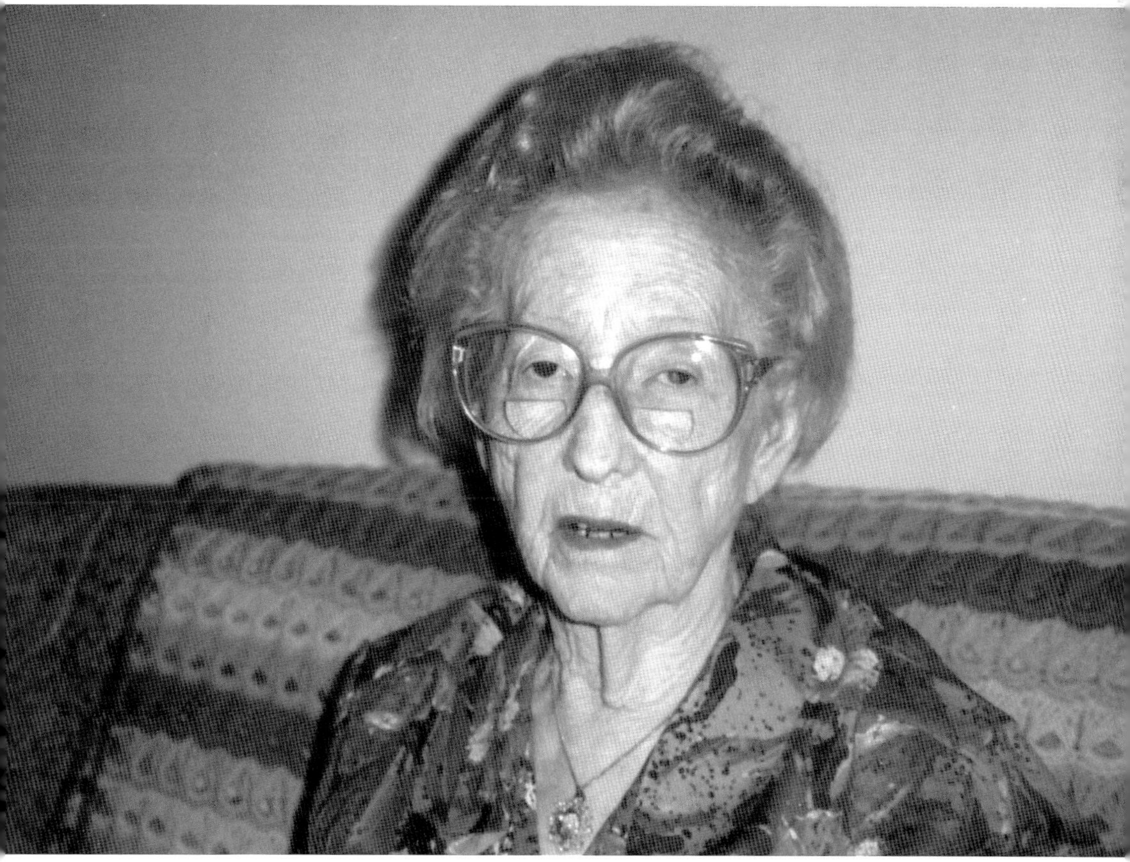

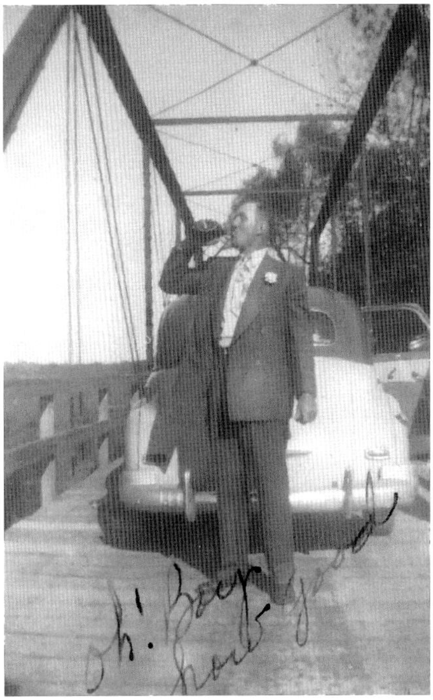

Cecil Dobecka Sr.

Cecil Dobecka Sr. was born in 1915 to Frank and Mary Dobecka. He was the eighth child born to the couple. In 1947, Dobecka married Mary Cervenka. The ceremony was a double wedding, with brother Tony marrying Mary's sister Pauline. Several months prior, their brother Johnny Dobecka had wed Mary and Pauline's sister Vicki. Cecil and Johnny went into business together, running a gas and grocery store in Carrollton. (Courtesy of Cecil Dobecka Jr.)

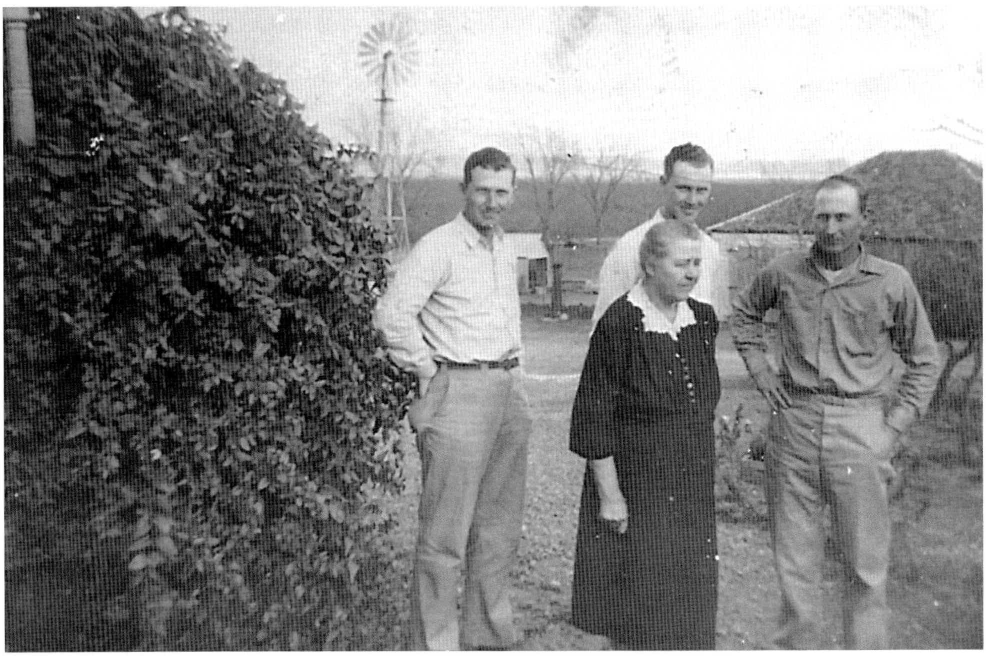

Cecil Dobecka

Cecil and Johnny Dobecka later began a dairy business on the family land. The property had been sold to Cecil Leslie, who leased it back to the Dobeckas. The two brothers remained in business until the late 1950s, when they sold to L.B. Ledbetter. Cecil also raised cattle, was a member of Coppell's volunteer fire department, and served as a Coppell city councilman. He passed away in 1967. (Courtesy of Cecil Dobecka Jr.)

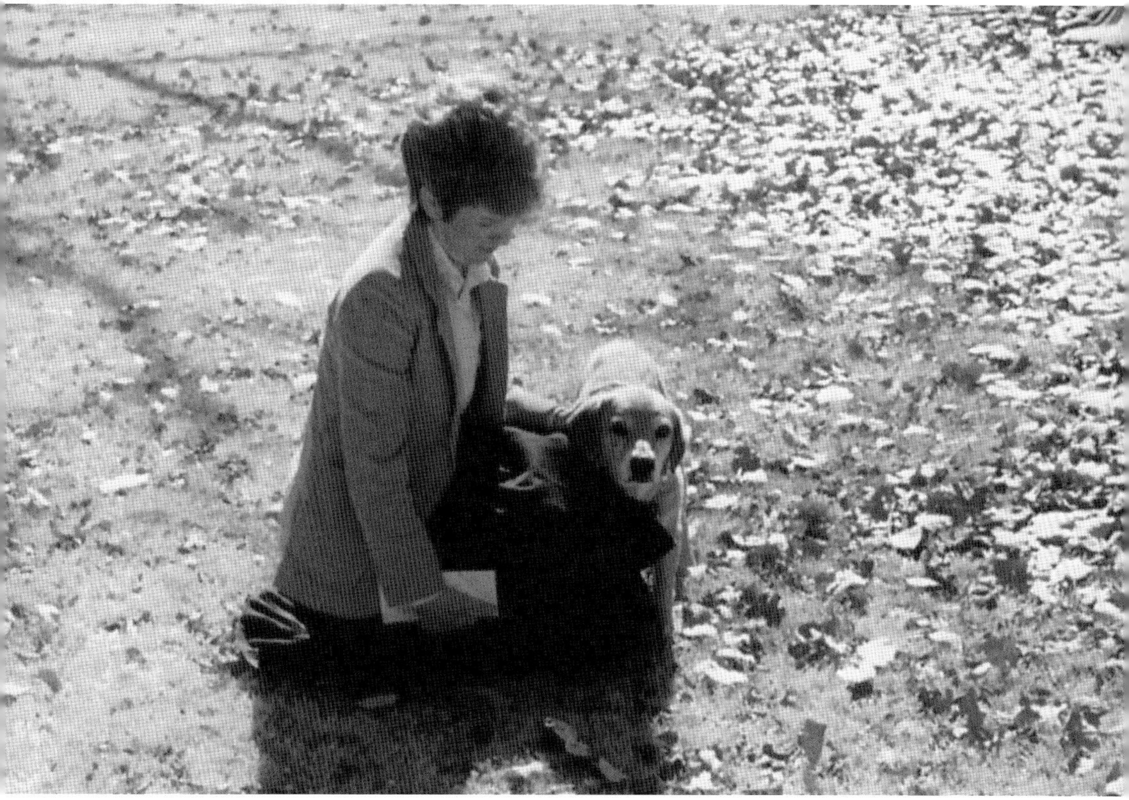

Pooch: The Firehouse Dog

Pooch began his life as a stray. No one knows exactly where he came from, but one day after school he followed Barbara Lee's son home and quickly became a member of the family. Each morning, he would walk with the Lee children to their bus stop and wait until it arrived. After the kids were gone, he would trot to the firehouse and remain there until returning home with the Lees at the end of the day.

Mayor Andy Brown Jr. passed a city ordinance that named Pooch the town's official fire house dog. Pooch was awarded a plaque, his own personal fire hydrant, and a medallion to wear around his neck. (Courtesy of Richard and Barbara Lee.)

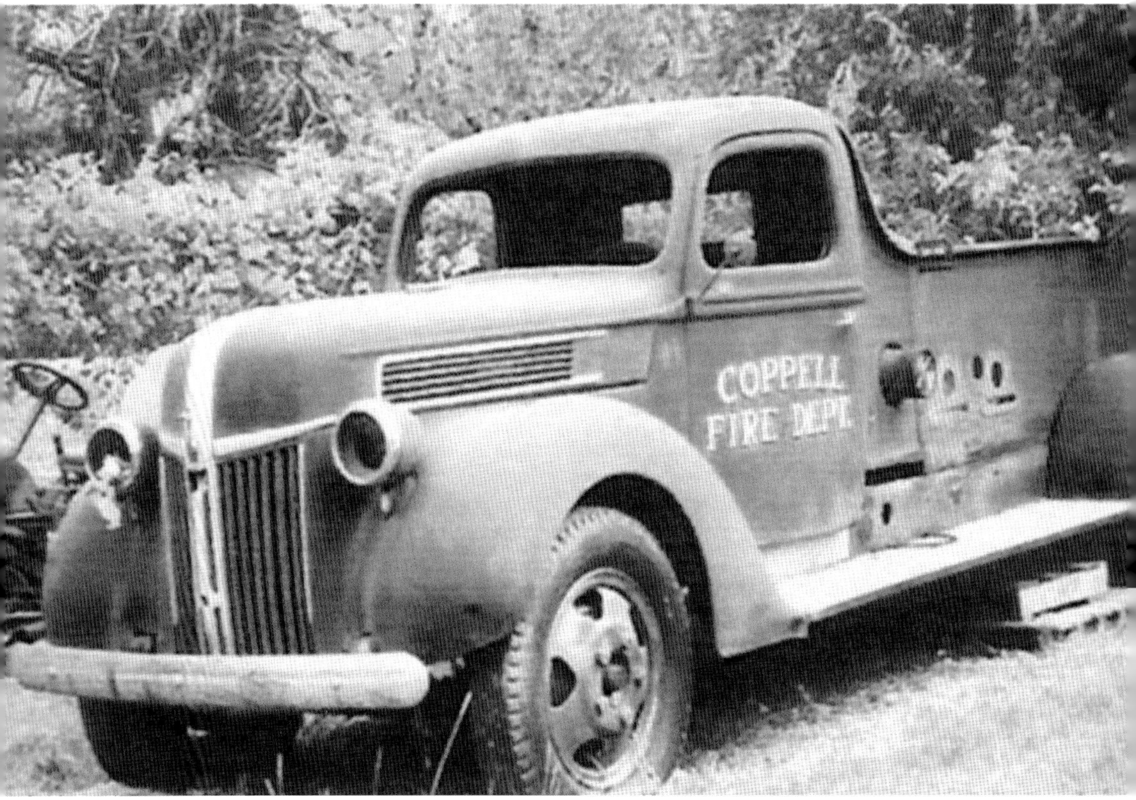
COPPELL
FIRE DEPT.

Old Red (OPPOSITE PAGE)
Old Red is a 1941 Ford that the City of Coppell purchased from Carrollton in the early days of the fire department. It was purchased with money raised by the fire department's volunteer force. After serving the city for years, the truck disappeared. It was eventually found rusted and in need of serious repairs. The firefighters went business to business, handing out flyers and free popsicles, to generate interest in restoring the vehicle. Jean Murph, editor of the *Citizens' Advocate*, wrote a song about the truck, which was recorded by a Nashville musician and released as a CD single to aid in the restoration fundraising.

The truck was fully restored and used in city parades and other events. It was also used as the hearse for former chief Earl Tinsley after his passing in 2014. (Courtesy of the Coppell Historical Society.)

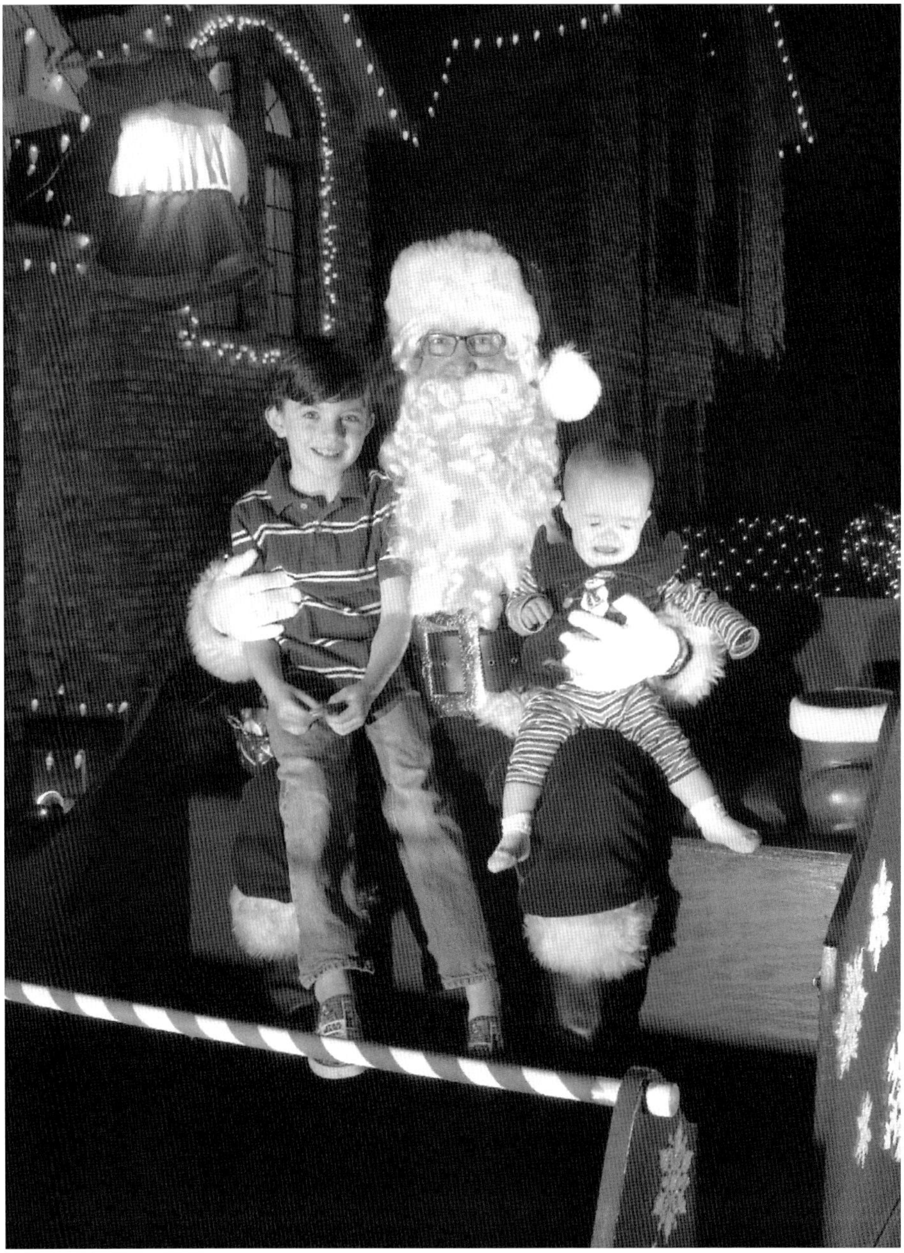

Danny Vrla

Since 1988, Danny Vrla has been the Santa Claus of Coppell. Each Christmas, he constructs a wooden sleigh in his front yard, dresses up as Saint Nick, and visits with children from all over town.

The tradition began as a way to entertain his seven-year-old son and now spans generations. Children sit on his sleigh, whisper their Christmas wishes, and receive a peppermint candy cane before being left with an admonition to always listen to their parents.

It is not unusual to see crowds waiting in front of his house each night during the Christmas season. He has been Santa for so long that children who visited him in their youth have returned to visit with children of their own. (Courtesy of Kara Jex.)

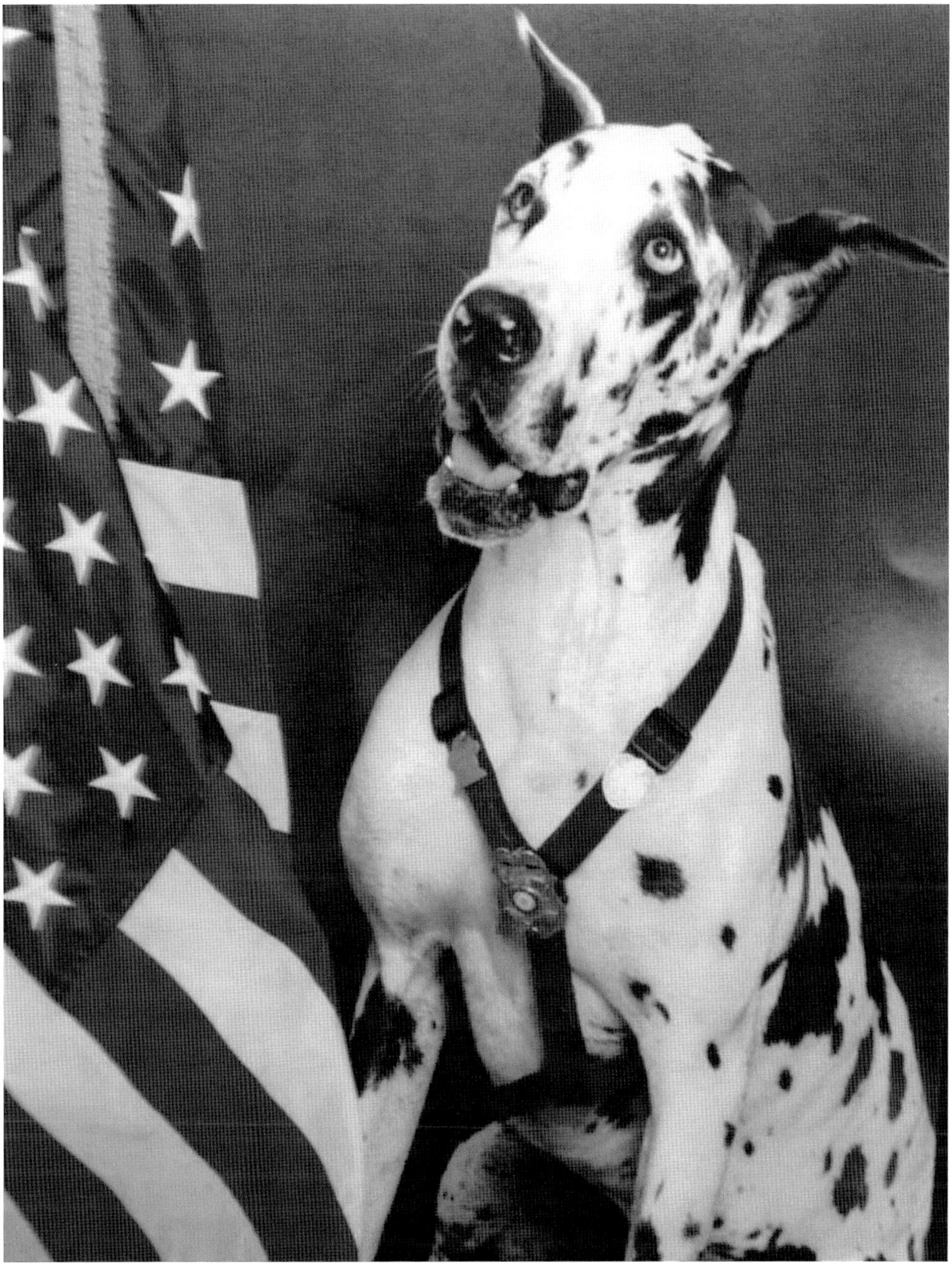

Dash

In 2000, Capt. Eric Greaser adopted a lumbering Dalmatian puppy from the nearby Coppell animal shelter and brought her to Coppell's Firehouse No.1. The dog was given the name Dash, after the Pierce fire engine. She became the department's mascot and was trained and cared for by the firefighters.

Dash remained with the department for three years before "retiring" to live on a ranch. During her time with the department, her main duty was to live as an unusually spoiled member of the firefighter family. (Courtesy of the Coppell Fire Department.)

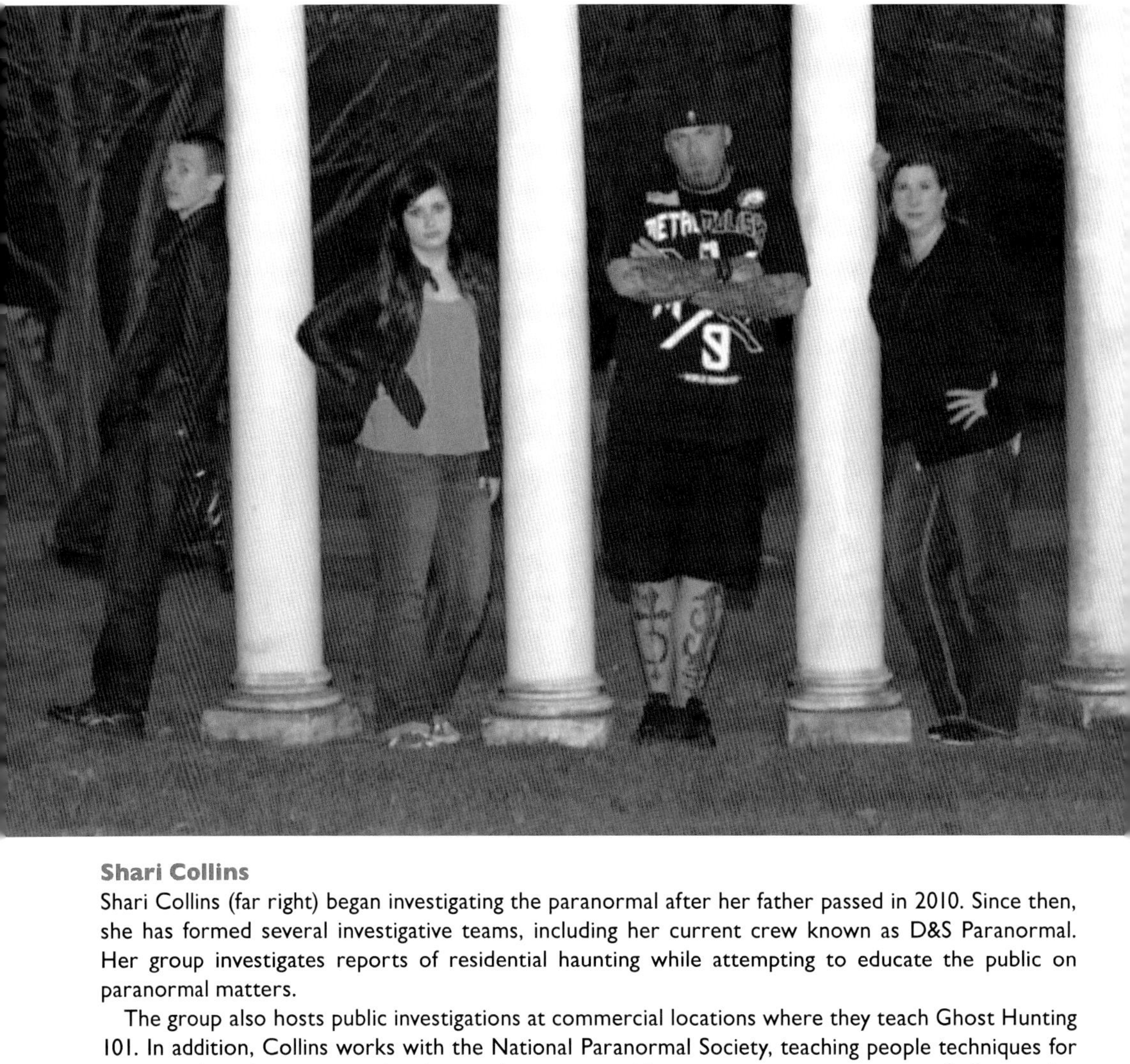

Shari Collins

Shari Collins (far right) began investigating the paranormal after her father passed in 2010. Since then, she has formed several investigative teams, including her current crew known as D&S Paranormal. Her group investigates reports of residential haunting while attempting to educate the public on paranormal matters.

The group also hosts public investigations at commercial locations where they teach Ghost Hunting 101. In addition, Collins works with the National Paranormal Society, teaching people techniques for photographing the paranormal and tips on how to assemble your own investigative team. Collins credits her team as being one of the few to employ and teach youth about the ghost hunting process. (Courtesy of Shari Collins.)

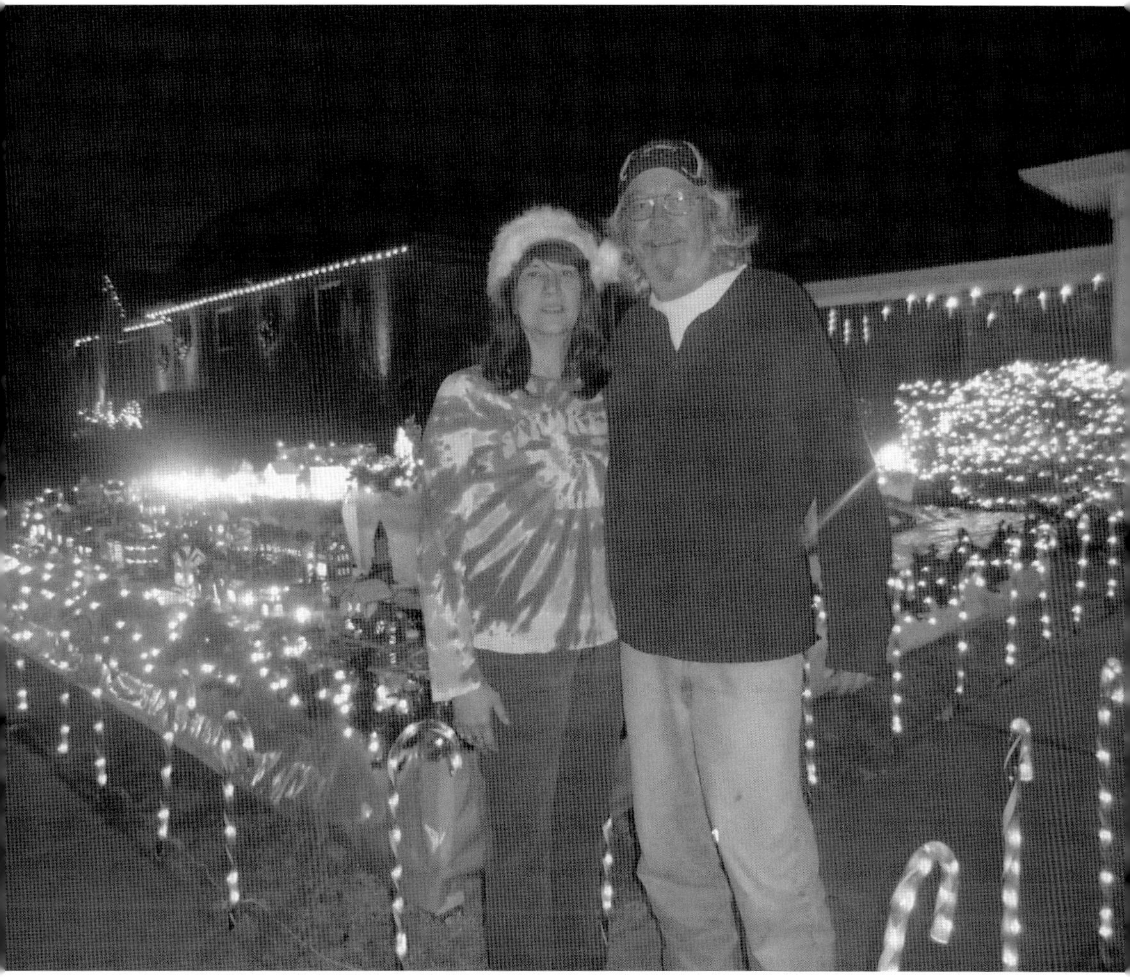

Jeff and Peg Hoogendorn
Following the terrorist attacks on September 11, 2001, Jeff and Peg Hoogendorn decided to do something to raise community spirits. The result is the Trains at Havencrest, an event turned annual Coppell tradition. The Trains is a sprawling display of Christmas lights and toy trains that wind through handmade settings of locations as diverse as New Orleans, Costa Rica, and the Sturgis Motorcycle Rally. Another portion of the display contains a life-sized nativity called The True Gifts of Christmas, a collection of parcels labeled with words like joy, peace, and forgiveness.

Peg credits her inspiration as the Christmas displays she saw in the store windows of her hometown of New Orleans when she was a young girl. The success of the event has led the Hoogendorns to add a Halloween display and neighborhood cookout. (Courtesy of Kara Jex.)

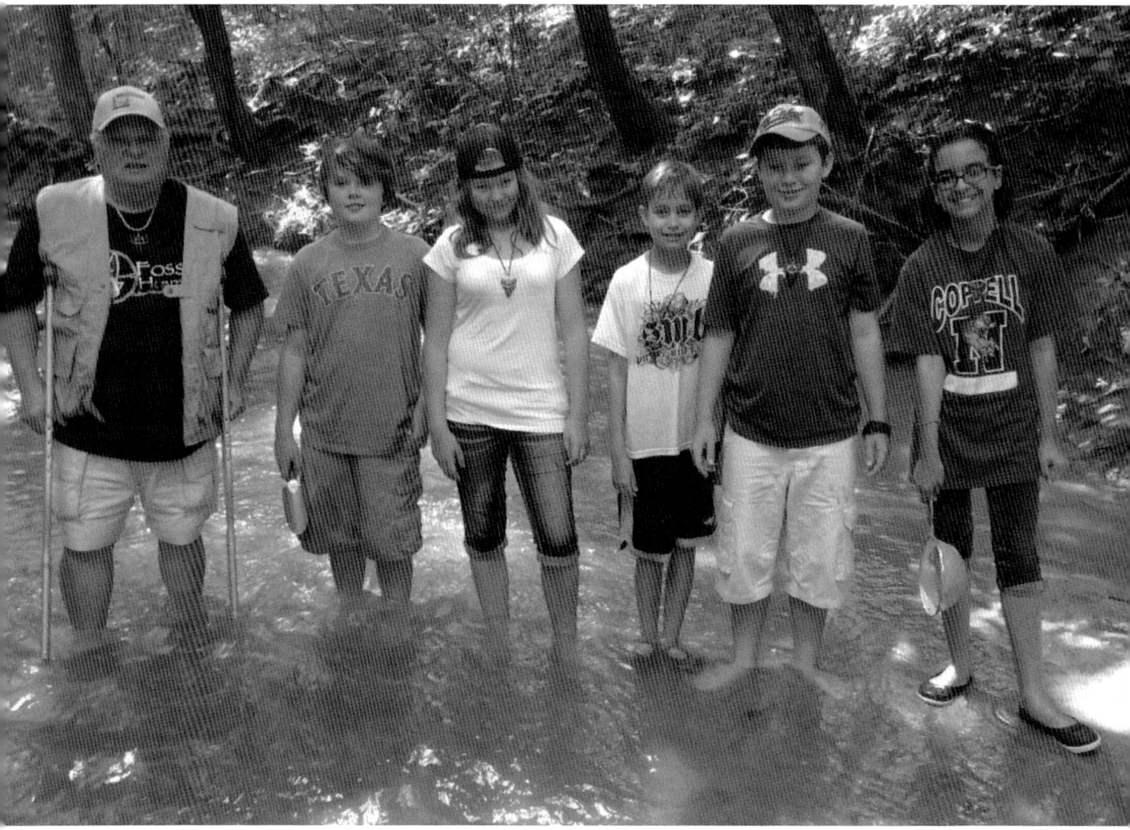

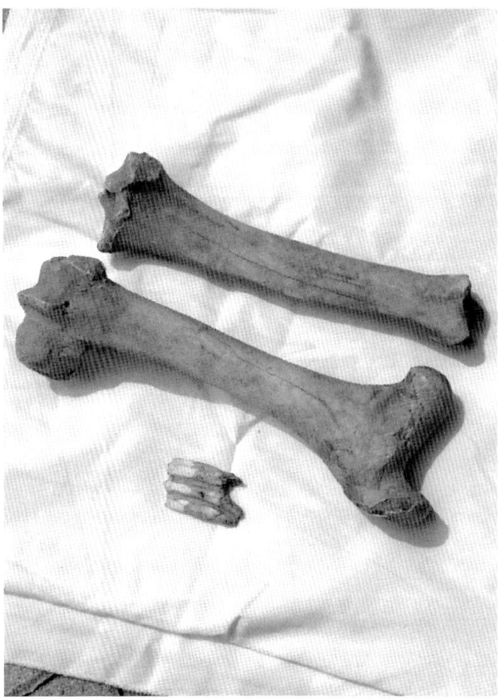

David Goodner

David Goodner spent 28 years in the oil industry before pursuing paleontology. He worked as a geologist for Mobil Oil from 1974 to 2000 and as president of the Texaco Central Area Division from 2000 to 2007. Goodner holds a bachelor's degree in science and master's in geology. As of 2015, he has a pending PhD in micropaleontology. He serves on the board of the Friends of Coppell Nature Park and is a Green Bay Packers shareholder.

Goodner leads geology and fossil camps at the Coppell Nature Park, presenting each of his students with a megalodon tooth at the end of the session. He also serves as a guest lecturer on geology and paleontology for Coppell schools.

Goodner has made significant discoveries in the Coppell Nature Park creek, including a number of 92-million-year-old oysters, ammonites, and fossilized bison bones dating back 20,000 years. (Both, courtesy of David Goodner.)

CHAPTER SIX

Government

On November 18, 1955, a group of 35 residents of Coppell signed a petition requesting that the town become incorporated. Several weeks later on December 17, a public vote was held, with the majority voting in favor. The land constituting incorporated Coppell was two square miles.

Immediately following incorporation, a new election was announced to select city leaders. Notices were placed outside of Floyd Harwell's barbershop and stores owned by residents English and Cooper. An additional notice was run in the *Carrolton Chronicle*. The election was held on January 6, 1956, and elected a mayor, five aldermen, a town secretary, and a town marshal.

Today, there is a general belief that the town's first mayor was William T. Cozby. A sign at the cemetery where Cozy is buried records him as such, as do a number of newspaper articles written over the years. Cozby, however, was not even a candidate.

The actual first mayor of Coppell was R.M. Johnson, who won in a landslide. City records show that Johnson captured 28 of the 40 total votes cast. Joining Johnson were Roy Liberto as secretary, Albert Hodge as marshal, and G.C. Lanham, C.C. Mitchell, W.E. Grave, and George Corbin as aldermen.

Johnson remained mayor until April 1960, when William T. Cozby took office.

In the years that followed, Coppell has had a number of colorful and significant political figures. Like any elected official, each has had ardent supports and equally passionate decriers. A quick review of old newspapers or city council minutes will reveal political battles and controversies, some of which grew so heated that residents voiced open concerns that violence could break out between the factions. Many of these divisions still simmer just below the surface, and passions still burn over decades-old feuds.

The profiles in the following pages will focus predominately on the positive contributions that the elected individuals have made to Coppell and the state of Texas.

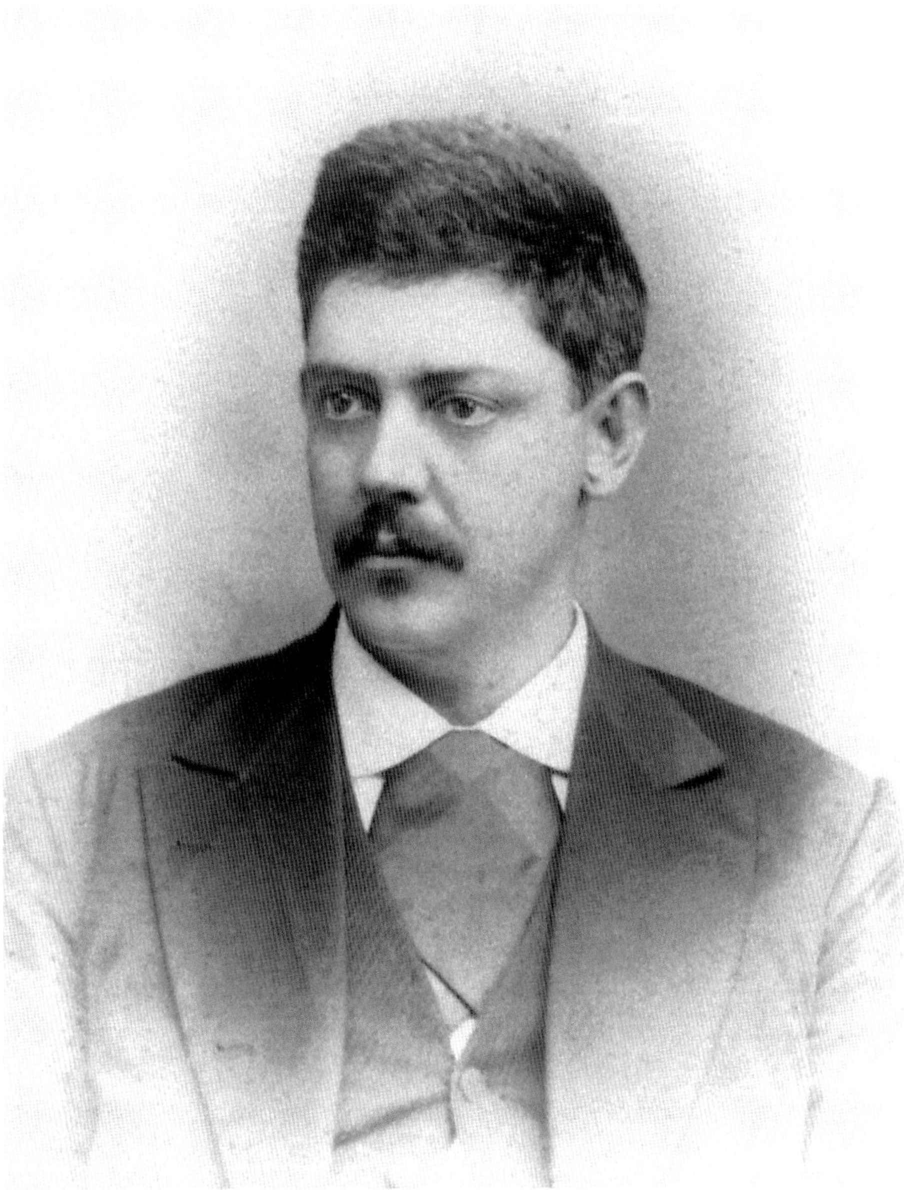

Barnett Gibbs

Prior to 1892, the city of Coppell was known as Gibbs. Though no one knows for sure, it is generally accepted that the name was in honor of Barnett Gibbs, a prominent attorney who started his practice in Dallas in 1873 after graduating from the Cumberland Law School. He served as the city attorney of Dallas before being elected to the state legislature in 1883. In 1884, he was elected lieutenant governor and briefly served as acting governor in 1885.

Gibbs was a populist who worked for legislation favoring farmers. This is often given as the reason the town chose the name Gibbs, despite the fact that he never lived in town. He was also known to defend railroad rights, though any connection to this and the naming of Gibbs would also be conjecture.

In 1904, Gibbs died and was buried in Dallas's Oakland Cemetery. (Courtesy of State Preservation Board, Austin, Texas; Photographer: Jesse Herrera, 8/18/94, post-conservation.)

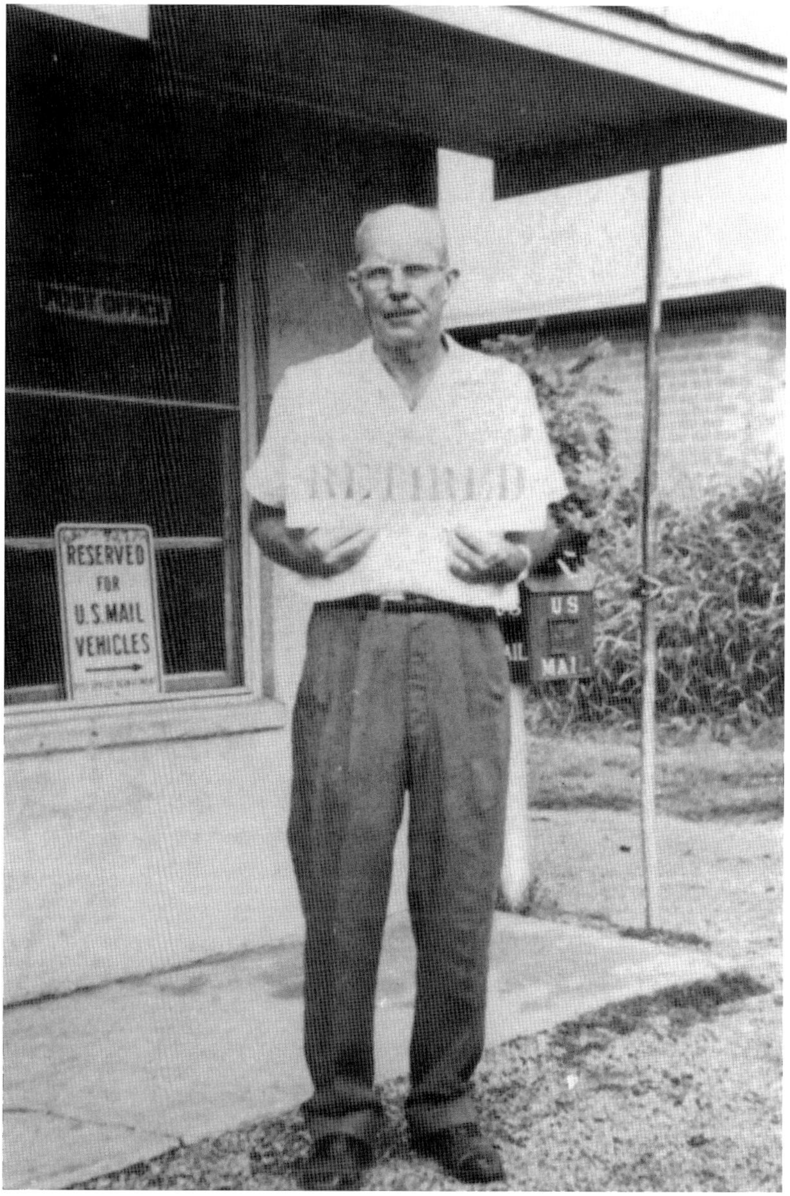

Clyde Parker

Clyde Parker was born in 1898 in Denton County to parents Dave Parker and Dora Nash. He spent the majority of his life in Coppell and was an active member of the town's Methodist church. Parker was married to Goldie Mae Robertson, and the couple had two children.

Parker spent many years as the Coppell postmaster, remaining in the position until his retirement in 1962.

Parker and his wife operated a small grocery business along with the post office. The post office was a small building, and Parker eventually had it rebuilt, doubling the size and making the new building from brick.

Parker was also known for building a domino hall in town, giving the old men who played in front of the general store another place to play. (Courtesy of the Coppell Historical Society.)

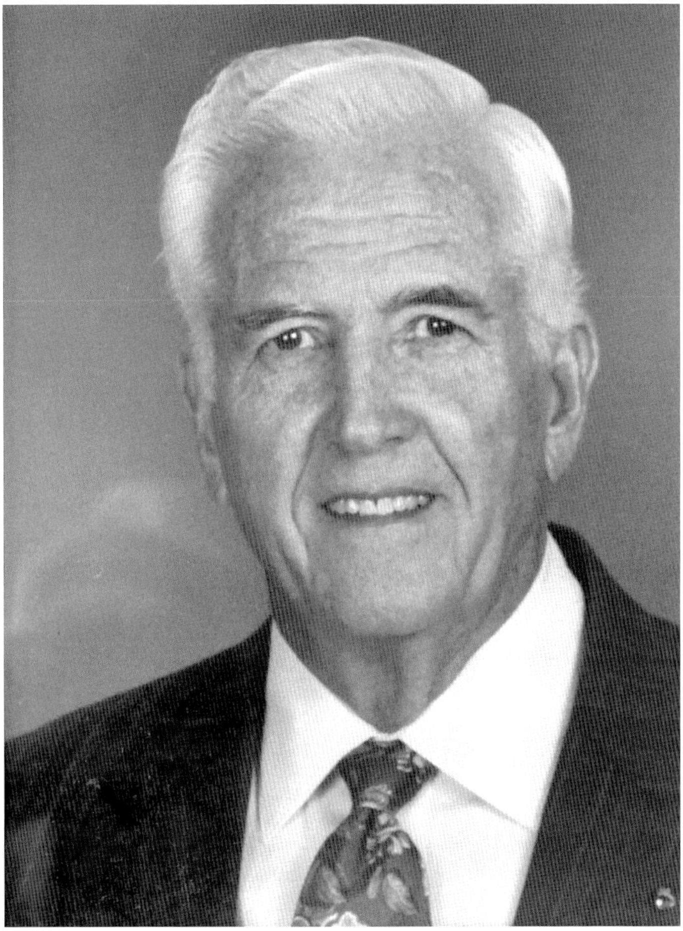

W.H. Wilson

In 1992, CISD opened W.H. Wilson Elementary. The school was named in honor of Wheelice H. Wilson Sr. Born in McKinney in 1921, Wilson was the son of a drugstore owner who later went into the dairy business. After high school, Wilson attended North Texas State University, where he majored in chemistry. A science degree led him to serve in the field of radar during World War II. He later worked for the Magnolia Oil Company, which was incorporated into the Mobil company in 1959. He worked as a computer specialist, building the first major analog computer the company used for research. He later worked as a data analyst.

He and his wife, Ruby Nell, purchased a home in Coppell that sits in the center of what is now known as Old Town. Wilson served on the town's water board, which created the first public water supply for Coppell. He later became a member of the school board, though the exact dates of his service have either been lost or were not recorded.

As the town began to grow, Wilson was elected to city council. His election came at a time of upheaval in town as factions clashed over issues of growth. The council was involved in numerous legal battles over issues of zoning and expansion of public utilities, among others. Despite the fierce resistance, Wilson and those in favor of change ultimately prevailed.

Wilson also served on the city's first historic commission in an attempt to preserve the town's past. In a fitting footnote to this legacy, Wilson's son Wheelice Wilson Jr. negotiated a deal with the city that will preserve Wheelice and Ruby's home in Old Town as a permanent part of Heritage Park. (Courtesy of Wheelice Wilson Jr.)

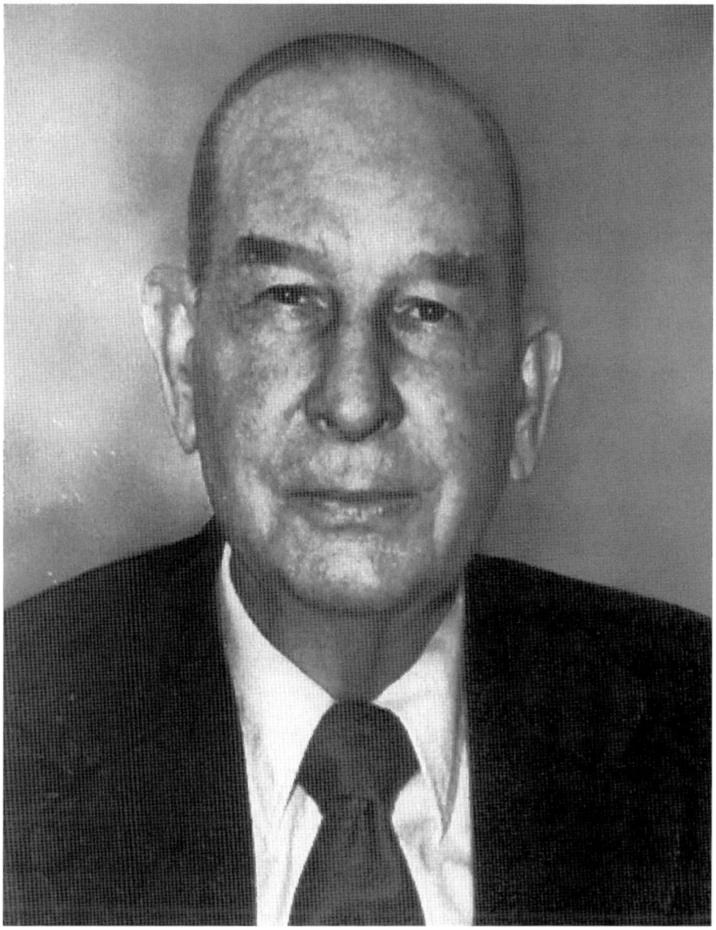

William T. Cozby

William T. Cozby was the second mayor of Coppell. He took office in 1960, four years after the town was incorporated. The era marked the beginning of Coppell's transition from a farm town to a suburb. The growth was met by fierce resistance from certain residents adamantly opposed to the increased taxation that came with incorporation and development.

In 1964, a town vote was held on the issue, with citizens voting on the option to disincorporate and dissolve the City of Coppell. The measure failed, but battles over the town's development continued. Lawsuits and delays abounded when passing city ordinances.

In the early years of Cozby's mayorship, he garnered local fame when he and a handful of residents appeared in the popular newspaper column *Tolbert's Texas*. In the piece, Cozby and others discussed the ferocity of the local chigger population. Cozby even invited scientists to come to Coppell and verify that the insects were in fact the largest chiggers in Texas.

In 1979, Cozby began working to protect the Bethel Cemetery. Research had uncovered that Cozby, who was related to several of Coppell's pioneer families, had relatives buried in the cemetery. He worked to generate interest in the cemetery, reaching out to other families who had relatives buried on the land. The process of raising money and getting the land protected took 10 years, and in 1989, the town held a dedication for the historic Bethel Cemetery. In addition, the location became listed on the register of historic places in the state of Texas.

In recognition for his lifetime of service to the city, Coppell's public library system is named the William T. Cozby Public Library. (Courtesy of the Coppell Historical Society.)

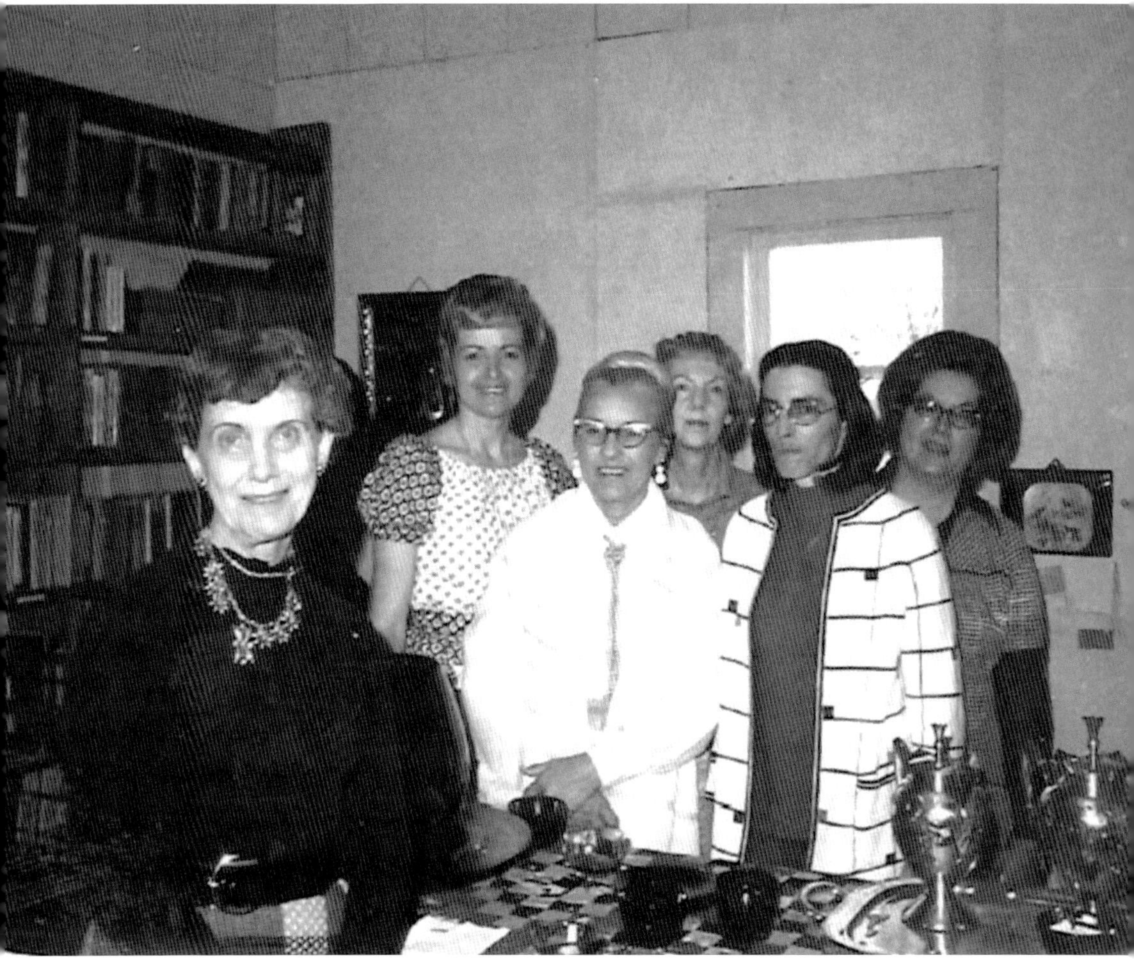

Jo Jackson

The first library in Coppell was operated from a small frame house in Old Town Coppell. It opened in 1974. The building was originally the residence of W.J. Russell before being remodeled by city volunteers.

The town's first librarian was Jo Jackson (second from right), known to many as the "Bird Lady of Coppell." She served her first year on a volunteer basis, receiving no pay for her work. Jackson suffered from polio and was remembered as always walking from her home to the library. She gained the nickname Bird Lady for her encyclopedic knowledge of and passion for birds.

In 1975, the library became part of the Dallas County library system, gaining a $140 per month salary for the librarian. Due to deteriorating health, Jackson initially recommended another for the position but ultimately remained until her resignation in 1979. (Courtesy of the William T. Cozby Library.)

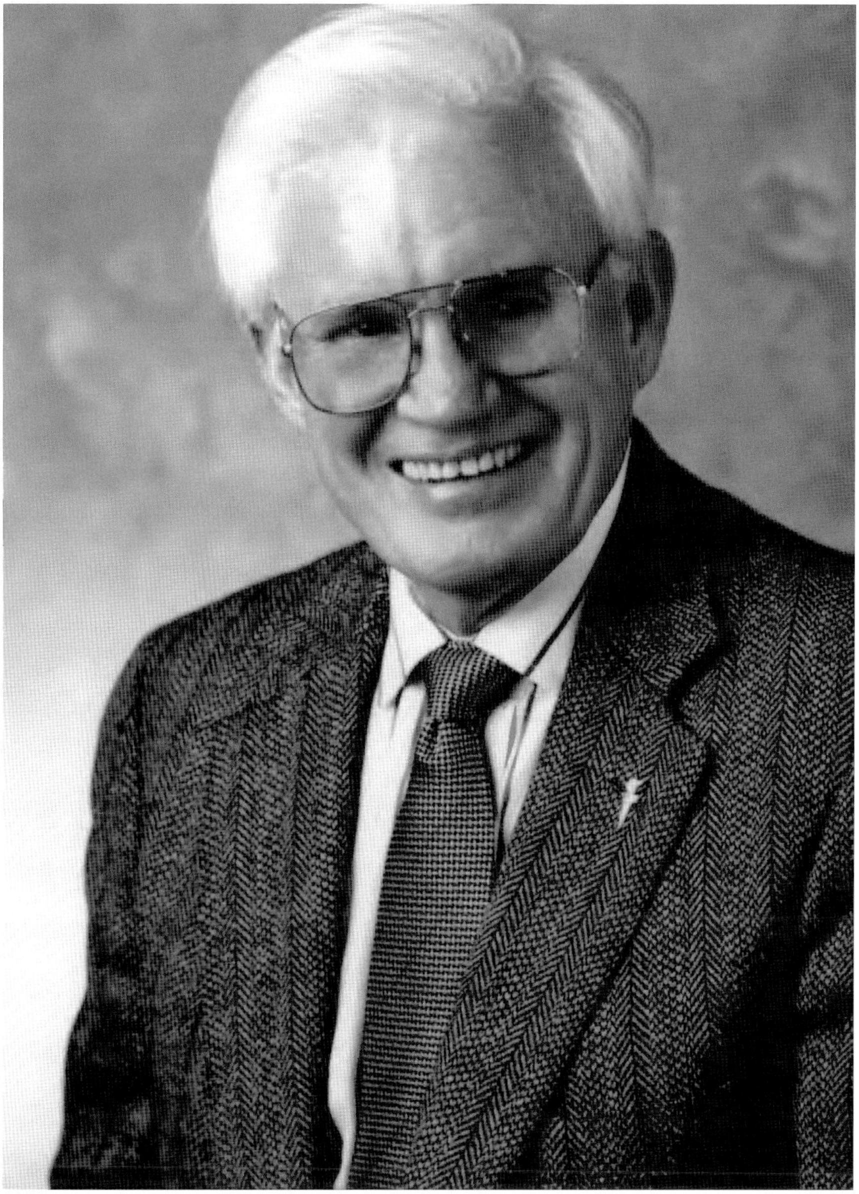

Don J. Carter

Don Carter was born to a poor family in Arkansas in 1933. The family struggled until 1957, when Carter's mother, Mary, created the business Home Interiors and Gifts. Carter helped his mother found the business, and by 1982 it had grown to an annual $400 million in sales. In 1987, Carter became president and CEO of Home Interiors before selling in 1994.

The success led Carter to found an expansion NBA team in 1980. Along with Norm Sonju, he started the Dallas Mavericks. Carter was a constant presence at games, sitting courtside in a cowboy hat.

Carter called Coppell home for many years, owning much of what is now the Lakewood and Carter estates. He was the owner of the First Coppell Bank. He also served as a city councilman and is credited with many of the concepts that developed the town throughout the 1970s. He now makes his home in Sarasota, Florida. (Courtesy of the City of Coppell.)

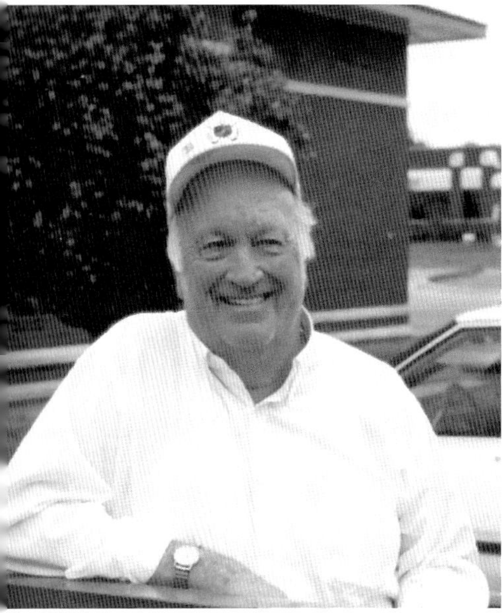

Walter Pettijohn

Walter Glynn Pettijohn served three terms as city councilman in Coppell during the 1980s. He was known as a political watchdog. He was outspoken in his views and defensive of his community. His views led him to challenge the practices of Mayor Andy Brown, setting off a chain of events that would eventually see Brown voted out of office.

Pettijohn was devoted to community service. A founding member of the Coppell Lion's Club, he was chosen as Lion of the Year and named to the club's roll of honor. He served in the US Army and was highly involved in the Northview Baptist Church in neighboring Lewisville. Pettijohn's wife Carole taught at Coppell High School. Walter worked as a teacher in the Carrollton Independent School District as the crafts teacher at Dewitt Perry Middle School.

He was also known for driving his John Deere tractor through town and offering to mow the lawns of anyone who needed help. (Both, courtesy of James Pettijohn.)

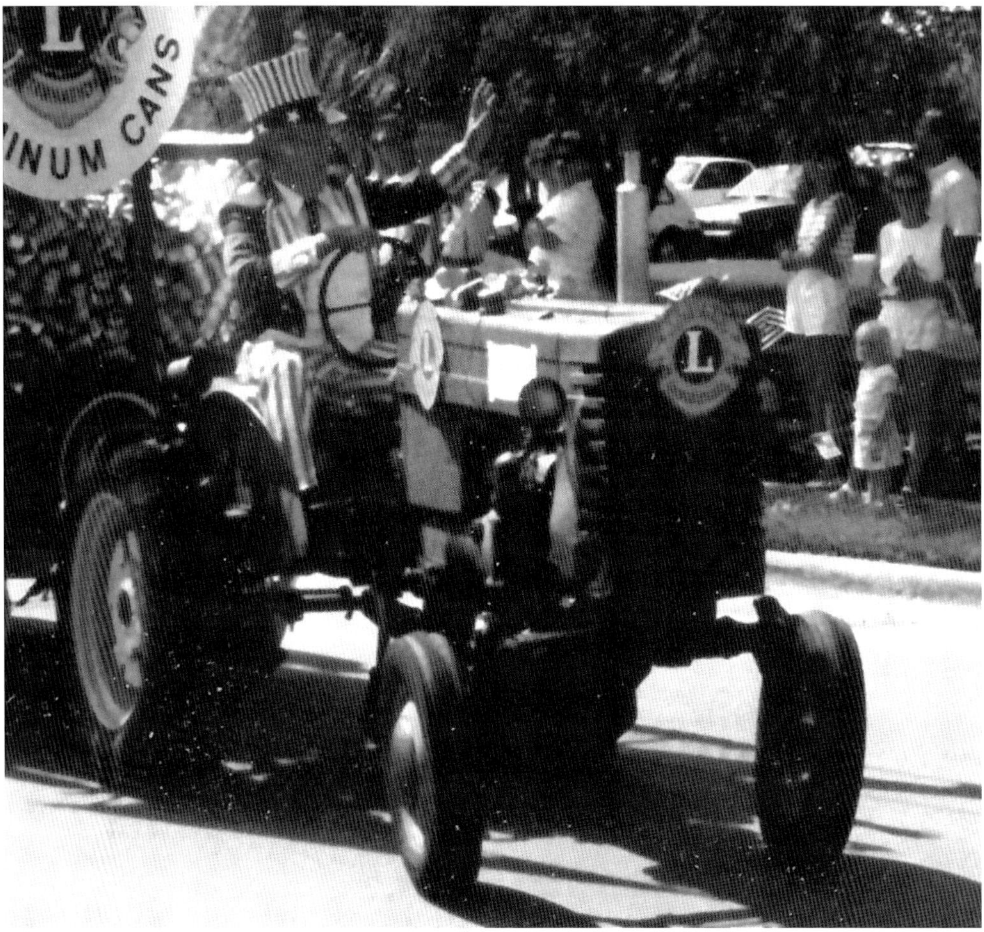

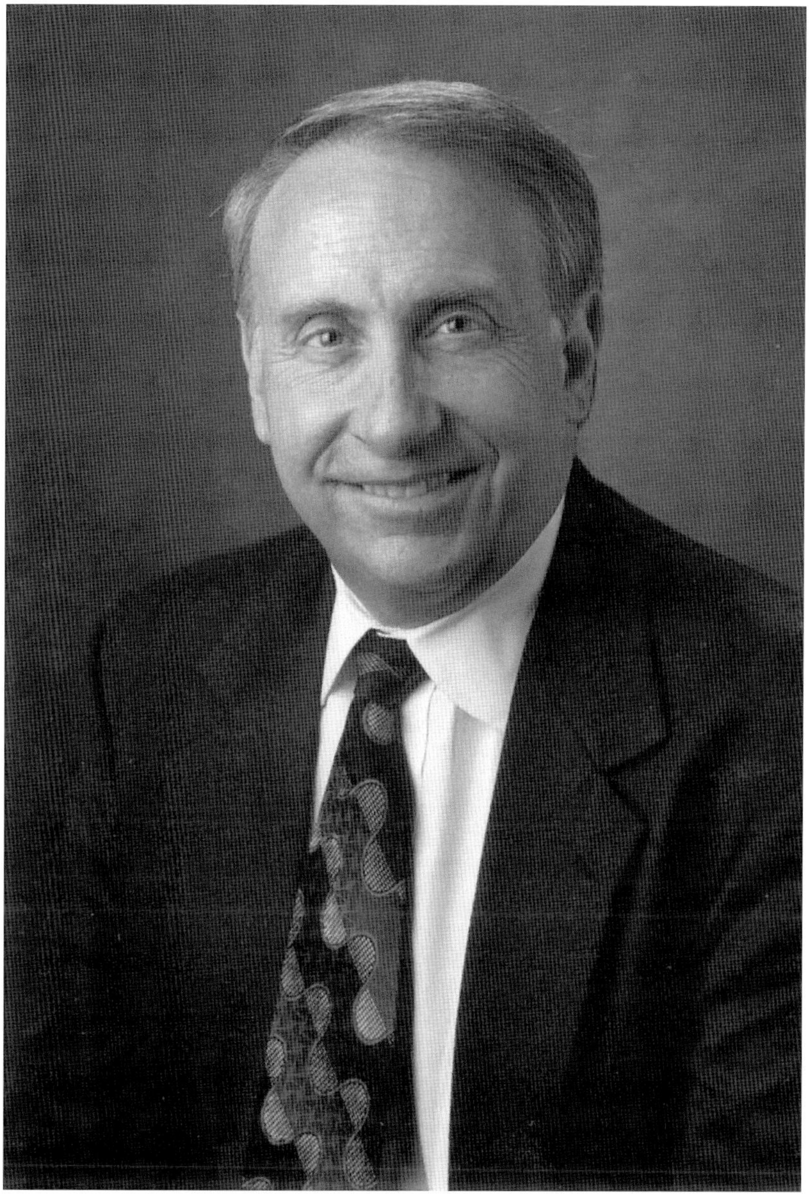

Andy Brown Jr.

Elected in 1979, Andy Brown Jr. championed the rapid growth and development of the town. He worked to annex land from the City of Dallas and worked extensively with developers to turn Coppell into a thriving suburb. He also laid out a detailed plan for city hall and what was pictured as a major commercial town center.

In 1985, Brown was defeated by Councilman Lou Dugan in a fiercely divisive election. Duggan captured 52 percent of the vote. After Brown's defeat, the city plan was changed, leading to a little-known quirk in city architecture. It seems that under Brown's plan, the city hall was designed to face out onto a row of shops that would create a new downtown area. However, the plan was later revised and the land was turned into a housing development and a small park. The back of the building was changed to the front, meaning that city hall is now always facing backward. (Courtesy of Andy Brown Jr.)

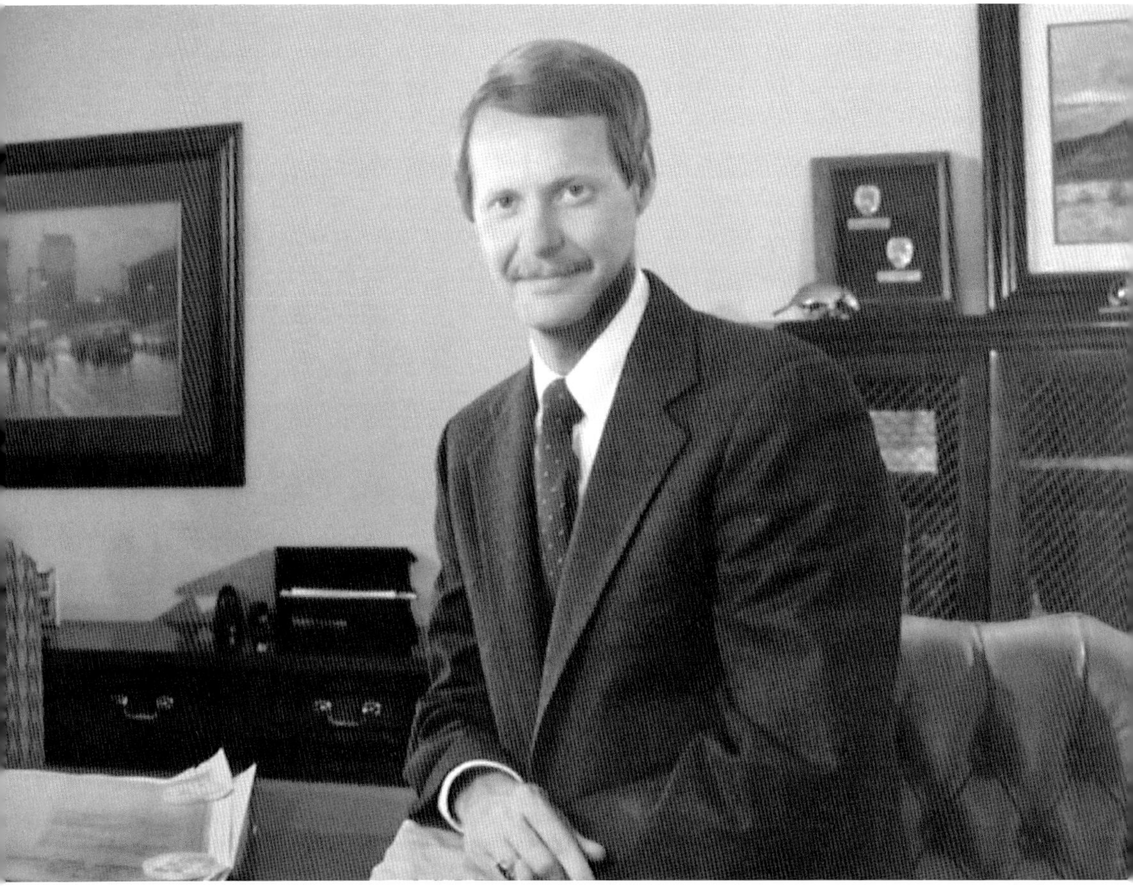

Lou Duggan
Lou Duggan began his service to the City of Coppell as a city councilman under Mayor Andy Brown Jr. At the time, the city was going through enormous changes. The Dallas–Fort Worth (DFW) airport had opened in 1973, and the effect was an explosion of growth that was turning the town from a rural area into a fully fledged suburb.

In 1984, Duggan began looking into irregularities at city hall reported by Jean Murph and the Coppell *Star.* Duggan decided to run for mayor on a reform platform. He won the election and set about creating greater transparency at city hall. Despite his victory, a good deal of Brown supporters remained in government, and Duggan even went on to name the public park system after Brown.

Duggan served several terms as mayor before declaring in 1988 that he would not seek reelection. He later went to work with Murph at her newspaper, the *Citizens' Advocate*. He also served as executive director of the Friends of Coppell Nature Park board for 10 years. In addition to his political work, Duggan has owned several companies and served on industry boards. He has a passion for Coppell history and has written a number of papers on the subject. (Courtesy of the *Citizens' Advocate*.)

Bill and Peggi Smothermon

Bill and Peggi Smotherman have been a strong community presence since moving to town in 1981.

Bill served as a city councilman for eight years and also served as mayor pro tem. As a councilman in the tumultuous 1980s, he helped vote on many difficult issues, including development, taxation, and the town's ordinance banning the sale of liquor. However, when asked about his time with the council, he wryly notes that they spent hours arguing about the color of carpets in the newly built city hall.

Not above getting their hands dirty, Bill and other city leaders like Mayor Lou Duggan volunteered to wash dishes to help the overworked staff at the grand opening of a local Italian eatery.

Bill is currently an active member of the town's Lion's Club and, with his daughter Mindy, serves at the club's community events like the annual pancake breakfast. He has served the club as president from 2012 to 2013 and for a time as treasurer.

In 2015, Peggi celebrated her 20th year as a teacher in the CISD. She has taught at a number of the district's middle schools and served a brief stint at the high school.

The family maintains an active presence in the Methodist church. Both Peggi and Bill sing in the church's choir. Peggi is a member of the church hand bells ensemble and occasionally sings as a member of the vocal ensemble known as the Sweet Adelines. (Courtesy of Bill and Peggi Smothermon.)

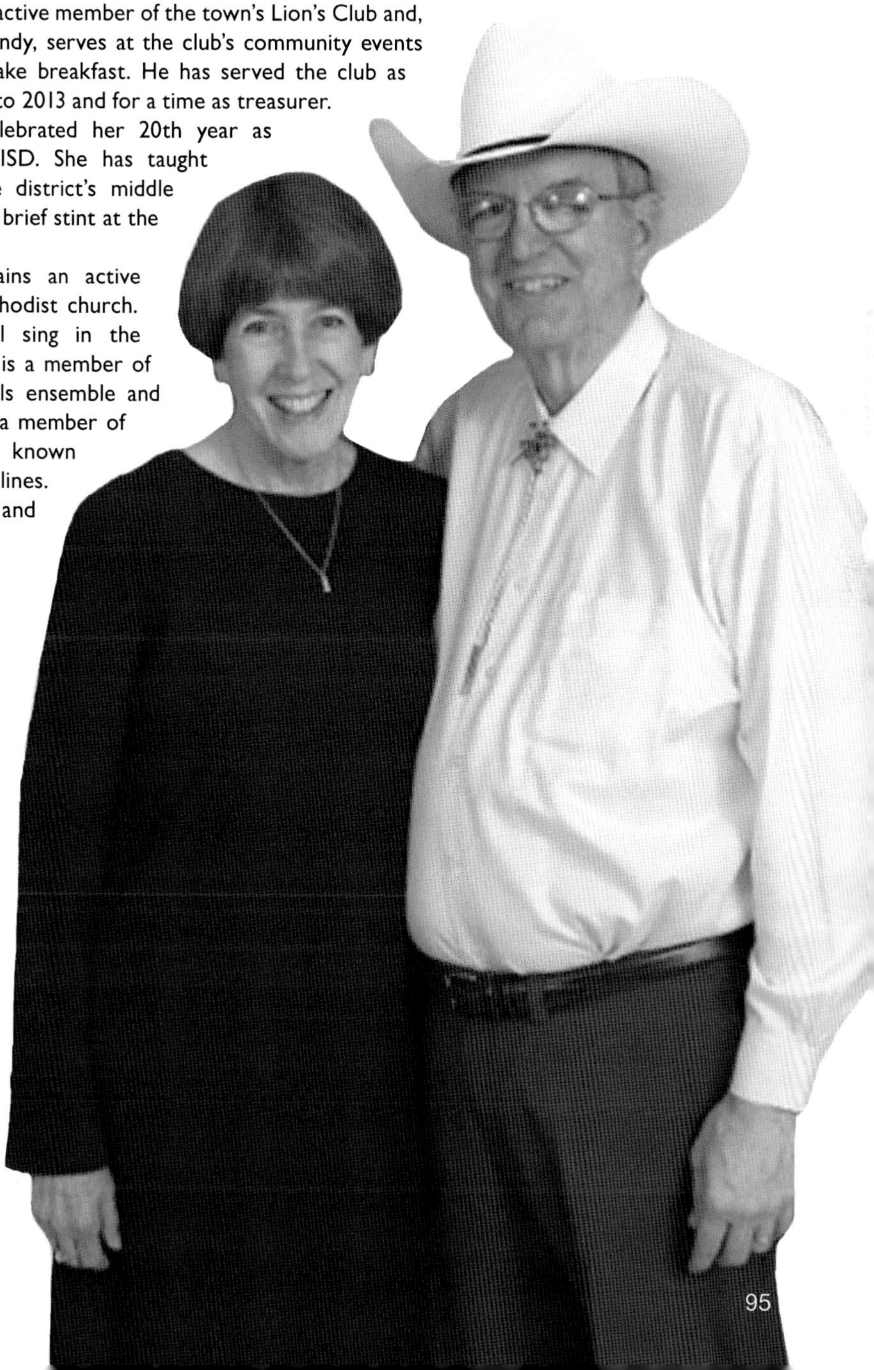

Bob Timmerman

Bob Timmerman served as the longtime on-market assistant for the Coppell Farmer's Market. He held the position from 2005 (two years after the market's opening) to 2012, when he retired. While in the position, Timmerman set up the market each Saturday morning and assisted market vendors with their various needs.

Timmerman also serves as a board member of the Friends of Coppell Nature Park and has completed the training for the Coppell Citizens Police Academy and the Coppell Citizens Fire Academy. (Courtesy of the City of Coppell.)

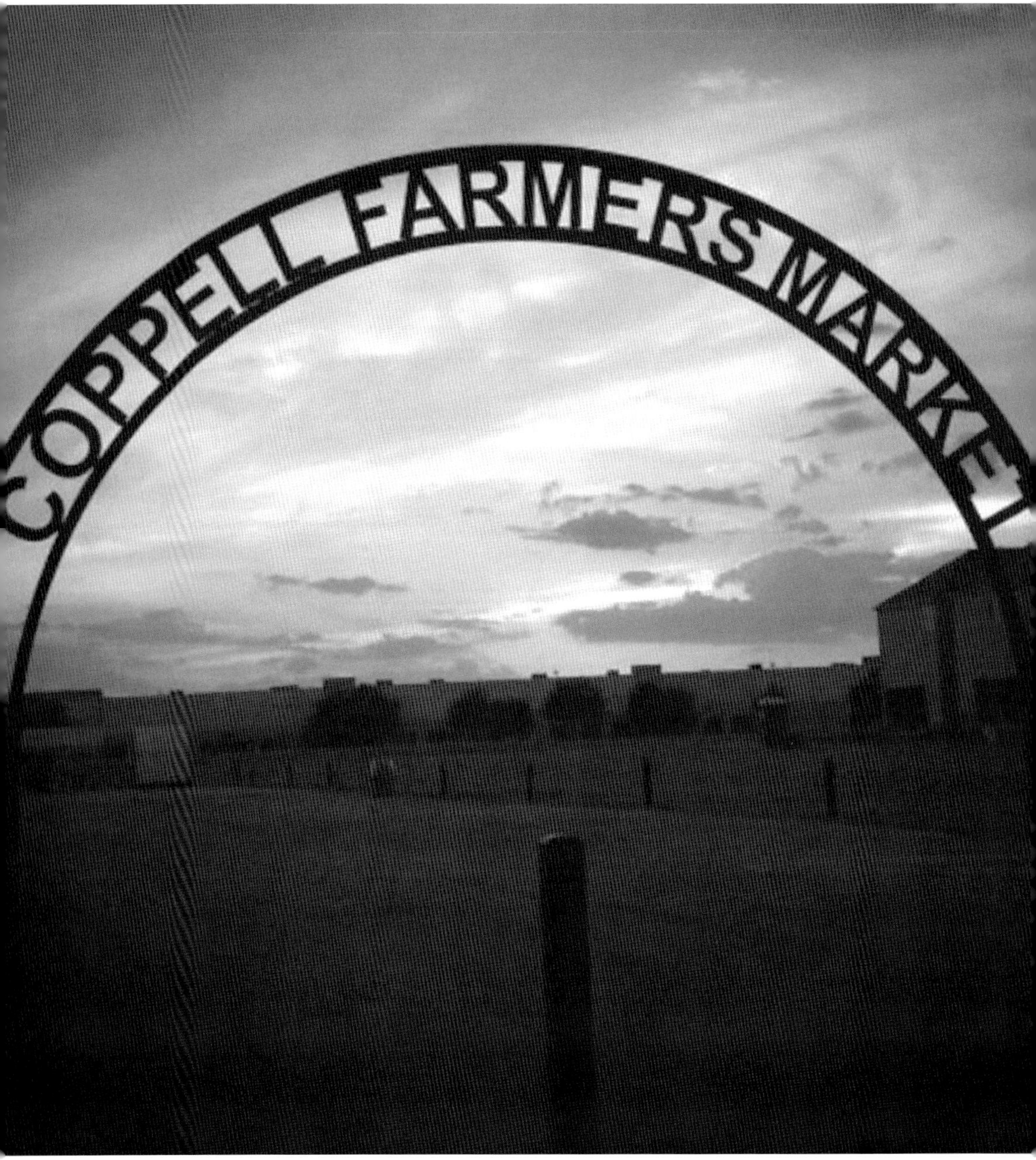

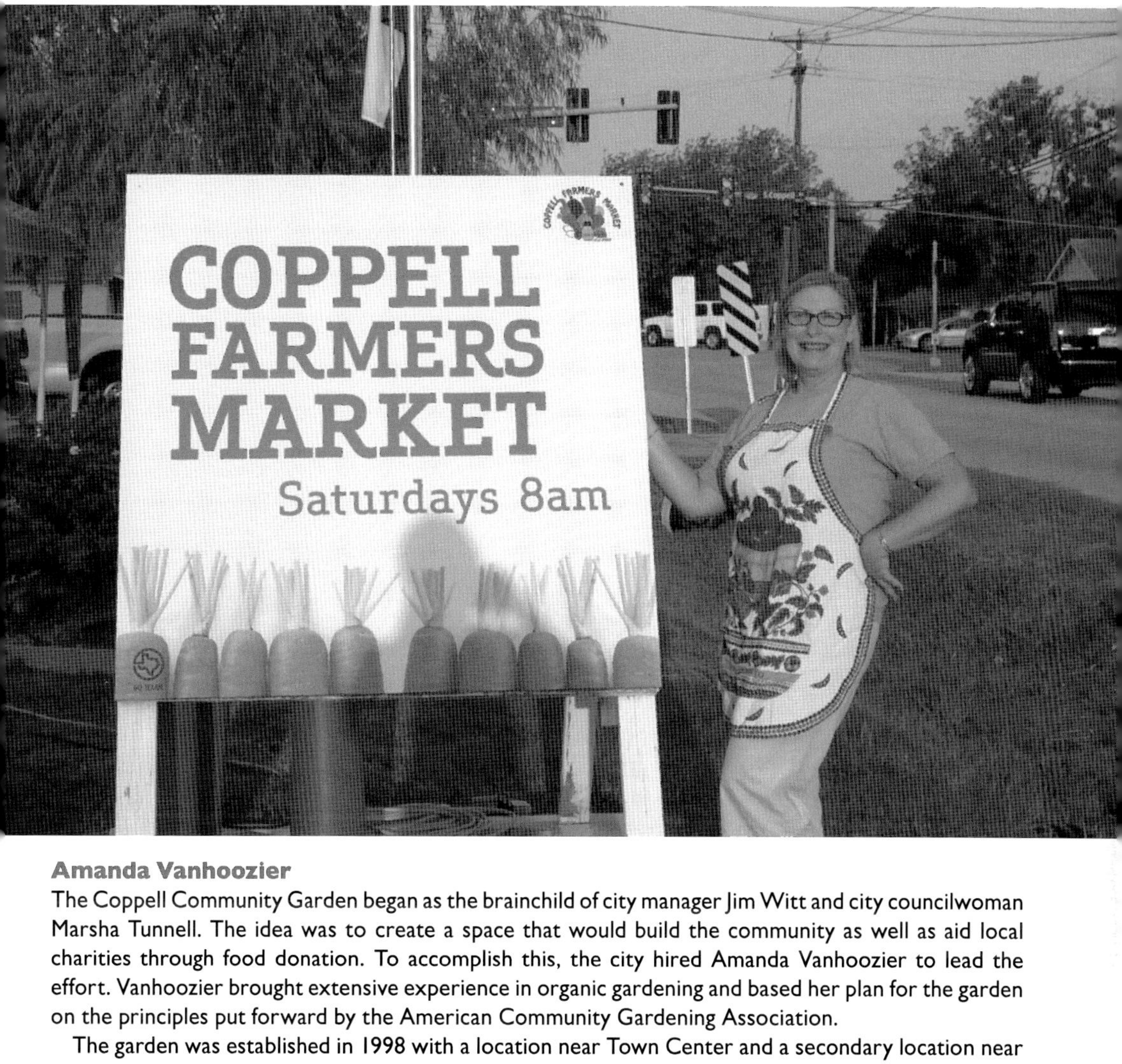

Amanda Vanhoozier

The Coppell Community Garden began as the brainchild of city manager Jim Witt and city councilwoman Marsha Tunnell. The idea was to create a space that would build the community as well as aid local charities through food donation. To accomplish this, the city hired Amanda Vanhoozier to lead the effort. Vanhoozier brought extensive experience in organic gardening and based her plan for the garden on the principles put forward by the American Community Gardening Association.

The garden was established in 1998 with a location near Town Center and a secondary location near the post office. Both gardens participate in the Share the Harvest program, which donates all crops grown to Metrocrest Services. To date, the garden has donated over 100,000 pounds of fresh produce. It also regularly hosts community educational events on sustainable living practices.

Vanhoozier also served the Coppell Farmer's Market from its opening until 2015. (Courtesy of the City of Coppell.)

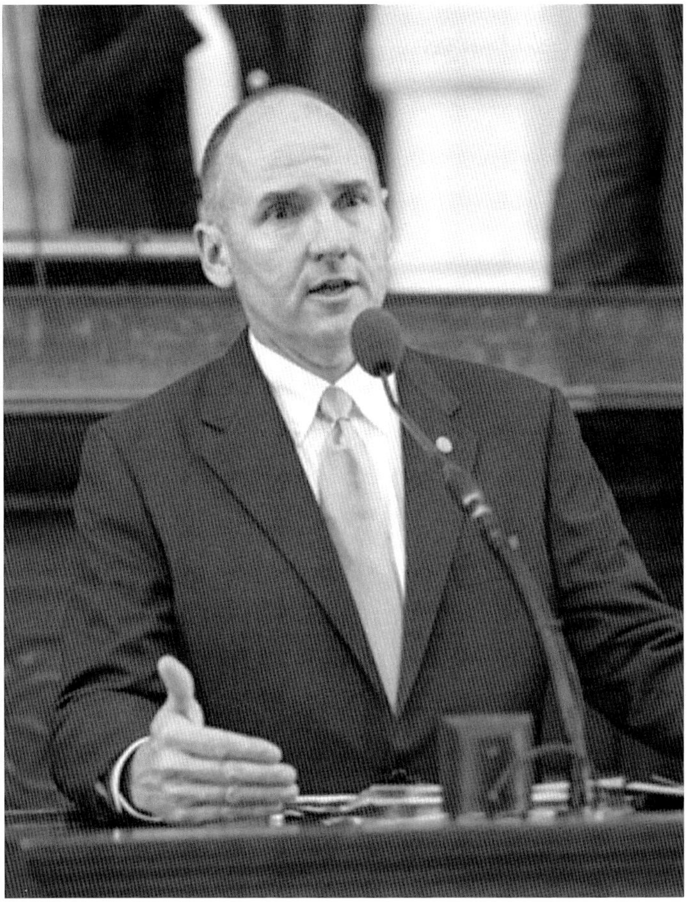

Bennett Ratliff

Bennett Ratliff was born into a political family. His father, Bill Ratliff, was a Texas state senator from 1988 to 2004, serving as lieutenant governor from 2000 to 2003. His brother Thomas is on the Texas State Board of Education. Bennett joined the family legacy in 2013, when he was elected into the Texas House of Representatives. He served in the legislature until January 2015.

Bennett was born in 1961 and, like his father, went on to study engineering at the University of Texas. In 1993, Bennett and his wife, Becky, moved to Coppell with their three children. In 2002, he opened the Ratliff Group LLC in Coppell and quickly built it into a highly respected engineering and construction firm. In 2013, Bennett received a distinguished engineering award from the Texas Engineering Foundation of the Society of Professional Engineers.

The Ratliff family has always been a strong proponent of public education. Prior to his House term, Ratliff served nine years on the board of trustees for CISD. In addition, Bennett helped found the Coppell Education Foundation. He acted as a sponsor for the high school's solar car team and engineering academy. He is also a regular volunteer for the Special Olympics, Challenger Baseball, and the Ironman for Angels program.

During his time in the House of Representatives, Bennett continued to champion education, earning a place on the legislative honor roll and the title of honorary life member from the Texas PTA. He was also named a legislative champion by the Retired Teachers Association.

After leaving office, Bennett began work on a new office for the Ratliff Group that will be located in Old Town Coppell and will replicate the facade of his family's historic Coppell business, the Harrison-Ratliff General Store. (Courtesy of Bennett Ratliff.)

CHAPTER SEVEN

Service

In 2009, Pam Cope was nominated for Texan of the Year for her work "rescuing trafficked children in Saigon, child slaves in Ghana, and AIDS orphans in Cambodia." This lifesaving work was done through Cope's Touch a Life Foundation, founded with her husband, Randy, in 1999.

The organization was created after the Copes traveled to Southeast Asia. While there they visited friends in Vietnam who ran an orphanage, and witnessed firsthand the area's gripping poverty. The experience left a deep impression on Pam Cope, who had recently suffered a tragedy of her own.

Only months earlier, Cope's son Jantsen died of an undetected heart ailment. He was 15 years old. By creating Touch a Life, the Copes hoped to create a legacy that would honor their son's memory.

In 2008, the Copes moved to Coppell. The next year, Pam published her book *Jantsen's Gift*, telling her story of grief and the work that it birthed. Touch a Life also began to make an immediate impact on Coppell.

New Tech High School partnered with Touch a Life in the fall of 2009. Students helped fund laptops for children in Touch a Life's Ghana program and sponsored a young girl named Comfort.

Though the Cope family moved from Coppell in 2013, their presence continues to be felt. New Tech graduate Maggie Gross serves as an intern for the Dallas office of Touch A Life, and resident Jonna Smith has helped Coppell's Methodist congregation combine with the organization for mission service.

The story of Coppell is filled with examples of selfless giving and service. Some, like Touch a Life, have received wide recognition for their work. Others are quiet, unassuming stories of giving that are easily overlooked. In every case, they are stories of people devoted to living for something greater than the self.

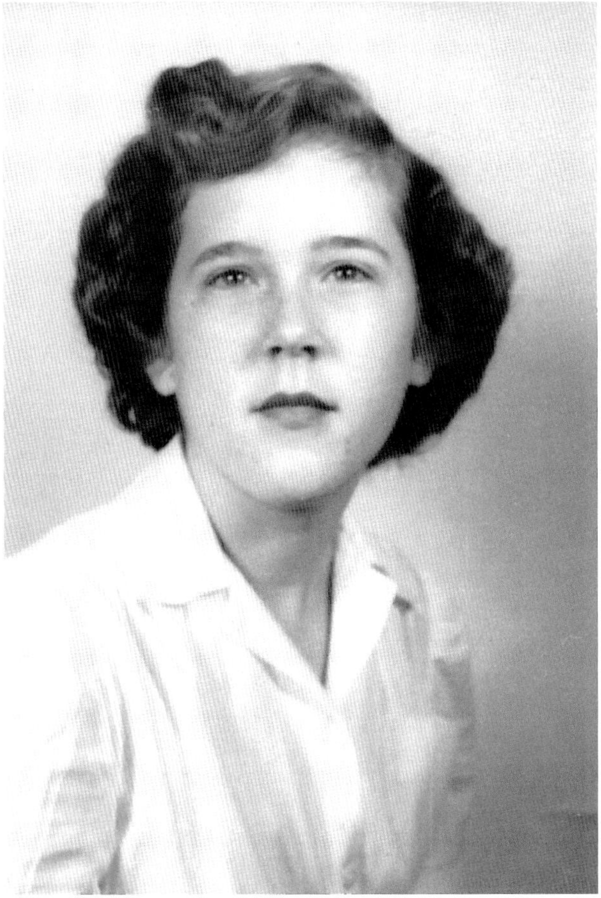

Barbara Lee

Barbara Jean Melton Lee was born in 1935 to parents Ernest Melton and Bernice Gentry. Her great-grandfather Alexander Gentry moved to the Coppell area from Alabama around 1880. He settled on a plot of land that ran by the old Highway 114.

As a child, Barbara made her home on land that was later covered by water when the Dallas Power and Light Company created North Lake. In 1943, her grandfather was struck and killed by a vehicle while riding a horse-drawn wagon. The family subsequently split the land into six parts, which remained in their possession until bought for the development of DFW.

Barbara attended the Coppell School and remembers writing letters to a Ms. Watkins, who would grade penmanship. During this time, Barbara became the school's student librarian. She recalls that there was no public library at the time, but each summer, the local grocery would receive books from the Dallas Bookmobile and convert one shelf in the store to a lending library.

She married Richard Lee in 1956, and the two moved to Oakcliff for a month before returning to Coppell. That month was the only time that Barbara has lived outside of town. The Lees had three children: Richard Lynn, Vanessa Gay, and Ernest Jeffrey. Richard was a member of the school board, and Barbara remembers typing the first cookbook for the school's PTA.

A lifelong member of First Baptist Church of Coppell, she has seen the church grow from a small white building on Bethel Road into the large congregation now known as GracePoint Church on Beltine Road.

Barbara has been a tireless worker in preserving the town's history. She served for numerous years as the president of the Coppell Historical Society and remains an active member, participating in numerous community events at the Historic Kirkland House. (Courtesy of Richard and Barbara Lee.)

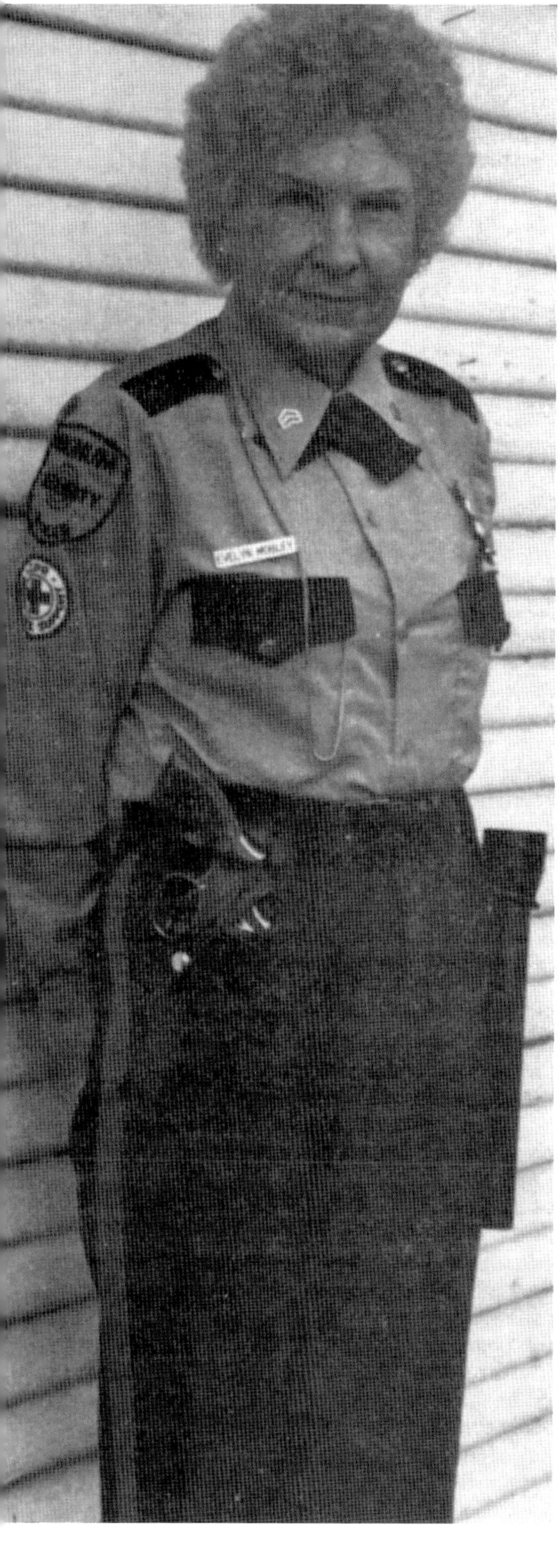

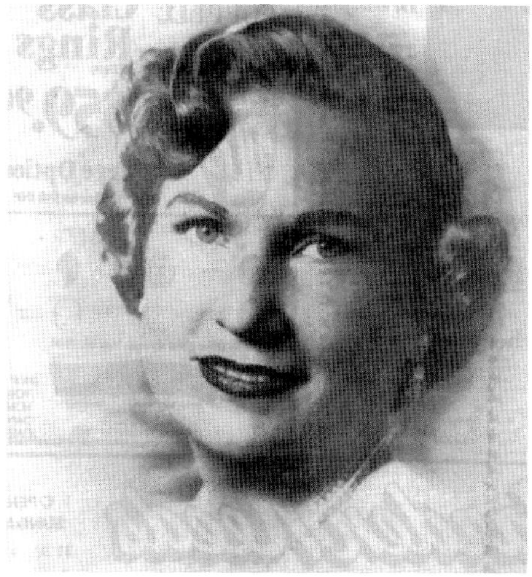

Mary Evelyn Mobley
On February 27, 1996, Coppell mayor Tom Morton read an official proclamation naming March 1 Ann McNear and Mary Evelyn Mobley Appreciation Day. The proclamation was acknowledgement for a decade of service to Coppell's library system. Two years previous, Mary Evelyn had been honored as Coppell's Woman of the Year.

In addition to her library work, Mary Evelyn was instrumental in the preservation of the historic Bullock Cemetery and the Bethel Cemetery. She worked for years as part of the Historic Bethel Cemetery Association. (Courtesy of the William T. Cozby Library and the Coppell Historical Society.)

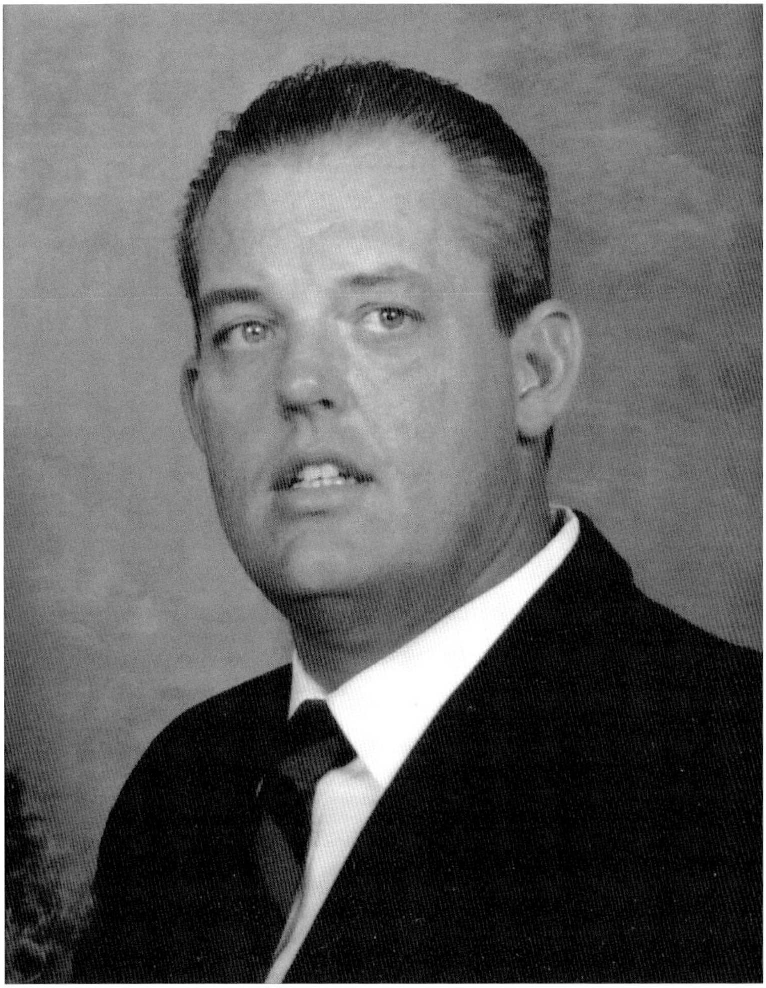

B.J. Smartt

B.J. Smartt was raised in Denton, where he played football and baseball, and participated in the school band. A star athlete, Smartt was recruited by the Kansas City Chiefs but was unable to pursue a career in football due to chronic back problems.

In 1984, Smartt moved to Coppell. He served in the Methodist church men's club and organized volunteers to tend to the church grounds. He was frequently seen riding a lawn mower to church, working the church coffee bar, or asking members for donations to various church ministries.

As a commercial construction worker, he proved vital in the building of the church. When funds ran low, Smartt organized volunteers and donated his services free of charge to the construction effort. The portion of the building that he constructed now bears the name Smartt Hall.

Smartt's wife relates a story that epitomizes his spirit of no-nonsense service. While speaking with Pastor John Rosenberg, Smartt learned that the church was interested in expanding the Rotunda Chapel. Smartt assessed that removing a wall would likely add space for as many as 100 seats. When the pastor expressed interest, Smartt immediately went home and returned to the church with a sledgehammer, ready to begin work.

In 1998, Smartt died of heart failure while visiting Branson, Missouri. He left behind his wife, Joy, and their three children. Joy reflected on Smartt's brief life, saying, "He did God's work in the time he had." (Courtesy of Joy Smartt.)

Fred and Judy Conger

Fred and Judy Conger moved to Coppell in 1980. A member of First United Methodist Church of Coppell, Fred served as treasurer in 1983, leading him to joke that he "paid for the new building," even if it was with other people's money. In addition, Fred and Judy served as the church's official historians. Judy also serves as a docent for the Coppell Historical Society at the Historic Kirkland House.

Fred played keyboard in a musical group called the Budget Blues Band with residents Kent Moore and Jim Shannon. The group performed regularly at the Methodist church and elsewhere. Despite their name, the band did not play blues but focused on 60s and 70s rock and roll. Fred is also a long-standing member of the Coppell Lion's Club, serving as its president since 2014, after being named the district's Lion of the Year in 2013. (Courtesy of Fred Conger.)

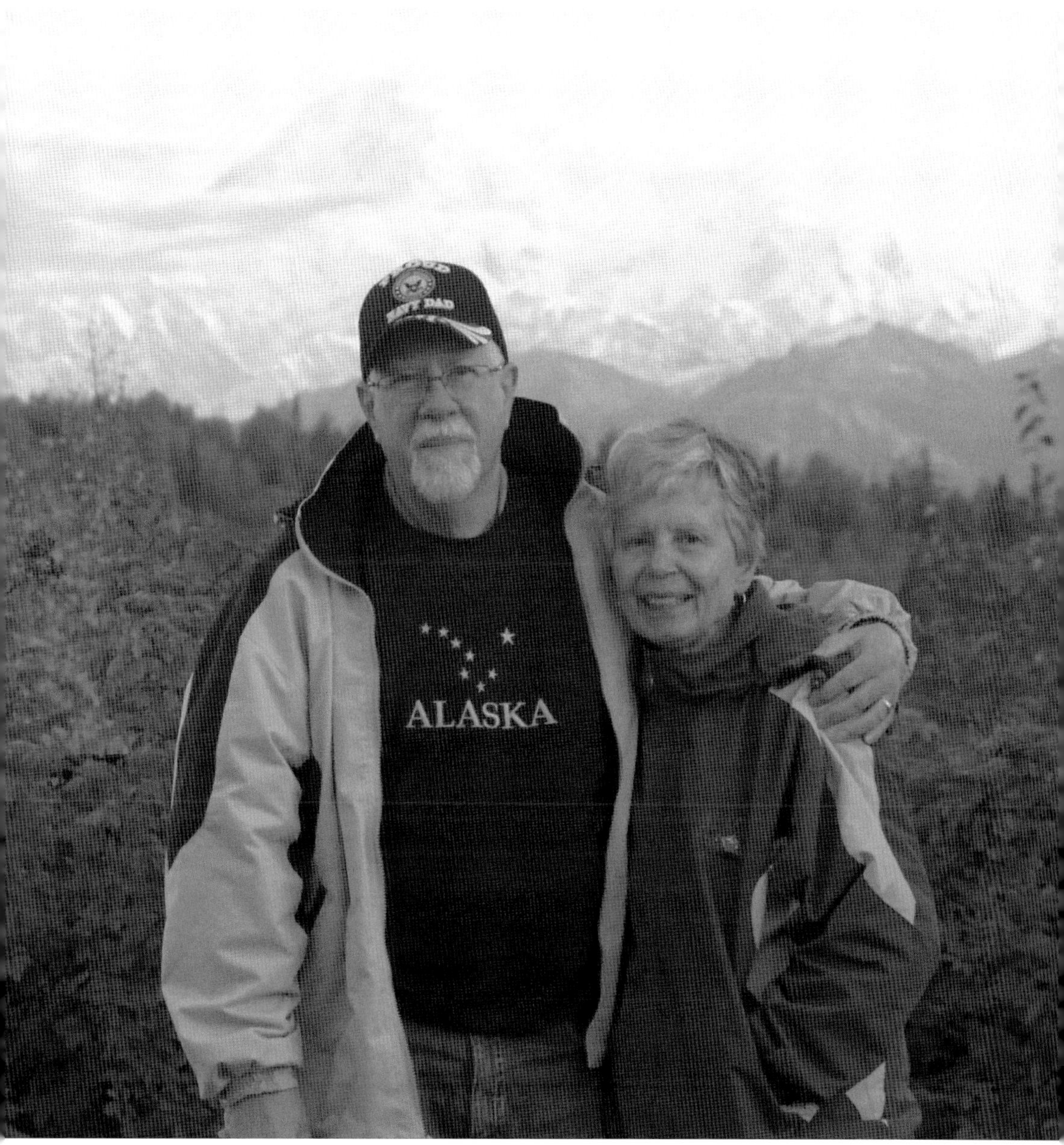

Todd and Tara Storch

Taylor's Gift Foundation was created in 2010, shortly after founders Todd and Tara Storch lost their 13-year-old daughter Taylor (far left) in a skiing accident. The organization was created to raise organ donor registrations and start conversations across the nation as well as provide financial support to families affected by organ donation through their legacy gift program.

The foundation also sponsors lodging for pre-transplant and post-transplant patients and awards scholarships to graduating high school seniors who demonstrate the "Outlive Yourself" spirit by making a difference in the world.

After Taylor's passing, her organs were donated and received by multiple people, including one lifesaving heart transplant. The experience is detailed in the Storches' best-selling book, *Taylor's Gift: A Courageous Story of Giving Life and Renewing Hope*. In November 2013, the book was named the nation's most inspirational book by Books for a Better Life in New York City.

The Storch story and Taylor's Gift Foundation have received international attention and touched the nation. One particularly touching moment occurred when the Storches were given the rare opportunity to listen to their daughter's heartbeat in the chest of the woman whose life Taylor saved. The story aired on *Good Morning America*, which launched a national platform for Taylor's Gift Foundation. Since then, the Storches have shared the importance of organ donation on national media such as the *Today* show, the *Ellen DeGeneres Show*, *People* magazine, and more.

Today, through the efforts of Taylor's Gift and its peers, Texas has had over five million new organ donor registrations. Todd and Tara hope to encourage people everywhere to "Outlive Yourself." Taylor sure did. Learn more at www.taylorsgift.org. (Courtesy of Todd and Tara Storch.)

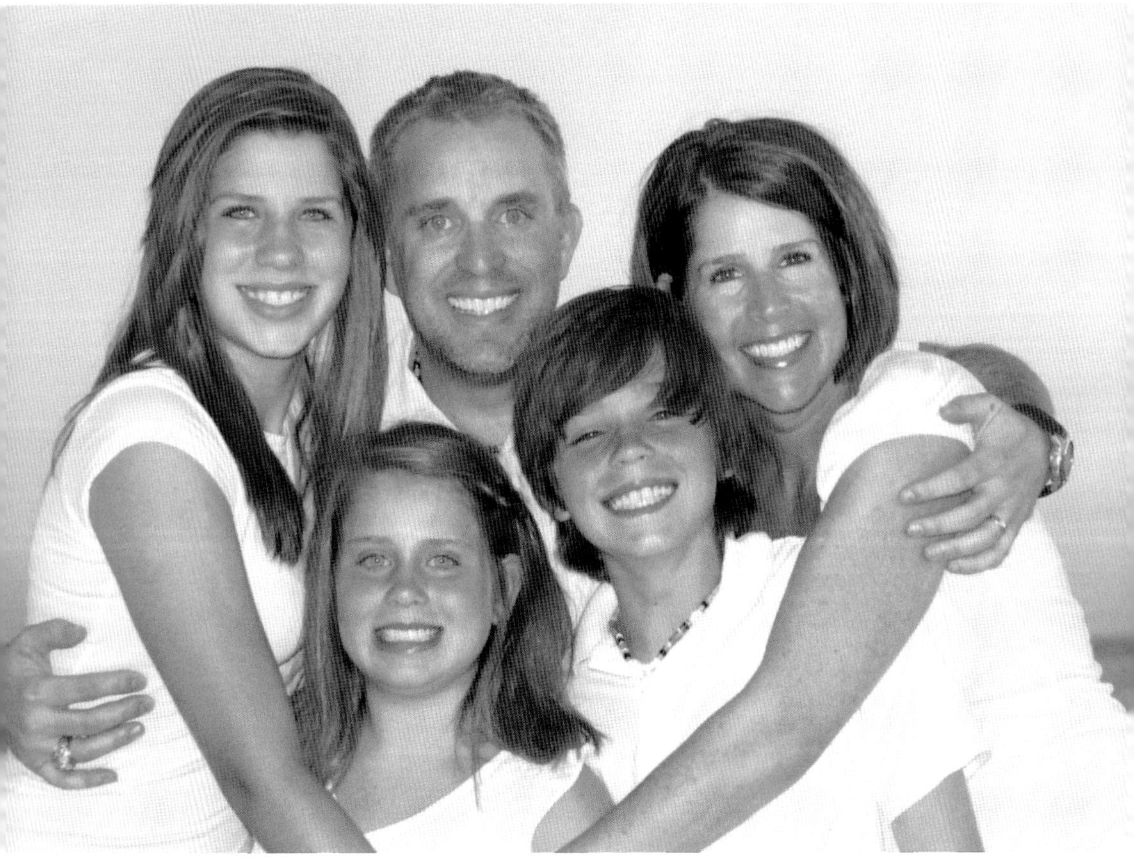

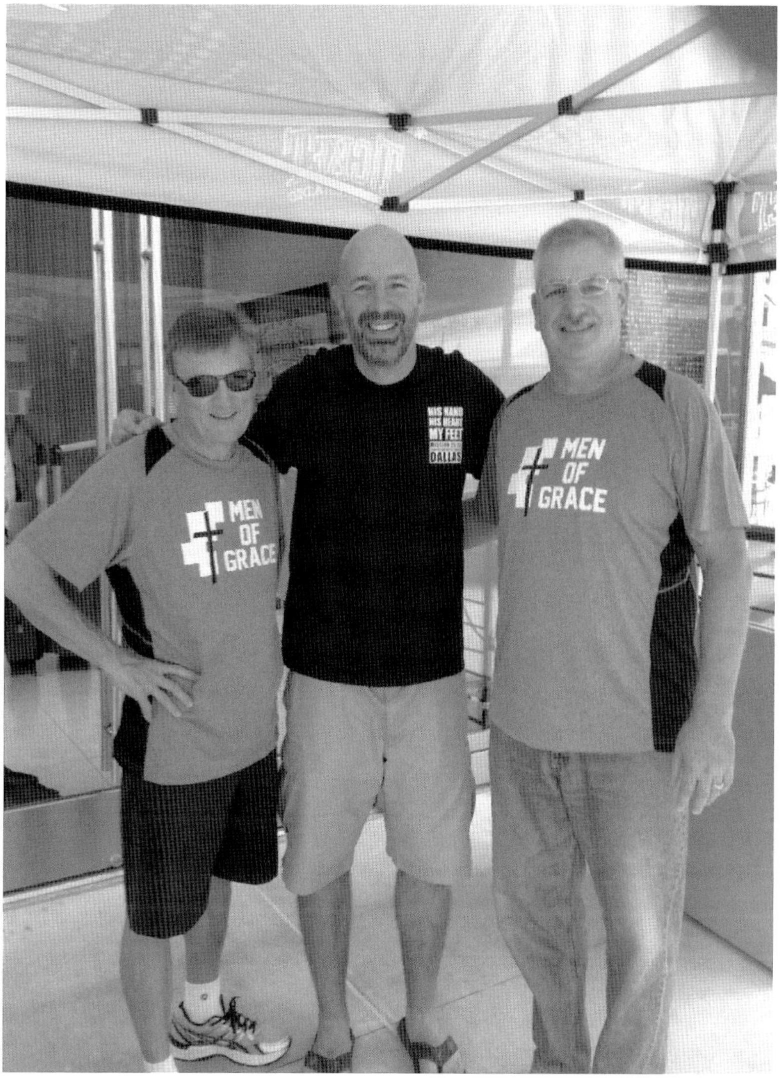

Bob Sturm

Bob Sturm (center) wants his listeners to know he is "not just some dude in the next cubicle over." As cohost of the popular *BaD* radio show on 1310 The Ticket, Sturm has brought an encyclopedic knowledge of sports to Dallas–Fort Worth listeners for over 15 years.

A native of Wisconsin, Sturm's fascination with sports began at a young age. Growing up in a strictly conservative home, Sturm was only allowed to watch television for sports. This led the young Sturm to devour any and every sporting event available.

Sturm went on to graduate from Liberty College and take his first broadcast job in Lynchburg, Virginia. In 1998, he moved to Coppell and began working at The Ticket. In 1999, *BaD* radio was created. Since then, Sturm has written a book about the championship season of the Dallas Mavericks and been named Dallas–Fort Worth's best sports radio personality by the *Dallas Observer.*

Sturm is also involved in regular ministry work, traveling to Guatemala on mission trips as well as using his radio platform to promote various charitable activities. His experiences in Guatemala led Sturm to the adoption of his son from Honduras. Sturm is an active member of Valley Ranch Baptist Church and has held speaking engagements at other local churches. (Courtesy of Bob Sturm.)

Jacob Logan

Driving down any Coppell street will reveal numerous cars with royal blue stickers emblazoned with the number 21 on their window or bumper. These stickers are tributes to Jacob Eli Logan.

Born in 1995, Logan was a star football player for the Coppell High School Cowboys. He played wide receiver and safety for the team. Logan was a popular student, both with his classmates and teachers. He was a three-year starter on the football team, but rather than letting the success go to his head, he was known for his modesty and a willingness to befriend anyone. While other players dreamed of NFL stardom, Logan planned to become an inner city coach in Memphis.

Logan was also known for his devout faith. In 2012, he posted on a social media site, "Jobs, sports, and people will fail you. God will not. He is a righteous Savior that has not and will never fail you." The post came less than one month before the swimming accident that claimed Logan's life.

The community rallied to honor Logan. When the Coppell Cowboys played their next football game, a large flag with the number 21 was carried on the field, and students dressed in royal blue, carrying signs that read "The hybrid. The legend. The guardian angel." Logan's sister Jordan donned his jersey and stood in for him as Captain. The players wore the number 21 on their helmets.

In the years since Logan's death, his family has carried on his legacy. His parents, Howard and Mona Logan, started the annual Jacob Logan Run for 21. The money raised from the event is then used to build homes for orphans in Zambia through the Family Legacy Foundation. In June 2014, Logan's LifeVision Home was opened and subsequently used to house eight boys. In December of the same year, his family began the push to build another. (Courtesy of Mona Logan.)

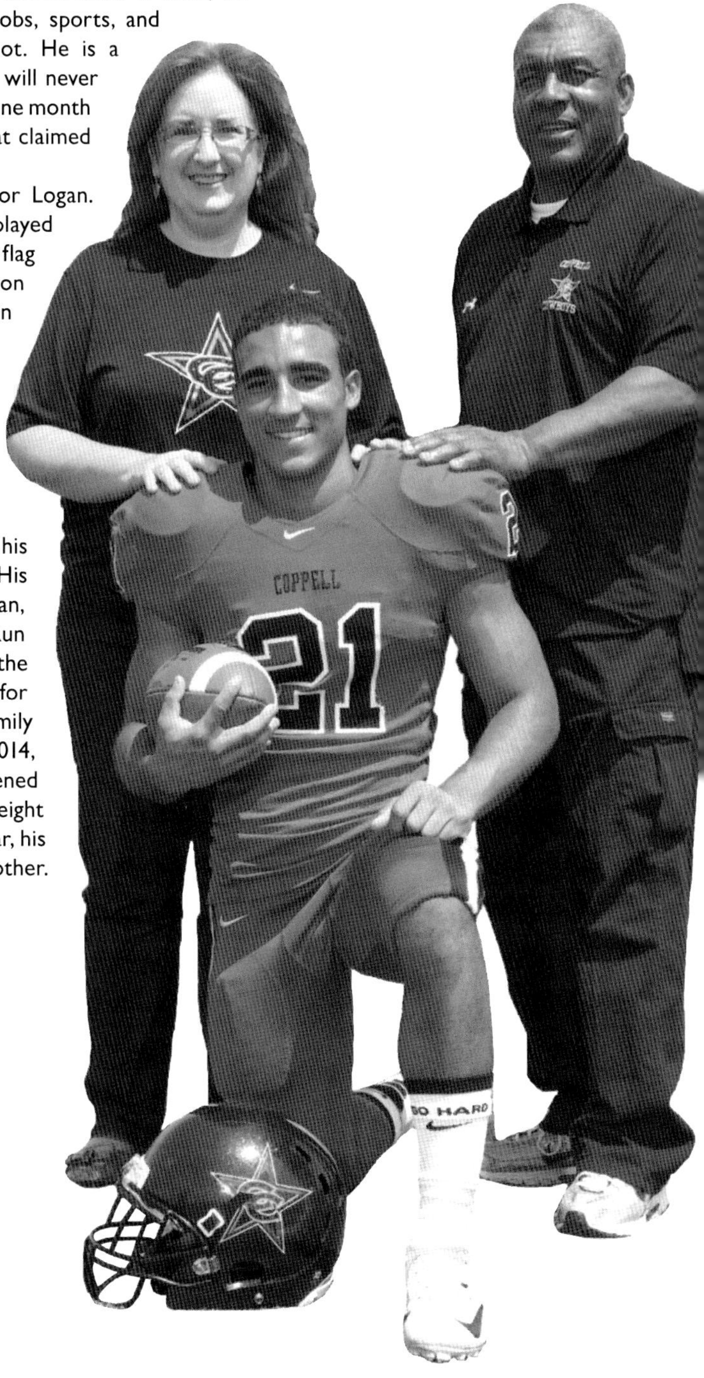

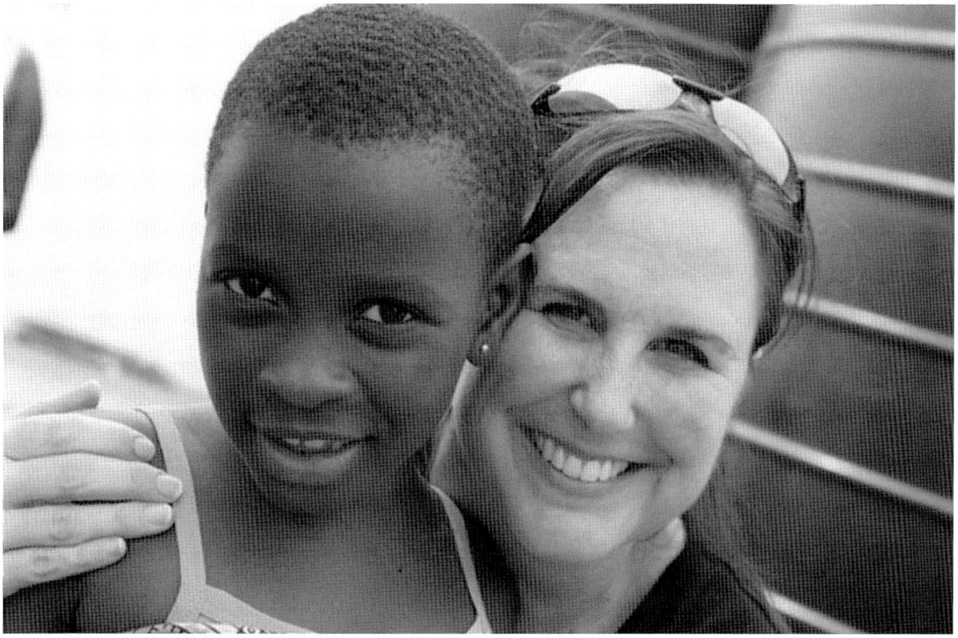

Jonna Smith

As a local business owner and mother, Jonna Smith had never considered traveling to Africa. That changed after reading *Jantsen's Gift* by Coppell resident Pam Cope. The book detailed her work rescuing children from child slavery in the Lake Volta region of Ghana. Within days of finishing the book, Smith found herself reaching out to Cope and arranging to sponsor a house for the rescued children. She named the house Taylor's House in honor of Taylor Storch, a Coppell teen who had recently passed away.

Since those early days, Smith has traveled to Ghana to work at Taylor's House and has become the Africa missions director for the Coppell Methodist church. She hopes to encourage others to take part in this lifesaving work. (Both, courtesy of Jonna Smith.)

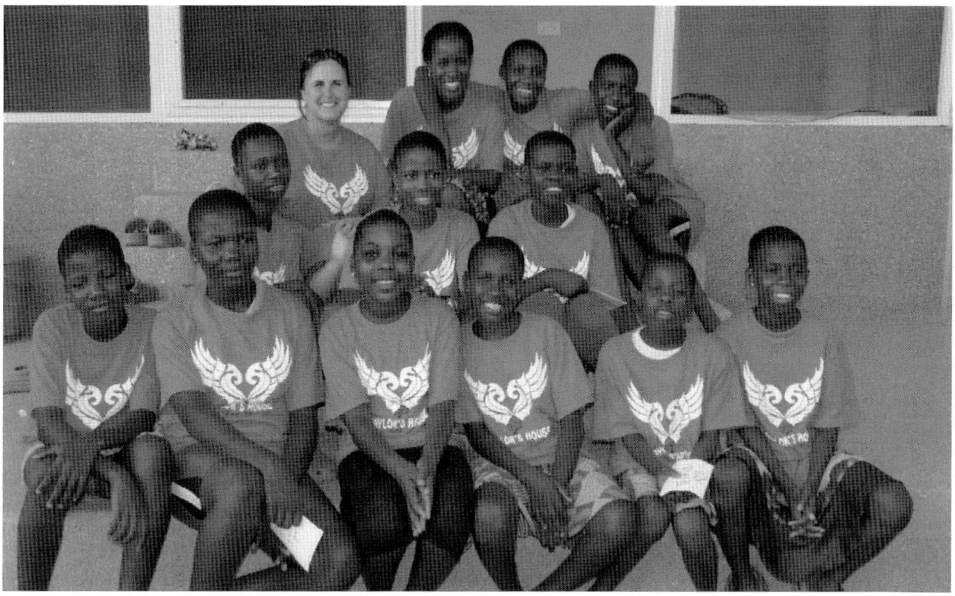

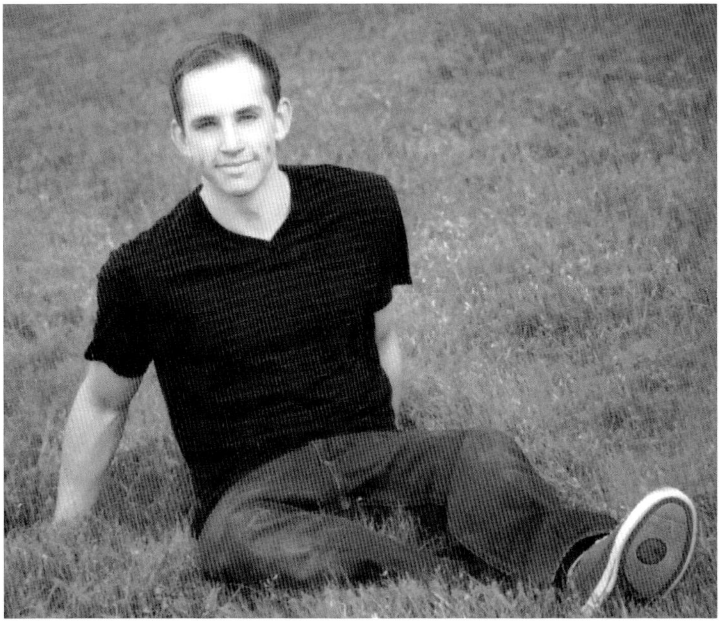

Zack Thompson

Zack Thompson was the middle child of Joe and Julie Thompson. Born in 1994, his all too brief life ended on November 8, 2013, for reasons that remain unknown.

Thompson was a graduate of Coppell's New Tech High School and was attending the University of Texas at Arlington at the time of his passing. He was an athlete who played baseball, basketball, and football. Thompson was also an avid online gamer. Thompson's father recalled that he was someone intent on following his own unique path through life.

After his death, Thompson's parents created the Zack Thompson Foundation as a place of comfort and support for families who have lost a child. The family also created Zack's Children's Garden at the Rolling Oaks Memorial Center. The centerpiece of the garden is the Angel of Hope statue, established as a place of memorial and respite for grieving families. (Both, courtesy of Julie Thompson.)

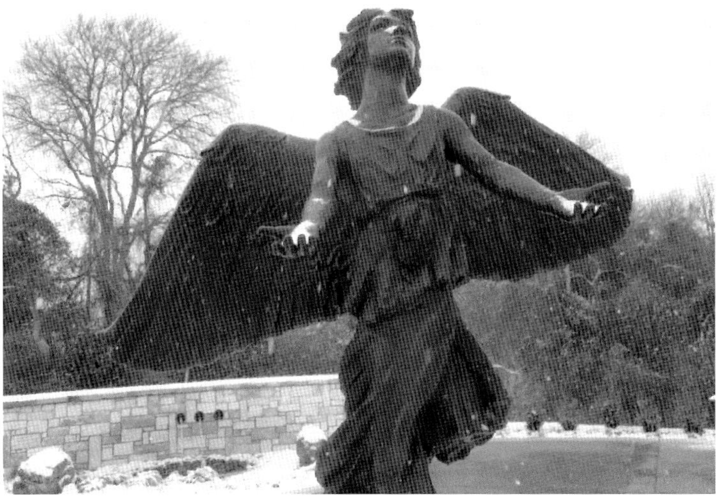

CHAPTER EIGHT

Heroes

The Coppell Fallen Officers Memorial sits just outside the entrance to the Coppell Justice Center on Town Center Boulevard. It is a simple monument of brick and concrete and only bears two names: Officer Don Swearingin and Officer Michael Johns. Beneath these names is engraved the letters EOW, an abbreviation of the phrase "End of Watch," a poetic and haunting reference to their deaths while on duty.

For Donald Swearingin, EOW came on December 12, 1972. Swearingin was in pursuit of a speeding vehicle when he hit a patch of ice on the Denton Tap Bridge. His vehicle struck a tree, and the young officer died of his injuries. He was 20 years old.

Swearingin joined the Coppell Police a short eight months prior, after serving for a year in his home town of Weatherford. From April to June 1972, he was Coppell's only officer. Locals called Swearingin "Big Don." He worked with local youth to prevent drug use and was commended in May for arresting a suspect linked to six Dallas area murders.

The *Irving Daily News* ran a story of the community in mourning. Resident Art Delong remembered that Swearingin frequented his store, and the two often joked about the startling quantity of microwave dinners that Swearingin consumed.

On December 19, seven days after Swearingin's death, Mayor Hulen Scott and the Coppell City Council made a resolution honoring Officer Swearingin and funding his funeral expenses.

Coppell's history, like any town's, is built from people like Swearingin who dedicate their life to the service of their community and country. In many ways, the soldiers, police officers, and firefighters make up the beating heart at the center of the community. Their stories help make all other stories possible.

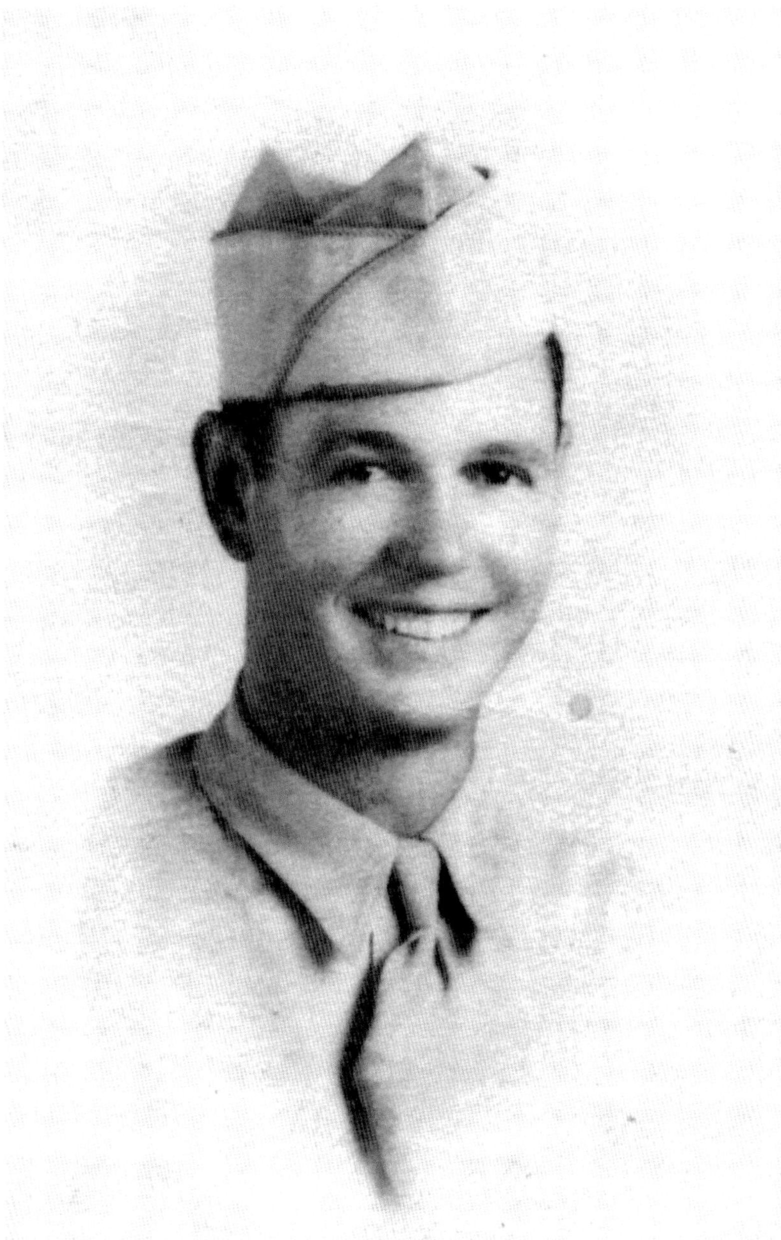

Carroll E. Kirkland

Son of John Kirkland and Edna Stringfellow, Carroll Kirkland was a true son of Coppell. Born and raised in the area, Carroll was a star athlete at Carrollton High School, lettering in baseball, basketball, and football. He married Francis Katherine Horn, and the two had one daughter named Beverly.

Kirkland went on to serve in World War II as an assistant automatic rifleman. He fought in Company A of the 18th Infantry. He was mortally wounded by machine gun fire while attempting to capture a hill in the Huttgen Forest near Heistern, Germany. He died the next day from his wounds and was buried in the American Military Cemetery at Henri Chapelle, Belgium. Kirkland was awarded the Purple Heart for his service. (Courtesy of the Coppell Historical Society.)

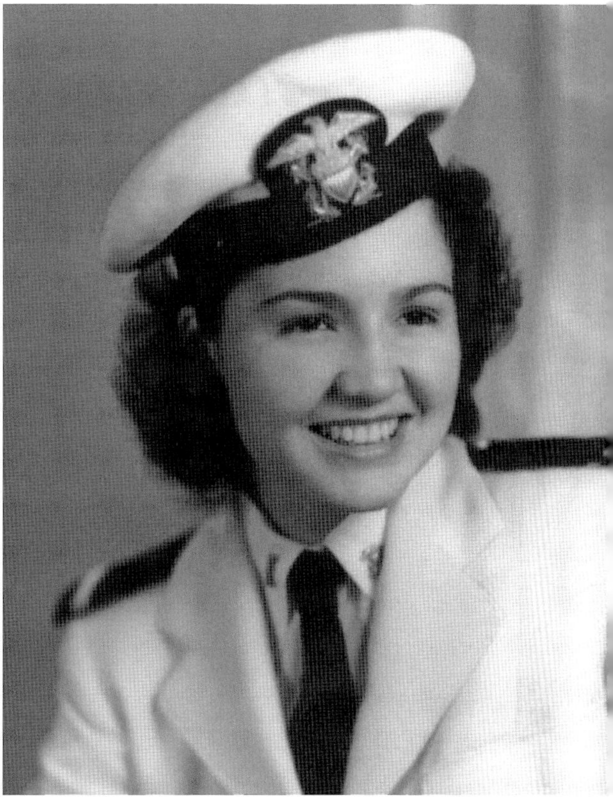

Geneva Burks

In 1944, Geneva Burks was serving as a Navy nurse in Portsmouth, Virginia. While serving, she began tending to a Navy mechanic named Mingus Preston Burks. The two were married on October 11, 1944. At the time, the Navy had a rule prohibiting nurses from marrying, and Geneva Burks was forced to leave the service. Two months later, the Navy changed the rule in order to stem the flow of departing nurses.

For nearly 70 years, there was virtually no record that could verify Burks's service. Burks and her son Walter attempted to find copies of her discharge papers without success. In 2013, she reached out to Congressman Kenny Marchant about locating the records. The process took approximately one year, but she was finally recognized for her service at nearby Carrollton's Liberty Fest. At the celebration, Marchant presented Burks with an honorable discharge, a World War II victory medal, and an honorable service button. (Right, courtesy of Geneva Burks; below, courtesy of the office of Kenny Marchant.)

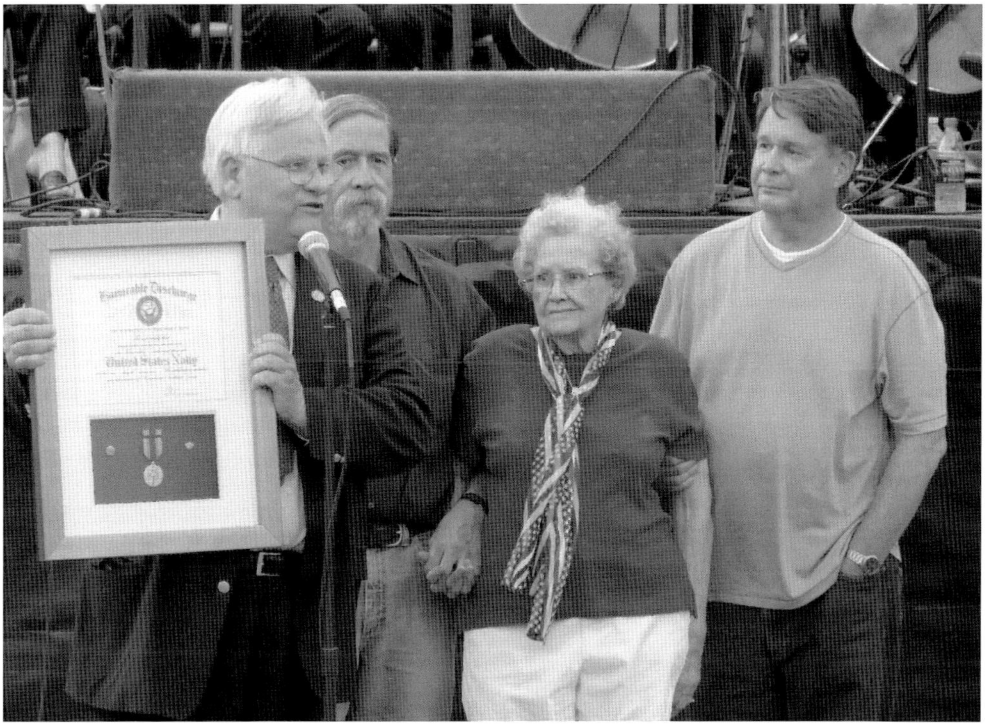

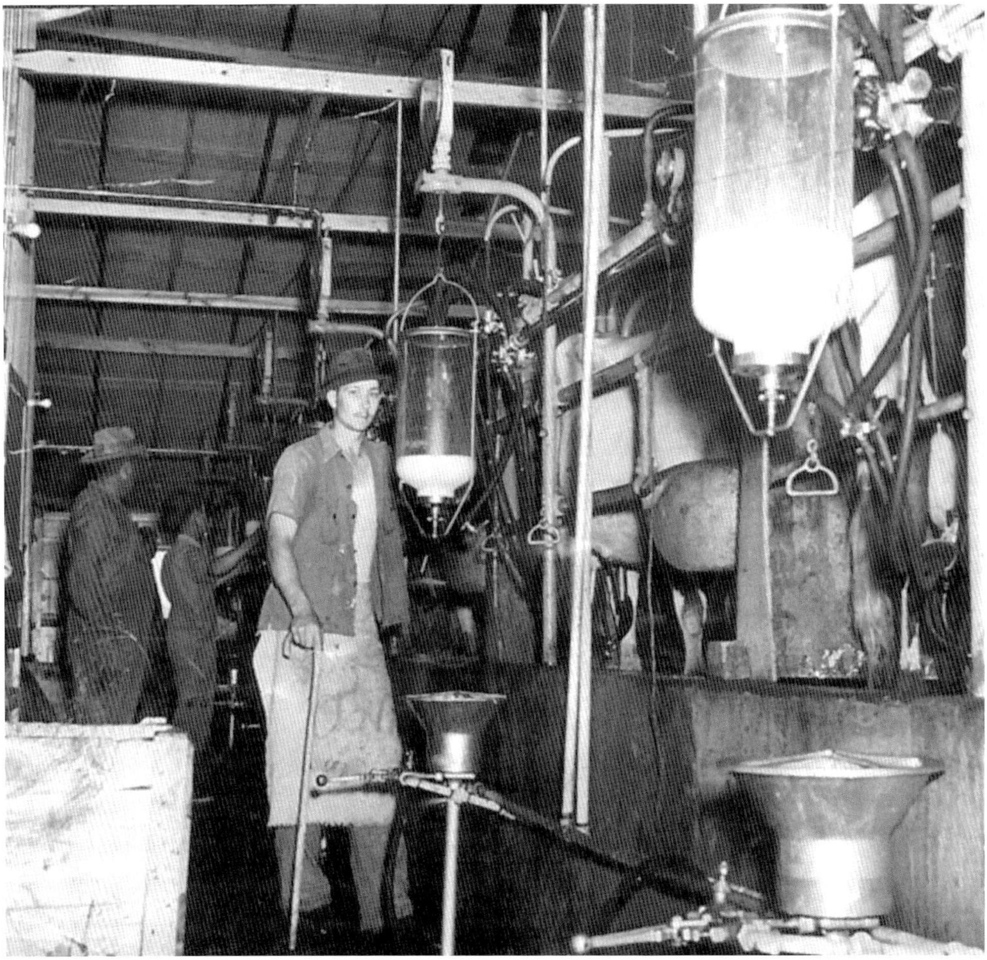

John Dobecka Sr.

John Dobecka Sr. was the ninth child of Frank and Mary Dobecka. He was born in 1917 and grew up on the family's large farm along the Trinity River. A member of the US Army, John served in World War II from 1942 to 1946 in the Pacific theater. He served with distinction and was awarded a Purple Heart with two oak clusters as well as the Bronze Star.

In 1946, John married Vickie Cervenka, a first generation American whose mother had come to the United States as an infant from Moravia. Through most of the 1950s, John ran a dairy business, selling the milk produced to the Metzger's Milk Company in Dallas. Along with his brother Cecil, John worked for the volunteer fire department. In 1967 he became a city councilman, filling the seat left vacant by Cecil's death.

John was a devout Catholic who, with brothers Cecil and Tony, helped with the creation of Mary Immaculate Church in Flower Mound. He also attended St. Ann Catholic Parish when it opened in Coppell in the 1980s. Over the years, John served the church as an usher while Vickie served as a eucharistic minister.

John also began a 4-H riding club in Coppell that participated in local parades and junior rodeos.

In March 2002, a publication of the Texas Czech Genealogical Society printed a story honoring the details of John and Vickie's 55-year marriage. In the article, it was related that Vickie had been giving John the same Valentine's Day card for 56 years, writing a new message in it every year. The two had been married almost 65 years when John passed away in 2011. (Courtesy of the Coppell Historical Society.)

Robert Lee Swofford

On November 14, 2014, a ceremony was held at Fort Sam Houston MacArthur Parade Field in San Antonio to present Robert Lee Swofford with the medal of knight in the French Order of the Legion of Honour. The ceremony was held three days after Swofford's passing.

Swofford was born on a sharecropping farm on April 19, 1922. From the age of eight, he dreamed of becoming a pilot. In 1939, Swofford joined the National Guard when he was only 17, lying about his age so he could sign up.

At the first opportunity, he signed up to become a pilot, training in Alabama and going through maneuvers in Louisiana.

As a B-24 pilot, Swofford was called to participate in the D-Day invasion of Normandy. Swofford led a 12-plane formation to the River Orne near the town of Caen, France, where his squadron bombed and destroyed a bridge. The bombing delayed German tanks from crossing and allowed the British to land their anti-tank guns.

Swofford earned two distinguished Flying Crosses with oak leaf clusters and six air medals. One of his missions was later depicted in the John Wayne classic *The Longest Day.*

Following the war, Swofford became a commercial pilot for Capitol Airlines (later part of United). Swofford remained a pilot for almost 37 years before retiring.

In October 2013, Swofford took to the skies again at a McKinney airshow that brought together a collection of World War II veterans. They flew in a B-24 and the only flying B-29 in the world. It was a fitting bookend to a lifetime spent slipping the surly bonds. (Courtesy of Kara Jex.)

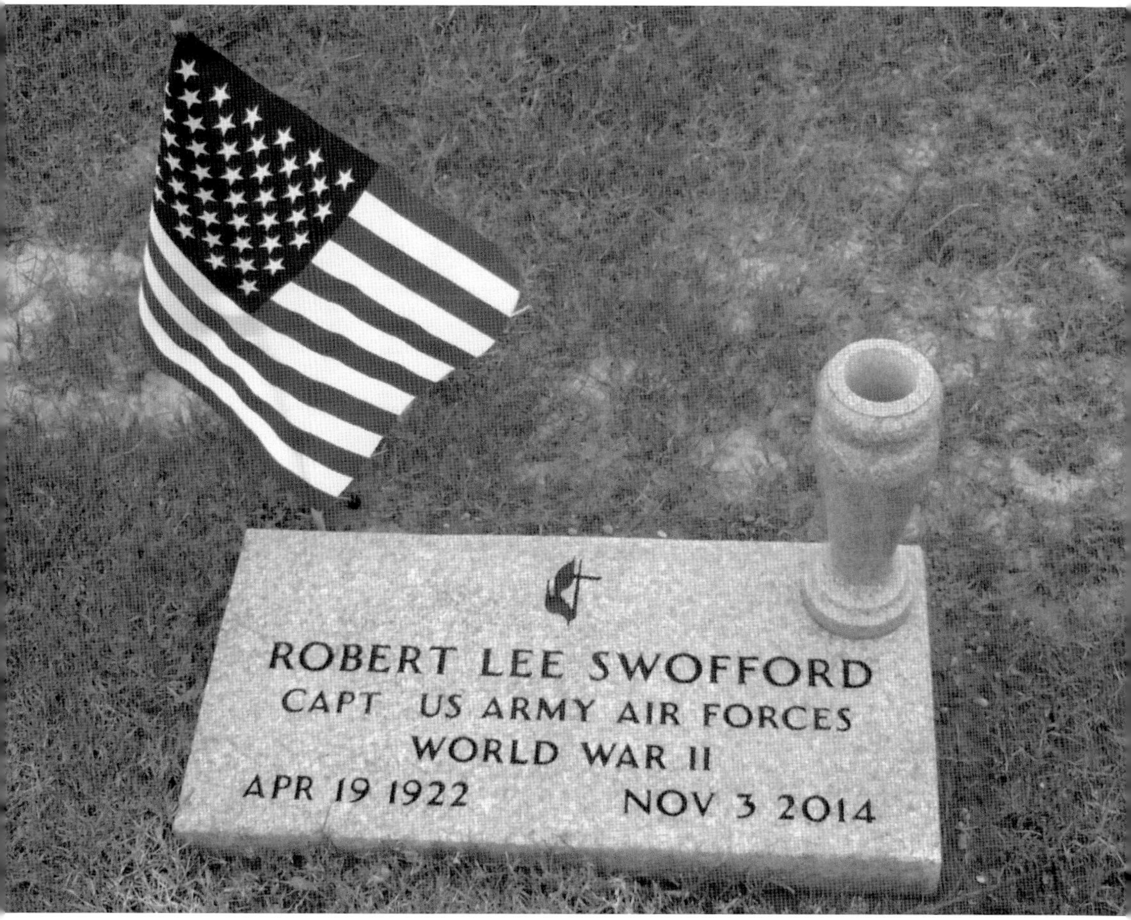

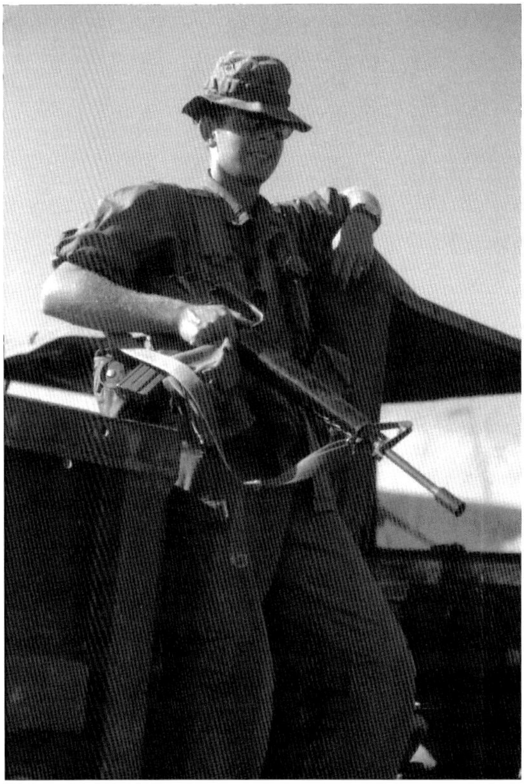

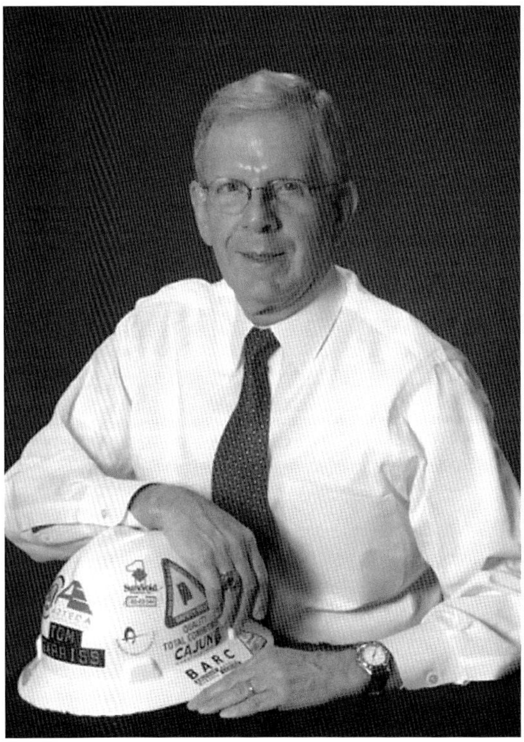

Tom Garriss

Tom Garriss was raised in Raleigh, North Carolina. He studied civil engineering at North Carolina State University and graduated in 1970. While in college, he was a member of the ROTC and, after graduation, was called up to active duty as an Army engineer officer.

Garriss served one tour in Vietnam, arriving in Cam Ranh Bay in July 1971. During his time in the service, he saw intense combat and recalls riding to LZ Dottie with the body of a fellow soldier wrapped in a poncho at his feet.

Following the war, Garriss continued serving for nine years in the Army Reserves. He continued a career in construction that included clients such as Muhammad Ali and involved working on the MGM CityCenter project in Las Vegas, Nevada.

In 1990, Garriss moved with his family to Coppell. After arriving in town, he became active in the Methodist church and was a founding member of the Boy Scout troop at St. Ann Catholic Parish. He is a member of the Coppell Lion's Club and has served as its president on two separate occasions. (Courtesy of Tom Garriss.)

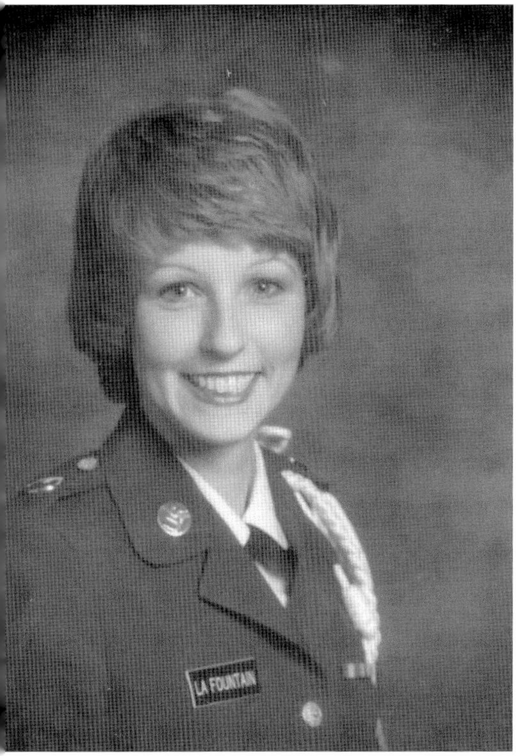

Michelle LaFountain

In 1999, Michelle LaFountain moved to Coppell, where she quickly became involved in the life of the community. LaFountain served regularly on the school PTO and worked on the Coppell Band Boosters board. She currently serves as the administrator for a popular social media page dedicated to the city of Coppell. In her free time, she crochets baby items that are provided to impoverished infants.

Prior to coming to Coppell, LaFountain was making history in her home state of Vermont. She was the first member of the Women's Army Corps to ever serve in the state. She enlisted in 1972 and performed basic training at Fort McClellan in Virginia. She then served active duty at Fort Monmouth in New Jersey before returning to the Reserve until her retirement. (Both, courtesy of Michelle LaFountain.)

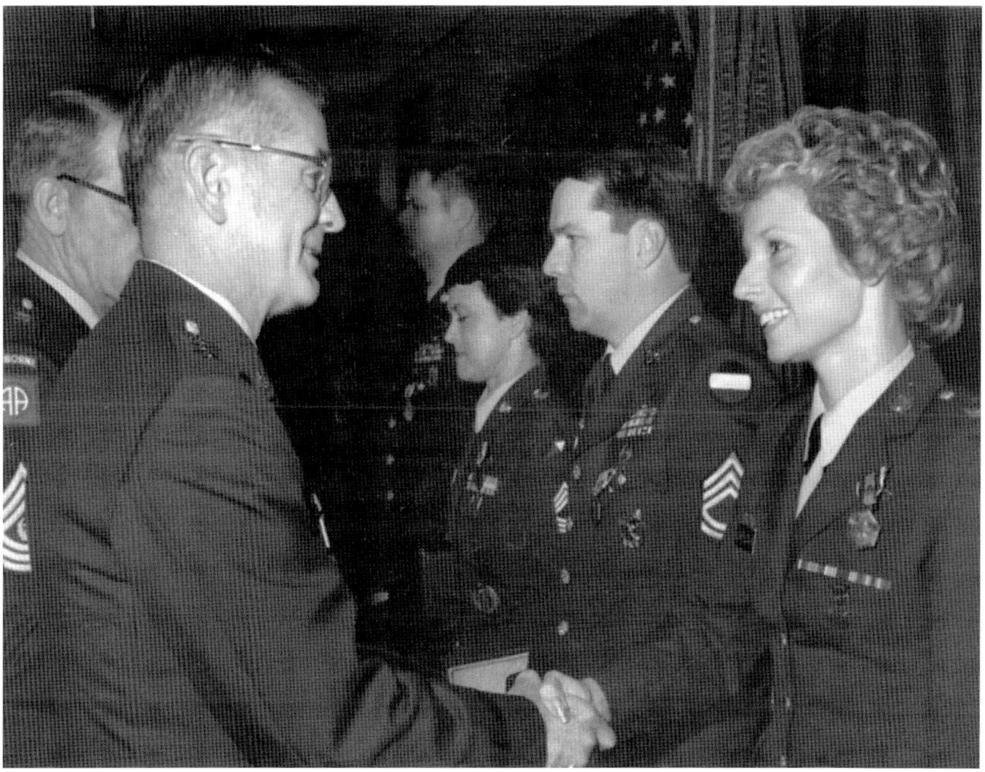

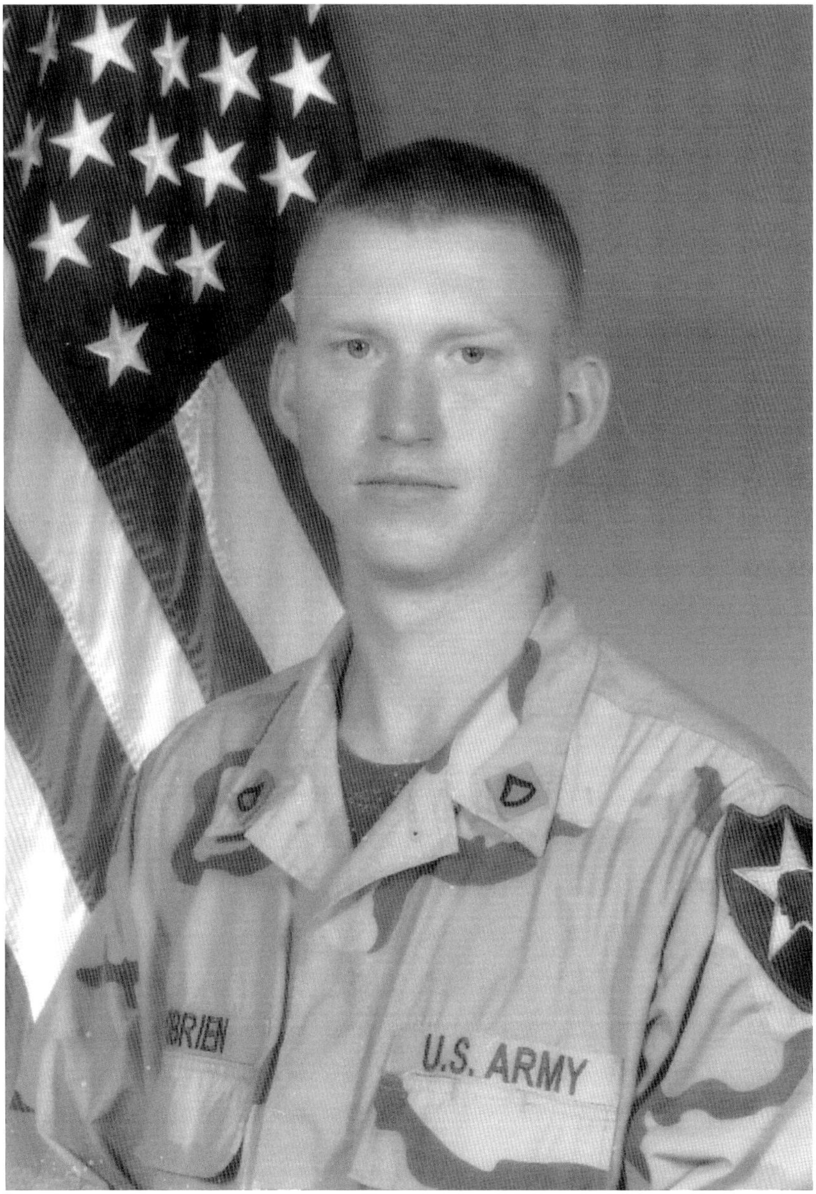

Heath O'Brien
Heath O'Brien moved to Coppell at the age of six. His family played a major role in the religious history of Coppell. His father served as the first bishop for the Coppell ward of the Church of Jesus Christ of Latter-day Saints.

A graduate of Coppell High School, O'Brien was a member of the school's soccer team and lettered in his junior year. After high school, O'Brien joined the Army, training at Fort Sam Houston before being sent to Camp Casey near the demilitarized zone of South Korea.

In 2004, he was deployed to the Anbar Province of Iraq, where he served as a combat medic for the 1st Battalion of the 503rd Infantry. While on mission, his vehicle hit an IED, killing the rest of the soldiers inside and leaving O'Brien severely wounded. He then spent 18 months in medical hold before receiving medical discharge. He was later awarded the Purple Heart for his service. (Courtesy of Tim O'Brien.)

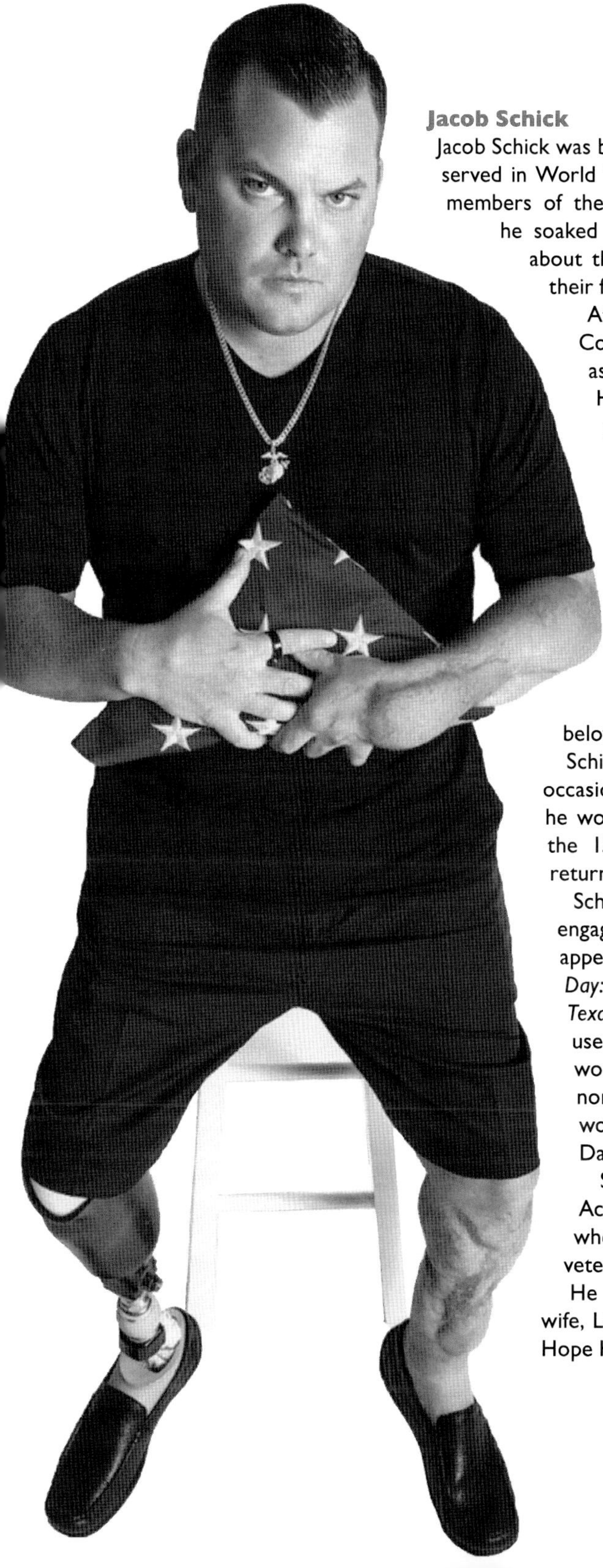

Jacob Schick

Jacob Schick was born into a military family. His grandfather served in World War II and his uncle in Vietnam, both as members of the Marine Corps. From the age of eight, he soaked up the stories his grandmother shared about their service and dreamed of following in their footsteps.

At age 14, Schick moved from Bossier City to Coppell, where he quickly established himself as one of the star players on the Coppell High School football team. By his senior year, he was team captain. That same year, he enlisted in the Marine Corps.

In 2004, Schick was deployed to Iraq as part of Bravo Company 1/23. On September 20, Schick was driving a vehicle that struck a triple-stacked land mine designed to destroy tanks. The resulting injuries included compound fractures in his left leg and arm, ligament and bone loss, partial loss of his left hand and arm, and amputation below the knee of his right leg.

Schick was offered the Purple Heart on several occasions but refused the award, indicating that he would not accept any commendations until the 156 soldiers he was deployed with had returned home.

Schick's story has spread through speaking engagements, articles, and television appearances (including the HBO special *Alive Day: Home from Iraq* and the *Good Morning Texas* special *Starting Over*). Schick has used the platform to advance the cause of wounded veterans. He also serves with the nonprofit organization Carry the Load and works for the Center for Brain Health in Dallas, Texas.

Schick made his acting debut in the Academy Award–nominated *American Sniper*, where he played the role of a wounded veteran.

He now makes his home in Dallas with his wife, Laura, and their son Jackson. (Courtesy of Hope Harrison Photography.)

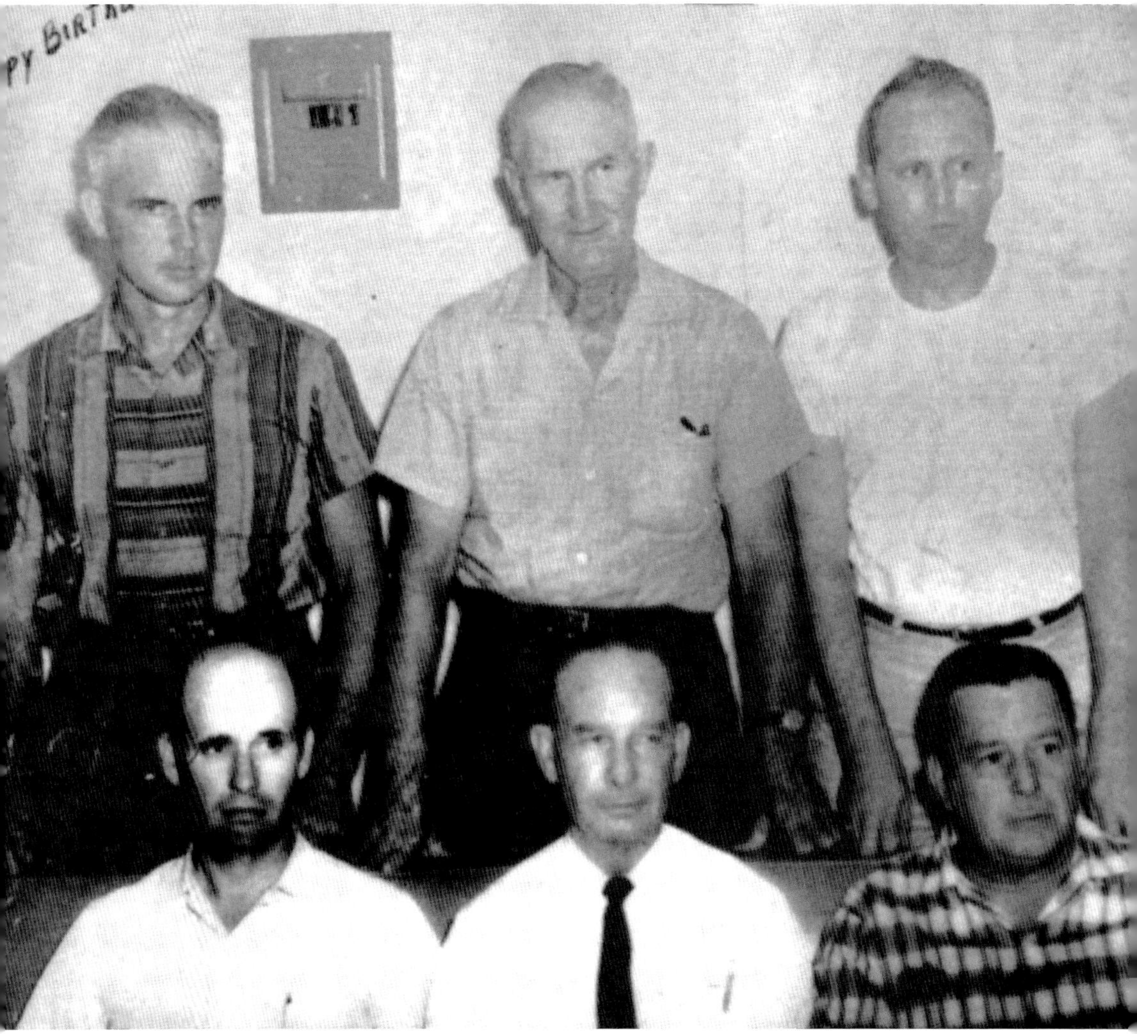

John Burns

John Burns's relationship with Coppell took a number of twists over the years. Burns moved to Coppell in 1938. At the time, the town was home to seven honky-tonks and no formal law enforcement.

In 1958, Burns became a city councilman as well as a charter member of the town's volunteer fire department. In 1964, he was named a deputy constable by Dallas County and served as the town's only law enforcement.

Burns later went into business with his son Johnny, who became mayor in 1977. Their business involved excavating sand and gravel, which was subsequently used to build a number of the roads north of present-day Sandy Lake Road.

In later years, Burns became a regular at Coppell's McDonald's, where he would gather with other Coppell "old-timers" like Walter Pettijohn and Johnny Dobecka. Together, the group would meet to share memories of Coppell and how they played a role in building it.

Burns is among those pictured here. (Courtesy of the *Citizens' Advocate*.)

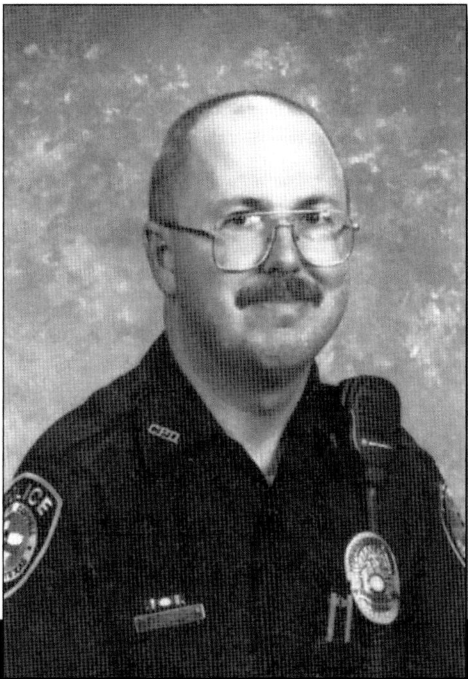

Michael Johns

In 2009, the Coppell Police Department began a motorcycle rodeo with the goal of raising money for a memorial wall that would honor Coppell's fallen officers. In the history of the department, only two officers have been killed while serving.

Originally from California, Michael Johns graduated from high school in Duncanville before pursuing his dream of becoming a police officer. Johns served for two years in Plano and nine in Desoto before joining the Coppell Police Department, where he served 10 years.

On December 28, 2001, Johns was attempting to stop a speeding vehicle when another vehicle collided with his motorcycle. Johns died of injuries shortly after.

The department's rodeo was a success, resulting in the 2010 dedication of the Coppell Fallen Officer Memorial. (Courtesy of the Coppell Police Department and Kara Jex.)

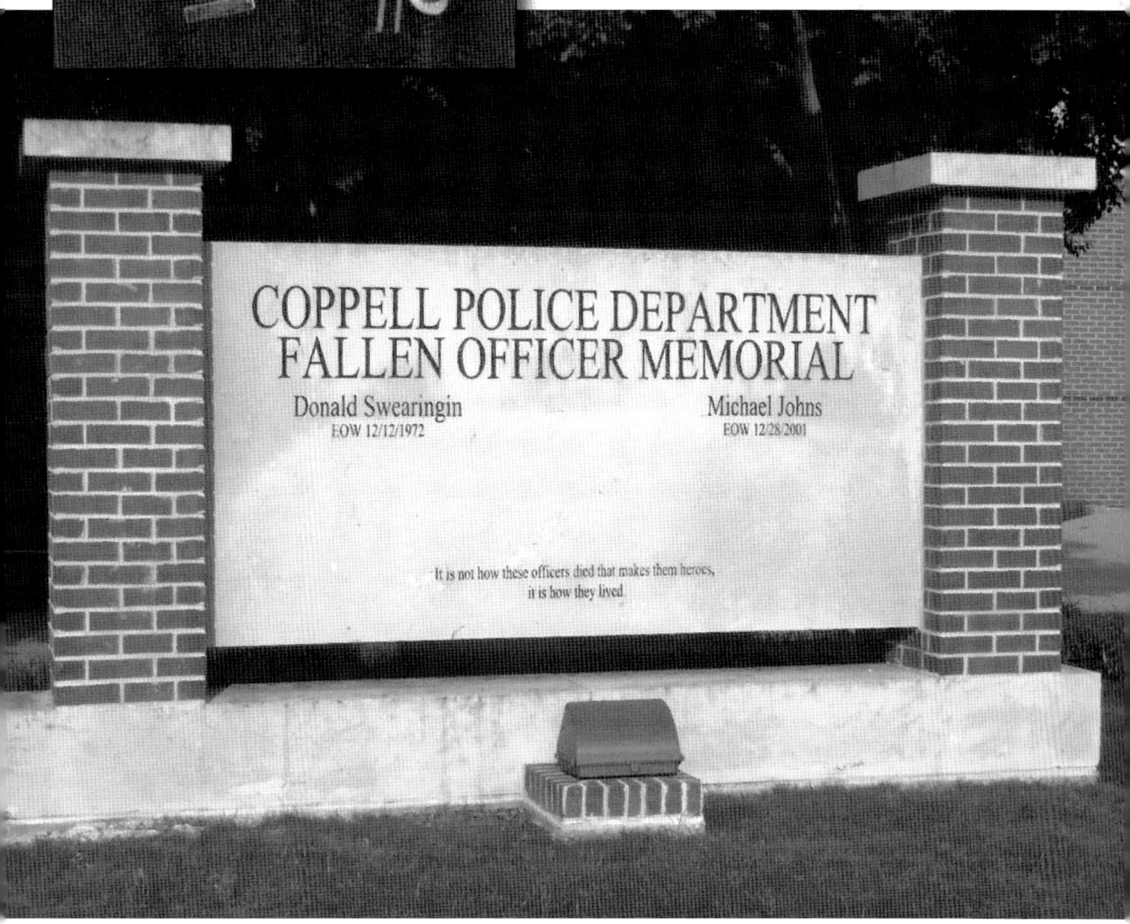

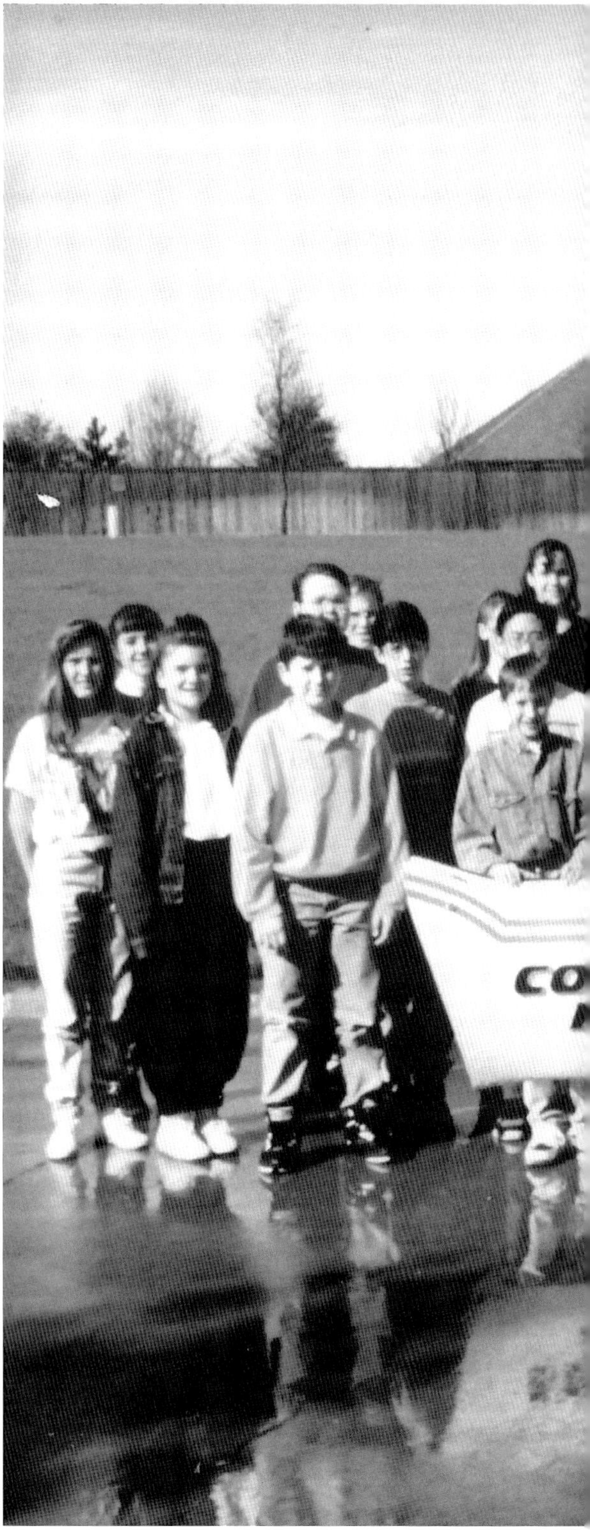

James Ledet
James Ledet began his law enforcement career in 1976 with the police department in Gladewater, Texas. In subsequent years, he served with the Kilgore Police Department and the Upshur County sheriff's office. Ledet then joined the Coppell Police Department, where he served for 20 years. In that time, he was twice honored as Officer of the Year, and in May 2010, he was honored with a community service award.

Ledet is most remembered for his time as school resource officer with CISD, where he served numerous campuses. Among his many duties, he helped put on an annual junior police academy during the summer months. Though joking that his job was "babysitter with a gun," Ledet also describes it as the most rewarding part of his career.

In 2012, Officer Ledet became Professor Ledet for the Criminal Justice and Public Administration programs at Tyler Junior College. (Courtesy of James Ledet.)

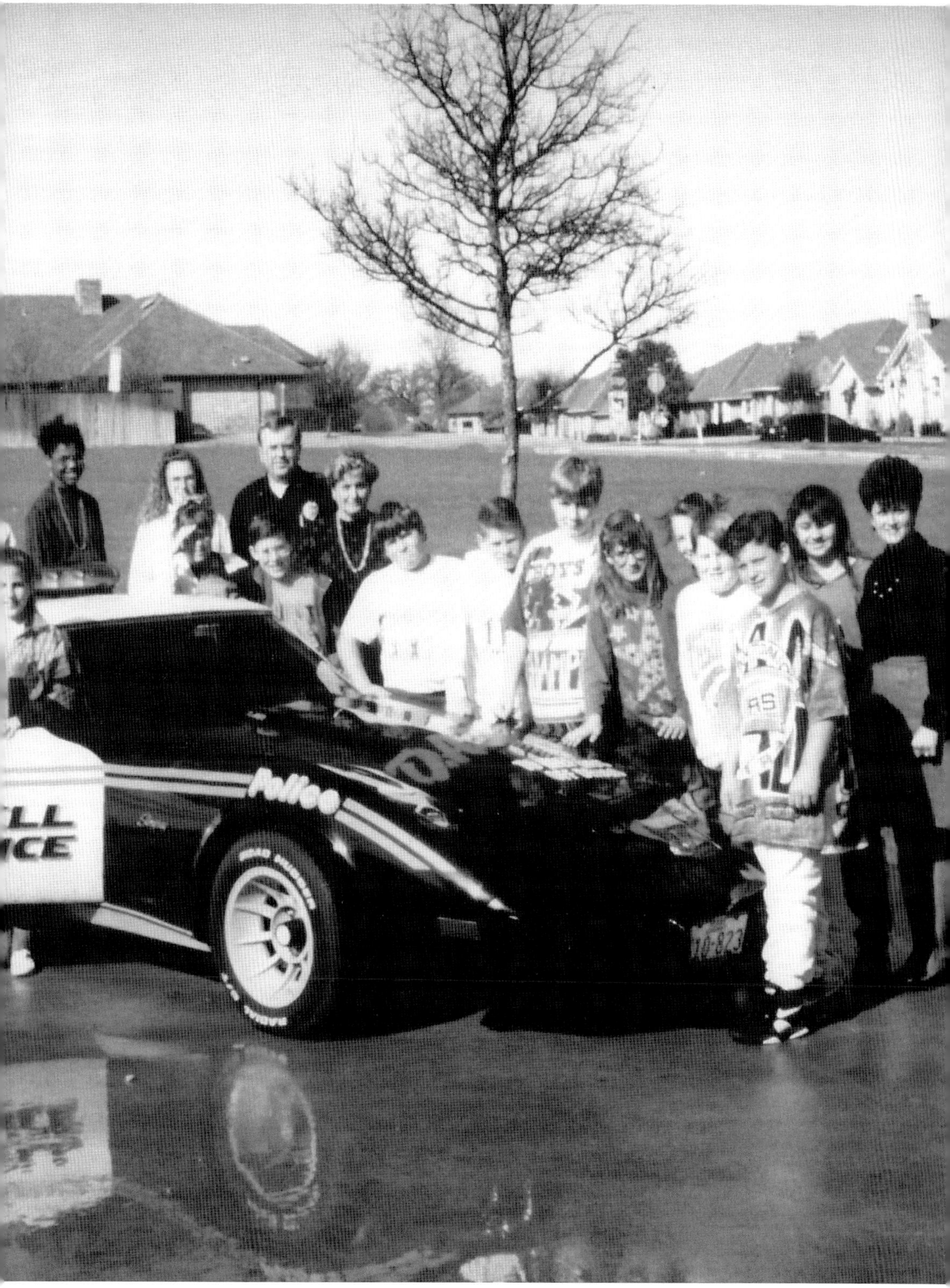
Police

Earl Tinsley

In 1957, Earl Tinsley became the first chief of the Coppell Fire Department. At the time, the fledgling group was made up entirely of volunteers.

Tinsley was a World War II veteran, serving in the Coast Guard and the Army Reserve. He was a police officer for the City of Dallas as well as a small business owner, operating a nursery and later owning and managing a number of Dairy Queen franchises.

Tinsley passed away in April 2014 in Tyler, where he resided with his wife. (Courtesy of the Coppell Fire Department.)

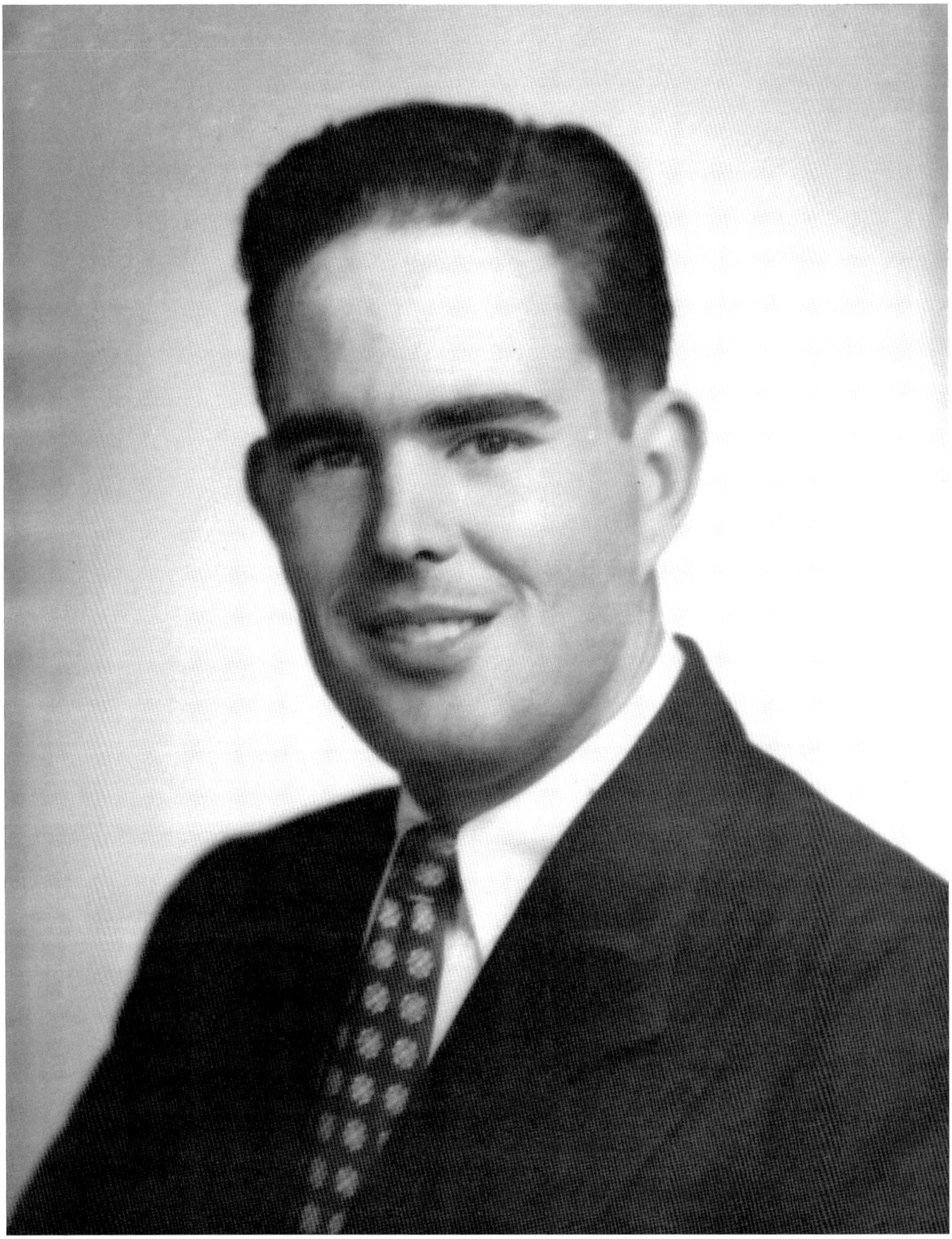

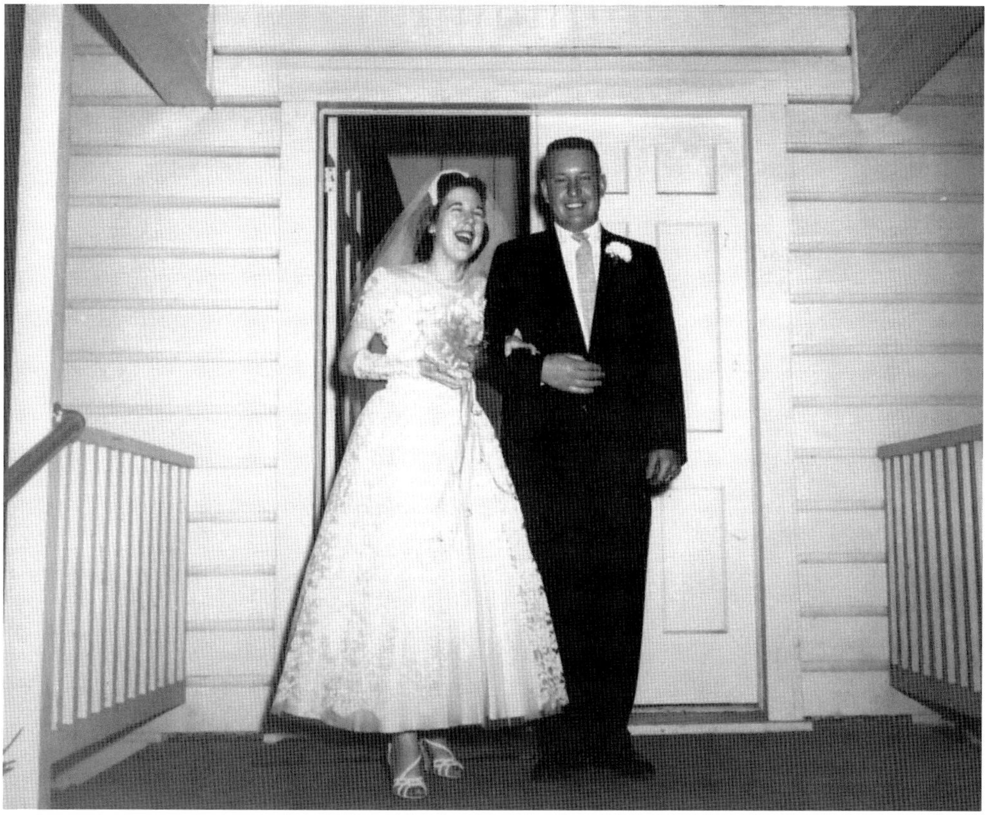

Richard J. Lee

Richard J. Lee was born in Dallas and moved several times with his family before settling in Coppell in the winter of 1945. He attended the Coppell School (now Pinkerton), where he met Barbara Melton, who would later become his wife. His eighth grade class held a total of 13 students.

In his seventh and eighth grade years, Lee woke at 3:30 a.m. to milk cows for "Boots" Leslie before going to school. He returned to round up the cattle and mix their feed each night.

In 1953, Richard graduated from Carrollton High School. Lee and Melton were married shortly after in 1956. In the early years of their marriage, the two had no phone and would receive phone calls through the neighboring Baptist parsonage.

A town tragedy would shape the direction of the rest of Lee's life. After returning home from work, Lee learned that a baby in a neighboring house had died. There was no emergency response or fire department in town, so Lee took the baby by car to Parkland Hospital in Dallas. In 1958, Lee, along with Earl Tinsley and Hal Hood, organized a volunteer fire department. They held their first meeting under a tree on the grounds of the Coppell School.

Lee became the department's fifth chief in 1967 and remained in the position until 1984. Because the early force was a volunteer department, the men were often at work and unable to respond to emergencies during the day. To aid the situation, Lee created a junior fire department that allowed high school seniors to respond to fires, provided they had completed a Red Cross safety course and had a driver's license. The program lasted roughly four years.

Lee served on the Coppell school board from 1962 to 1982, the longest term ever held for a trustee. A new elementary school, opened in 1983, was given the name Richard J. Lee Elementary. The school remained open until 2008, when the campus was transformed into New Tech High School. However, in 2014, Coppell opened the country's first net-zero energy elementary and named the new school Richard J. Lee. (Courtesy of Richard and Barbara Lee.)

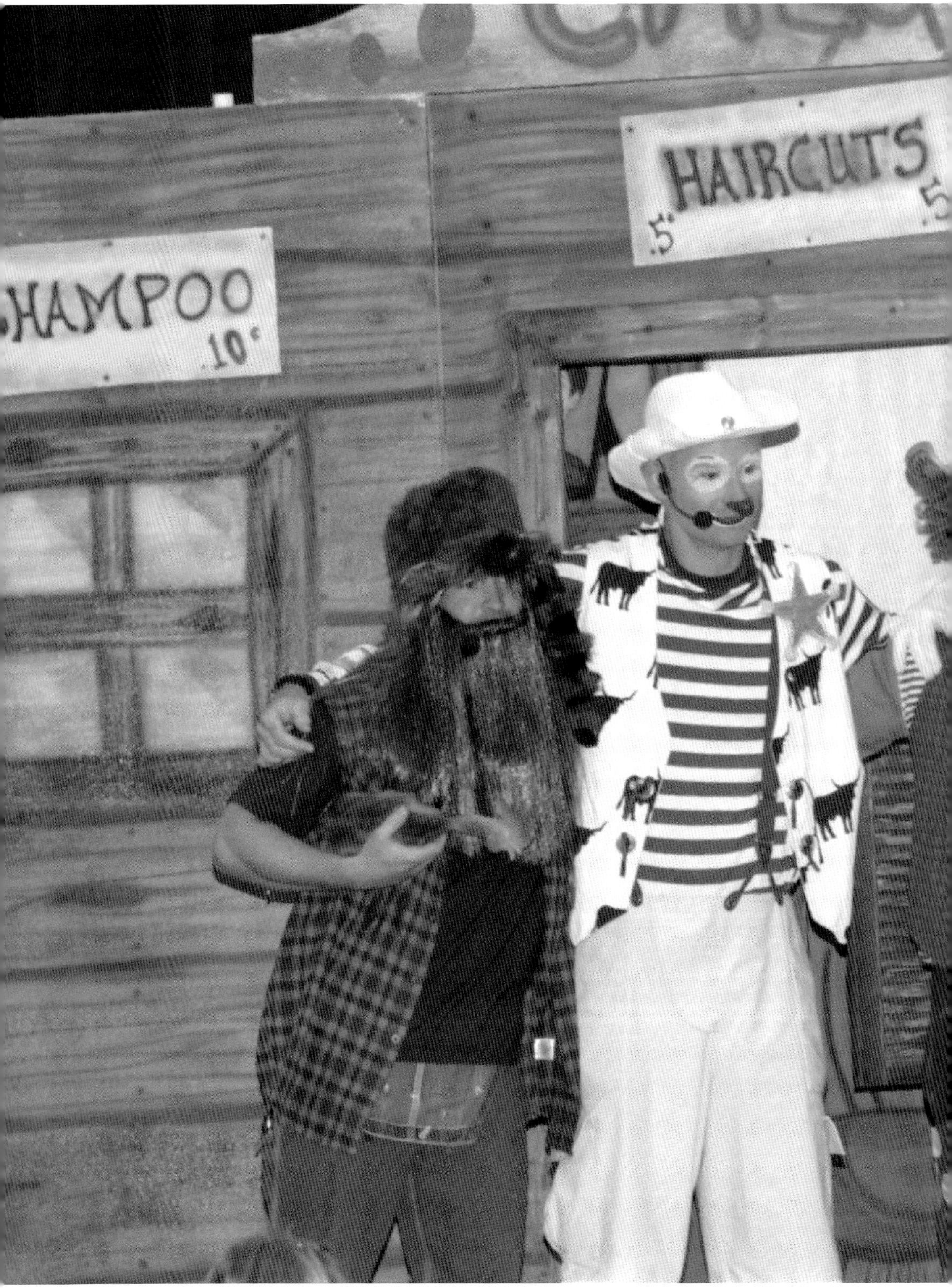
HAIRCUTS
5¢
HAMPOO
10¢

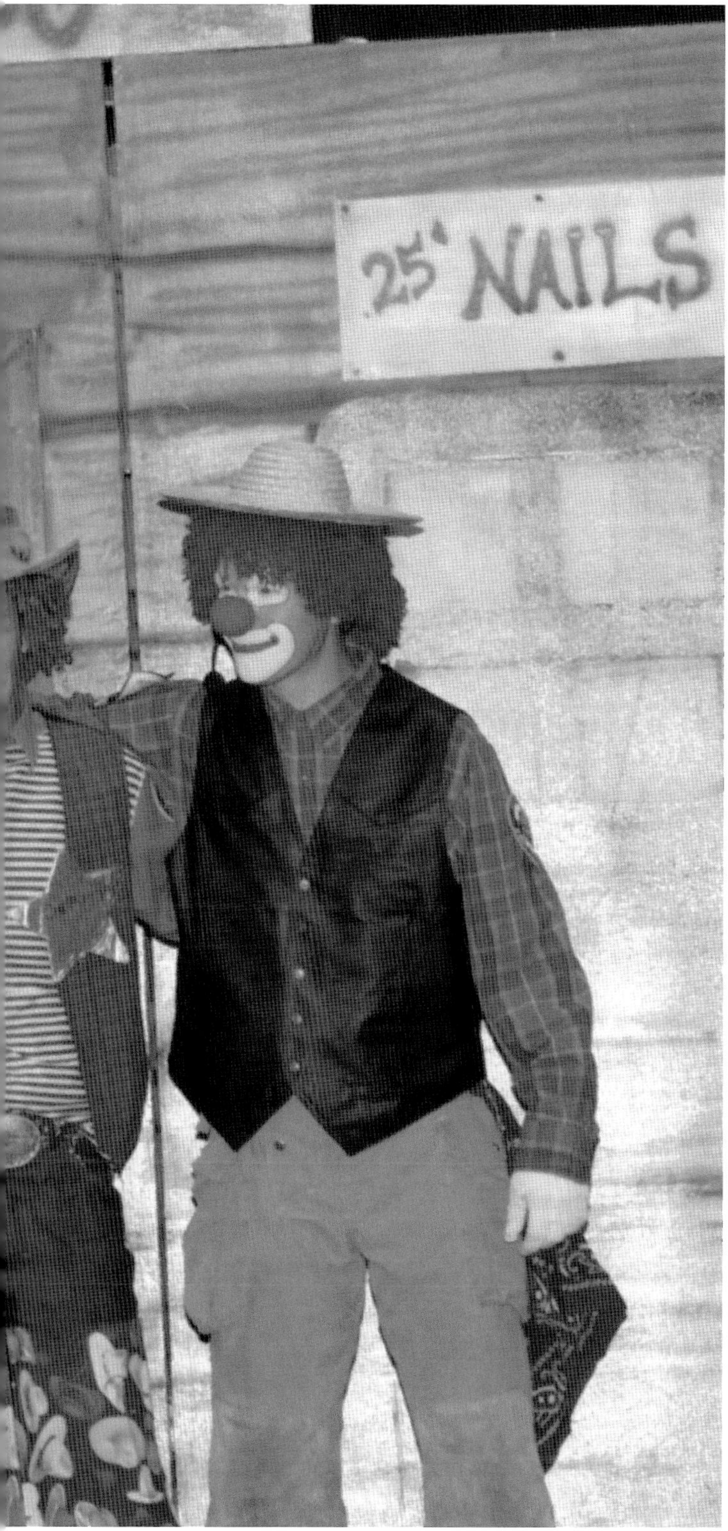

Coppell Fire Department Clowne Troupe
In 2004, the Coppell Fire Department Clowne Troupe began performing in local elementary schools. The group is composed of volunteer firefighters, who build and paint their own props, and design shows that reflect the annual themes put forward by the National Fire Protection Association. The troupe runs its show through the month of October, which is Fire Prevention Month.

The original cast included firefighters and paramedics David Green, Brian Stacy, James Daily, Dennis Cobb, Chris Holland, Chris Price, and Heather Dingfield. The current cast rotates regularly. Several of the members have taken part in professional clown classes and current member John Dabbs was awarded the 2012 Brian Collins Memorial Award for dedication to fire safety awareness. (Courtesy of the Coppell Fire Department.)

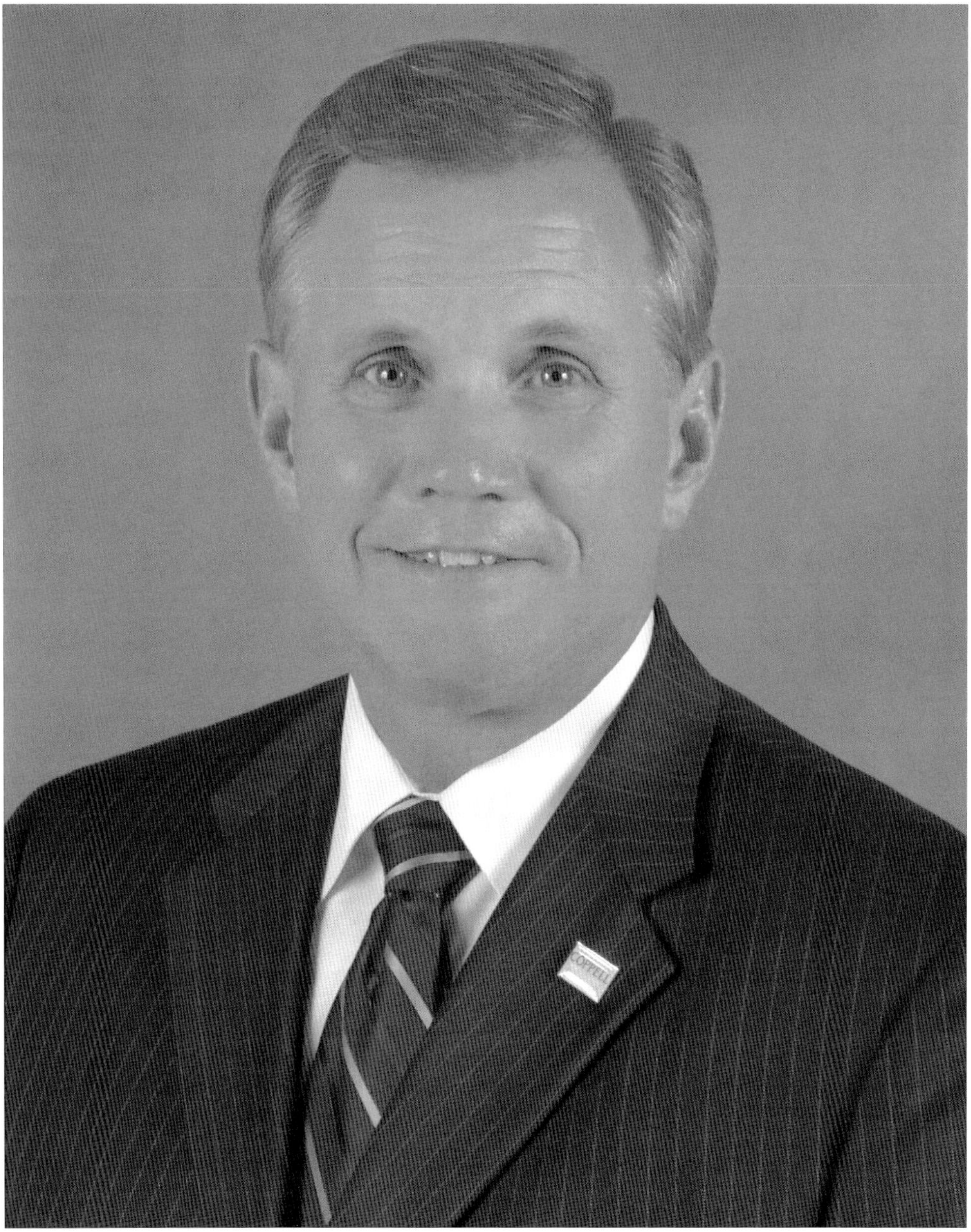

Clay Phillips
Clay Phillips is a lifelong resident of Coppell. In 1978, he graduated from Coppell High School as valedictorian.

He has served the city in numerous capacities since 1991, when he became fire chief for the Coppell Fire Department. Since that time, he has served as assistant city manager, deputy city manager, and his current position of city manager.

A member of Coppell's First Baptist Church (now GracePoint), Phillips serves in the music ministry and as an elder. He was also a member of the Gospel Quartet First Four, which toured through Texas and neighboring states and recorded several albums. (Courtesy of the City of Coppell.)

INDEX

Austin, Barbara S., 36
Bennett, Dr. Jesse C., 13
Bowen, Anita, 39
Bowen, John, 39
Braem, Kathy, 55
Brandenburg, Ryan Kate, 30
Brightwell, Frank, 21
Broderick, Fr. Killian, 53
Brown Jr., Andy, 93
Brown, Josh, 44
Bullock, W.C., 65
Burks, Geneva, 111
Burns, John, 118
Carter, Don J., 91
Chalwell, Dr. Robert, 2
Citizens' Advocate, 18
Collins, Shari, 82
Conger, Fred, 103
Conger, Judy, 103
Cook, Beth, 42
Cope, Pamela, 99
Coppell Fire Department Clowne Troupe, 124–125
Coppell, George, 11
Cozby, William T., 89
Darwin, Kent, 25
Dash, 81
Demske, Alice, 26
Demske, Hilary, 26
Dobecka Sr., Cecil, 76
Dobecka Sr., John, 112
Dobecka, Frank P., 66
Dobecka, Gay, 41
Duggan, Lou, 94
Dupey, Michael, 9
Echols, Buddy, 45
Elbert, Emily, 28
Flesher, David, 23
Flesher, Don, 23
Franzioni, Tiffany, 22
Garriss, Tom, 114
Gentry, Ernest, 69
Gibbs, Barnett, 86
Goodner, David, 84
Hall, Jim, 59
Handley, Ruby, 35
Harrison Ratliff General Store, 12
Harwell, Clayta Plumblee, 74
Harwell, Floyd, 14
Hightower, J.E., 50
Hoogendorn, Jeff, 83
Hoogendorn, Peg, 83
Houston Campsite Oak, 60
Howell, Burrell B., 64
Jackson, Jo, 90
Johns, Michael, 119
Johnson, R.M., 85
Khorrami, Jay, 19
Kirkland, Carroll E, 110
Kirkland, Edna, 67
Kirkland, Jewel, 75
LaFountain, Michelle, 115
Layton, Foy, 51
Ledbetter, Buren, 71
Ledet, James, 120–121
Lee, Barbara, 100
Lee, Richard J., 123
Leone, Larry, 29
Logan, Jacob, 106
Mason, Scott, 46
McBride, C.A., 52
McBride, Carol, 52
McDowell, Ruby, 70
Minyard, Gretchen, 17
Minyard, Lisbeth, 17
Mobley, Mary Evelyn, 101
Nichols, Dena, 40
O'Brien, Heath, 116
Old Red, 78–79
Ottinger, W.A., 68
Parker, Bettye, 15
Parker, Clyde, 87
Parrish, James, 61
Peters, William S., 10
Pettijohn, Walter, 92
Phillips, Clay, 126
Pinkerton, Faye G., 1
Pinkerton, Woodrow Wilson, 34
Pooch the Firehouse Dog, 77
Ratliff, Bennett, 98
Record, John, 63
Record, Josiah, 63
Redden, Mary Jean, 33
Rejoice Lutheran Pumpkin Patch, 56–57
Rucker, Lisa, 31
Rucker, Robert, 31
Salerno, Gloria, 24
Schick, Jacob, 117
Shirley, Joe, 20
Simmons, Jack, 32
Smartt, B.J., 102
Smartt, Joy, 43
Smith, Jonna, 107
Smothermon, Bill, 95
Smothermon, Peggi, 95
St. Ann Carnival, 54
Stearman, Dr. William, 16
Storch, Tara, 104
Storch, Todd, 104
Stringfellow, John, 48–49
Stringfellow, Sara, 48–49
Strong, Juanita, 72
Sturm, Bob, 105
Swearingin, Donald, 109
Swofford, Robert Lee, 113
Thomas, William Ewing, 62
Thompson, Martha, 47
Thompson, Zack, 108
Thweatt, J.C., 73
Timmerman, Bob, 96
Tinsley, Earl, 122
Turner, Elaine, 58
Turner, Jay, 58
Vanhoozier, Amanda, 97
Vrla, Danny, 80
White, Vonita, 37
Williams, Una, 27
Wilson Jr., Wheelice "Pete," 38
Wilson, W.H., 88